WISDOM, MADNESS AND FOLLY

The Philosophy of a Lunatic

by

JOHN CUSTANCE

with a Preface by

DR. C. G. JUNG, F.R.S.M., M.D.D.Sc., D.LITT., LLD.

Dr. es Lettres, formerly of the Eidgen. Techn. Hochschule, Zurich,
Professor Ordinarius of Medical Psychology, University of Basel.

with a Foreword by

CANON L. W. GRENSTED

formerly Nolloth Professor of the Philosophy of the Christian Religion
in the University of Oxford

PELLEGRINI & CUDAHY
NEW YORK

PREFACE

When I was working in 1906 at my paper "On the psychology of Dementia Praecox" (as schizophrenia was then called), I could scarcely be expected to dream that in the succeeding half century psychological investigation of the psychoses and their contents would make virtually no progress whatever. The dogma, or intellectual superstition, that only a physical cause can be really valid still blocks for the psychiatrist the way into the psyche of his patient, and causes him rather to make the boldest and most incalculable interferences in the most delicate of all organs than to allow himself even to think about the possibility of genuine psychical relationships and effects, although these are completely obvious to an unprejudiced understanding. All that is necessary is to devote attention to them, but it is precisely this which is prevented by materialistic prejudices, even in people who have seen the futility of such metaphysical associations. The organic, even when it is not known at all but is purely hypothetical, is more convincing than the truly psychical, since the latter still does not exist in its own right, but is regarded as a secondary exhalation, as it were, arising out of the albumen-based scheme of things. How on earth do people know that the only reality is the physical atom, when this cannot even be proved to exist at all except by means of the psyche? If there is anything that can be described as primary, it must be the psyche, certainly not in any circumstances the atom, which, like everything else in our experience, is only directly given as a psychical model or picture.

I still remember vividly the great impression made upon me when I succeeded for the first time in deciphering the apparently completed nonsense of schizophrenic neologisms. It was an infinitely easier task than deciphering the hieroglyphs or cuneiform characters. While the latter make possible for us the authentic insight into the intellectual culture of ancient man, an achievement which is certainly not to be underestimated, the deciphering of the products of insanity and all other forms in which the Unconscious expresses itself discloses for us the meaning of far older and more fundamental psychical occurrences, and thus gives us entrance into the underworld of, or world behind, the soul, which is not only the matrix of the products of the ancient intellect but also of the ordinary modern consciousness itself. But this latter seems quite uninteresting and, moreover, to have least of all to do with the psychiatrist; more or less as if it were extremely important to know precisely whence and out of which quarries the stones were extracted to build our medieval cathedrals and, on the contrary, completely unimportant to know the purpose and meaning of these buildings themselves.

Half a century has not sufficed to make the psychiatrist, the "doctor of the soul," even in some small degree acquainted with the structure and contents of the psyche.

Nobody needs to write an apologia for the meaning of the brain, since it can actually be put under a microscope. The soul, on the other hand, is nothing, because it is not sufficiently physical to be hardened and colored. People still despise what they do not know, and what they know least of all they claim to know best, so that even the attempt to bring some sort of order into the chaos of psychological experience is regarded as "unscientific," since the criteria of physical actuality cannot be directly applied to the psychical. The evidence of *original documents,* which is fully recognized in the study of history and in jurisprudence, seems still to be unknown in psychiatry.

For this reason precisely a book like the present one should be particularly welcome to psychiatrists. It is a "document humain," unfortunately one of few. I do not know more than half a dozen of such autochthonous descriptions of psychosis; of these this is the only one to be derived from the domain of manic-depressive disturbance, all the others being derived from schizophrenia. At any rate in my experience it is quite unique. Certainly there are innumerous case-histories, with comparable descriptions of experience by the patient, which, however, never reach the light of day in the form of a printed publication; and,

in any case, probably none of these could approach the auto-
biography of our author in respect of clarity of expression, general education, wide reading, deep thought and self-criticism.
The value of this book is unusual, and all the greater since it
represents a discovery, or better a re-discovery, of certain fundamental structures and types of the psyche, uninfluenced by literature. Although I personally have for decades studied these very
phenomena, and have repeatedly described them, it was for me
nonetheless a novelty as important as it was unexpected to see
how the delirious flight of ideas and lack of restraint of the
manic state removes the threshold of consciousness towards the
Unconscious to such an extent, that the latter, as in the "abais-
sement du niveau mental" of schizophrenia, is exposed and thus
rendered intelligible. What the author has discovered in the
manic state agrees precisely with what I myself have ascer-
tained. I mean by this chiefly the *structure of the opposites* and
its symbolism, furthermore the type of the *anima,* and finally
the unavoidable coming to terms with the reality of the soul. As
is well known, these three main points play an important part in
my psychology, with which, however, the author did not become
acquainted until afterwards.

More especially for the expert in this field it will be of particular interest to see what kind of a total picture arises when the
inhibitions exerted by consciousness on the Unconscious are
removed in mania: the result is a crude and totally unmitigated
system of opposites showing itself in the play of all kinds of col-
ors and forms and reaching out into all heights and depths.
The symbolism is predominantly of a collective and archetypal
nature, and is therefore strongly mythological or religious. Clear
indications of a process of individuation are lacking, since the
dialectic unfolds itself in the spontaneous and interior con-
frontation of the opposites in the presence of an experiencing
and reflecting subject. The latter is not in any dialectical relationship with an opposite number; in other words there is no
dialogue. For that reason the values sketch themselves mainly in
an undifferentiated black-white system, and the problem of
more or less differentiated functions is not posed. For this reason

also, clear indications of the *process of individuation* are lacking since, as is well-known, this has as a necessary prerequisite intensive relations with other individuals and a coming to terms with them. The relation, that is to say the Eros, thus appears nowhere as a problem. Instead of it, psychical reality, which the author very rightly translates as "actuality," receives all the fuller appreciation, the value of which cannot be denied.

In accordance with the impressive content of his psychosis the author is correspondingly deeply affected. This runs through his book as a main motif from the beginning to the end and makes it a monologue and confession to a circle of anonymous listeners as well as a coming to terms with the also anonymous spirit of the age (Zeitgeist). Its intellectual horizon is wide and does honor to the "logos" of its author. I do not know what sort of impression the "normal" layman, who has never had anything from the other side of the barrier thrust upon him, will receive from this book. I can only say that both the psychiatrist and the practical psychologist owe the author the greatest possible thanks for the illumination which he has given them by his efforts. As a contribution to the knowledge of those important psychic contents, which either appear in pathological conditions or underlie such conditions, his book is both valuable and rare.

C. G. Jung

FOREWORD

I CAME TO know Mr John Custance while he was in Oxford during an interlude in the experiences which he has here described and interpreted. Nobody could have told at that time that he was the victim of the mysterious and alarming disorder known as manic-depressive insanity. Since then I have known him and talked with him during one of his escapes from hospital, when, as he assured me, his mind was racing at manic level. It was very striking that he was at the same time capable of a freedom of judgment which was, if the words mean anything, wholly rational and sane.

He has now done me the honour of letting me read this illuminating record of his experiences and of asking me to add a foreword. I do so very gladly indeed, not only because I count him among those for whom I have both friendship and respect, but also because of its intrinsic interest. Written, as he himself explains, during various phases of his recovery from acute attacks of mania, and while still passing through the different wards of a mental hospital, it is nevertheless marked throughout by a singular detachment and objectivity. It is in fact a first-hand document for the study of this type of psychosis, written by a singularly clear-sighted and honest observer who stands, unlike the doctors and psychologists generally, within the barrier and not outside. This gives his book the character of an authentic document and only secondarily that of a scientific study. It is all the more important that those who have charge of patients in mental hospitals should have inside knowledge of this kind brought vividly before them. Much of what Mr Custance has to say is highly relevant to the whole management of such hospitals, and the suggestions which he makes are those of a man of considerable practical experience as well as education. The plea for greatly extended occupational treatment is not new, but in most hospitals of this kind it has certainly not been met with adequate sympathy, patience, and imagination. Still less have the hospitals solved the difficult problem of enabling patients still shaken by their experiences to make a new start under suitably tempered conditions in the outer world.

The setting of the whole discussion is the inter-relation in the hospitals between patients, ward attendants and doctors. In this connection the material included in the Appendix is of importance. Some of it, indeed, is disturbing, but it rings true to anyone who has had any experience of such hospitals. What is significant here is that that is how the relation actually appears to the patient, and one of the most striking features of this book is the complete absence of any note of resentment. The situation is described with an understanding of both sides which is something of an achievement in fairness and objectivity. The same objectivity, perhaps with rather more indication of resentment, marks the account of the actual procedure when a patient is certified insane. It is a procedure which I have discussed with magistrates who have had the unpleasant duty of taking part upon these occasions, and who have told me of their profound discomfort in the whole affair. This record of the sense of helplessness and unfairness left in the mind of the patient is one which those who have this duty would do well to bear in mind. For certification, though sometimes necessary, has as one of its two main ends the protection and cure of the lunatic, and that end is not helped where a sense of unfairness lingers on.

A second feature of this book is its insight into some of the deeper problems with which metaphysics and religion have to deal. Those who have had to deal with lunatics and acute neurotics often find themselves startled by the curious clarity with which their minds work. It is as though their approach to some of the profoundest problems has been simplified by their loss of touch with what we supposedly sane folk regard as reality. Most of us, in fact, are too much aware of complex circumstances and factors to reach any clear and recognisable pattern of truth. But the approach of the lunatic has in many cases something of the child's directness and simplicity. His vision may be complicated in other ways, by delusions of reference or by distortions of imagery, but the radical truth which he is trying to express is often very well worthy of attention. Sometimes indeed it constitutes a challenge to our accepted notions, but it is not a challenge which it is wise to ignore.

In the final chapter Mr Custance (still writing in hospital) propounds a philosophical theory of Actuality which is of considerable interest. It is actually in line with a good deal that has been written in recent years under the label Existentialism, and it is, to say the least, an interesting fact that Kierkegaard, from whom the modern use of the term derives, had also gone through a long experience of the manic-depressive type. I am profoundly thankful that the writer knew little or nothing about Existentialism when he wrote this chapter. As it stands it is both more true and better put than much that has been written under that greatly abused title. The actuality of all experience, even the maddest, is an obvious truth and the problem of its relation to reality is one of which the difficulty lies on the side of reality, and not on that of actuality as it is here understood. This "Philosophy of a Lunatic" is put with disarming simplicity, but some at least of our professional philosophers would be none the worse for studying it, and taking it, in principle if not always in detail, very seriously indeed.

L. W. Grensted

CONTENTS

CHAPTER I

MEANING AND MANIA

I. *Introductory*

"WHATSOEVER ROAD you may explore, you will not reach the limits of the soul, for the soul has no limits." Twelve years or so ago these words of Heraclitus would have meant little or nothing to me. I might even have disputed the existence of a "soul". An active, energetic life, in which enjoyment of work and play seemed a sufficient reason for existence, left little place for metaphysical or ethical speculations, or even for religion.

Like so many others of my generation, I had embraced a comfortable agnosticism. On the one hand it was much simpler to leave the more awkward moral problems alone and retain a convenient elasticity of conscience. On the other hand it is by no means easy to reconcile traditional Christianity with the outlook of an age brought up on Bernard Shaw and H. G. Wells, whom the late Lord Keynes once described in a brilliant article in *The New Statesman* as the Divinity and Stinks masters of his generation. And traditional, orthodox Christianity was all I knew. The great idea of Evolution, of life, through man, consciously mastering the Universe, which Thomas Hardy expressed so well in a line which for once transcended his usual pessimism:

"Consciousness the Will informing, till
it fashions all things new"

captured my imagination as a young man and formed the basis of such philosophy as I possessed. I had no idea of the work of the Modernist movement in the Church towards bringing the evolutionary conception within the scope of Christianity. Unfortunately the evolutionary philosophy seems made for the healthy-minded, to whom crises of the soul are unknown. In my own case its limitations soon became apparent.

When the devil was well, the devil a saint was he. The soul is not unlike the body in that as long as it is well one is barely conscious of it. Let something but go wrong with its mechanism, however, and the whole aspect of things alters in a moment. In my middle thirties I was attacked by a not uncommon nervous disease known as manic-depression.

The gloomy wood in which I thus found myself, appropriately enough "in the midway of this our mortal life",* proved to be the entrance to regions of whose existence I had not the least suspicion. The depths of the inferno I was thus compelled to explore have been well described by William James:—"Desperation absolute and complete, the whole universe coagulating about the sufferer into a material of overwhelming horror, surrounding him without opening or end. Not the conception or intellectual perception of evil, but the grisly, blood-freezing, heart-palsying sensation of it close upon one, and no other conception or sensation able to live for a moment in its presence." †

As James says, only religion, and a strong religion at that, can help in the presence of such a consciousness. The soul that is well may succeed in ignoring all that is comprised in the word "God", the soul that is sick meets gods and devils at every turn. Psychologists may explain such phenomena as atavistic relics, deposits as it were of primitive superstitions left in the human soul in the course of the ages by the stream of consciousness of the race, but they are none the less factors which have to be dealt with. They constitute what has been described as "psychological truth",‡ and it is they which have led even fundamentally sceptical psychologists such as Jung and his disciples to make the re-establishment of a religious outlook an essential part of their therapeutic method.

A religious outlook! Have I achieved one at last? I do not

* Dante, "Inferno", Canto I.
† James, "Varieties of Religious Experience", p. 162.
‡ Jung, "Psychology of the Unconscious", p. 9.

know. I cannot even say whether I am Christian or pagan at heart—if Christianity and paganism are really opposites, as they are usually assumed to be. But I can claim that through my illness I have been compelled to face those problems of ethics, conscience and religion which I had tried to evade, and this book is in part an attempt to come to terms with them.

Manic-depression brought to me—as it does to nearly all who suffer from it—an intense emotional religious experience, very foreign to the temper of staid Anglicanism in which I was brought up. Is it true? Perhaps the question is wrongly put, and so unanswerable. But I cannot set it down as meaningless and go on as though it had never been. It is far too intimately a part of me; it is the unforgettable and inescapable. On my strange journey there were giddy heights as well as depths, and even the wildest flights of heated imagination are an essential part of the process of which I shall try to give some account here.

There is a phenomenon known as "anaesthetic revelation" which sometimes affects persons inhaling ether or nitrous oxide, notably the latter. It bears some analogy to the experiences of alcohol and drug addicts, but is much more intense. Depth beyond depth of truth seems revealed to the inhaler, and although this truth fades unaccountably on coming-to, the sense of profound meaning persists. Many experiments have been made by psychologists and others with such drugs, and all seem to agree that while the trance persists an extraordinary clearness and certainty appears to be attained regarding the whole construction of the Universe. The sceptics, however, point out that the recipients of this ineffable revelation are quite unable to give any clear account of it on returning to normal consciousness. Sir Humphry Davy, for example, after trying nitrous oxide could only explain portentously and with the most intensely prophetic manner that "nothing exists but thought".* William James, on the other hand, stressed the unity of the revelation. Its keynote was invariably a reconciliation. "It is

* Quoted by Leuba, "Psychology of Religious Mysticism", 274.

as if the opposites of the world, whose contradictoriness and conflict make all our difficulties and troubles, were melted into unity. Not only do they, as contrasted species, belong to one and the same genus, but *one of the species*, the nobler and better one, *is itself the genus, and so soaks up and absorbs its opposite into itself.* This is a dark saying, I know, when thus expressed in terms of common logic, but I cannot wholly escape from its authority." *

The analogy between certain phases of manic-depression and the nitrous oxide trance is striking. Again and again during the "manic" or "elated" periods of the illness, I have felt this sense of a revelation of ultimate harmonies; in some degree it persisted throughout the periods. In fact it was under the influence of this feeling that I determined to write this book, and I was encouraged in the idea by a psychiatrist who once treated me. "You need not imagine", he said, "that you have solved the ultimate problems of the Universe, but as a human soul your experiences cannot fail to be of some value."

It has been alleged against the validity of the "anaesthetic revelation" that it sometimes takes precisely the opposite form, of disharmony rather than harmony, of something horrible rather than of something ineffable.† This seems particularly to be the case when the anaesthetic is light and the operation painful. Here again there appears to be some analogy with the phenomena of manic-depression, in this case those of the depressive or melancholic periods.

Needless to say, I am not claiming a quality of "revelation" for any of my own experiences. The great authority of William James, however, gives me courage to maintain that they may not be altogether destitute even of metaphysical value. And they are in any event facts of consciousness, "psychological truth" in Jung's sense. Thus the attempt to make some sort of sense out of them is, I hope, not wholly

---

* "Varieties of Religious Experience", p. 388.
† R. F. Thouless, "An Introduction to the Psychology of Religion", p. 62.

futile. It may furnish some useful material to psychologists and psychiatrists and perhaps also be of value to fellow-sufferers who have been through the same strange recesses of the soul. In some degree, too, I am attempting to psycho-analyse myself in the hope that when my devils are really neatly pinned and labelled like butterflies and moths in a collection they will leave me alone for good.

2. *Abnormality and Mysticism*

Although the use of abnormal mental conditions for the study of human psychology as a whole has often been attacked, like most great steps in scientific method, its validity can now be regarded as established. It has been well compared with the use of the scalpel and the microscope in studying the anatomy of the body. Abnormal or insane conditions, in fact, enable special factors of mental anatomy to be isolated and inspected, unmasked by their more usual surroundings.* Most of the advances of modern psychology seem to have resulted from this method. The whole vast and imposing edifice of Freud and the psycho-analysis arose out of the observation of a few curious cases of hysteria, and few psychologists today repudiate the debt psychology owes to Freud. Whatever else they may be, the manifestations of nervous disorder are clues to what is hidden in the "Unconscious" or the "Subconscious Mind".

This book does not pretend to be a scientific treatise on psychology, so I may perhaps be excused from giving a precise definition of a conception about which there is still so much controversy. It is at any rate common ground that a vast range of influences, motives and tendencies which profoundly affect human actions are not fully present to normal consciousness. In the words of Robert Bridges

"conscient reason . . .
Is to the unconscious mind as the habitable crust
Is to the mass of earth; this crust whereon we dwell
Whereon our loves and shames are begotten and buried
Our first slime and ancestral dust."

* Cf. William James, op. cit., p. 22.

I shall therefore use the word Unconscious in the widest possible sense, much the same sense in which Myers and James used the word "subliminal". In any case the metaphor of Bridges seems to me peculiarly apt. It corresponds to what I have actually felt and imagined under the influence of my illness. It seemed to me as though irresistible impulses coming from outside myself forced me through a crust of normal consciousness and drew me through illimitible unexplored caverns of the soul in which the hidden springs of being were somehow revealed in thoughts, fantasies and feelings.

It is also possible to reverse the metaphor and to say, like one of Jung's patients, that the thoughts, fantasies and feelings "thrust themselves through me". Everybody knows the state between sleeping and waking, in which half-realised and half-seen thoughts and images follow one another in endless succession without any conscious volition of the individual. The reverie of Mrs Bloom at the end of James Joyce's *Ulysses* is a good case in point. This state has been called by a French psychologist * the "Outcropping of the Subconscious". If I may generalise from my own experience, abnormal mental conditions consist largely in an intensification of this state of reverie. Instead of being vague, however, the thoughts and images are vivid and often so overpowering that they cause marked physical sensations.

A point in this connection which seems to me to throw some light on the working of the Unconscious is the fact that often the physical sensations make themselves felt well in advance of the corresponding thoughts, and sometimes even without the thoughts becoming conscious at all. Thus at the onset of phases of manic excitement I have sometimes noticed the typical symptoms, the pleasurable tingling of the spinal chord and warm sense of well-being in the solar plexus, long before any reaction in the mental sphere occurred. The same thing happens with the sinking feeling of fear and horror which accompanies extreme depression. Not

* M. Baudouin, in "Suggestion et Auto-Suggestion".

very long ago, when I was fighting an incipient attack of depression, the physical symptoms appeared again and again, at times in an extreme form, without really depressing or fearful thoughts reaching the surface of my consciousness. The subconscious horrors were very close, ready to break through at any moment; they had as it were sent out their spearhead of sensation into the nervous system; but their main body of conscious thoughts was kept at bay.

Jung, in his *Psychology of the Unconscious*, divides all thought into two kinds; directed thinking and phantasy thinking. Directed thinking is thought directed to definite ends, to exerting a practical influence on reality. It is a comparatively late evolutionary acquirement and its greatest achievement is the modern conquest of nature by science. Phantasy thinking, on the other hand, is the series of images which follow one another not only in the half-awake state mentioned above, but in all kinds of day-dreaming; James calls it "a sort of passive dream state of which the higher animals are also capable".* Here belong all make-believe, all castles in the air, all wish-fulfilments which turn away from reality. It is the thinking of the nursery as well as of the lunatic asylum, but many of the greatest achievements of poetry, art and literature are based upon it. Its predominance is characteristic of primitive man, and Jung maintains that it played a much greater part even in the classic civilisation of Greece and Rome than it does today. Myths, the dreams of the race, are its typical product. All this type of thinking is largely governed by unconscious influences, which it serves to illustrate.

While Freud in his exploration of the Unconscious traces its origins mainly to the childhood of the individual in the nursery, Jung lays his chief stress on the childhood of the race. He develops a theory of a Collective Unconscious which is "the sediment of all experience of the Universe of all time, and also an image of the Universe that has been in process of

* Quoted by Jung, op. cit., p. 21.

formation for untold ages".*   Potentially latent in the structure of the human brain are not merely all the instincts and intuitions of our primitive ancestors but the forms in which they found expression. This explains the virtually identical form of old themes and legends all over the world and also the curious fact that mentally deranged people are able to produce precisely the same images and associations as are known to us from old manuscripts. "Inasmuch", he writes, "as through the Unconscious we have a share in the historical collective psyche, we naturally dwell in a world of were-wolves, demons, magicians, etc., these being things which have always affected man most profoundly."†

Certainly my own experience bears out Jung's theories. I found in the caves of the Unconscious demons and were-wolves, strange faces of forgotten gods, and devils, while my mind played unceasingly on everything it remembered of myths and magic. Folds of the bedclothes suddenly became the carven image of Baal; a crumpled pillow appeared as the horrible visage of Hecate. I was transported into an atmosphere of miracle and witchcraft, of all-pervading occult forces, although I had taken no interest whatever in these subjects prior to my illness.

One of the most striking features from this point of view was a strong tendency to anthropomorphism. The sun came to have an extraordinary effect on me. It seemed to be charged with all power; not merely to symbolise God but actually to be God. Phrases like "Light of the World", "the Sun of Righteousness that setteth nevermore" and so on ran through my head without ceasing, and the mere sight of the sun was sufficient greatly to intensify this manic excitement under which I was labouring. I was impelled to address the sun as a personal God, and to evolve little rituals of sun-worship. The moon had a similar effect, though less intense,

* I have been unable to trace the original of this quotation, which is given in Jastrow, "The House that Freud Built", p. 99.
† Quoted from Jastrow, "The House that Freud Built", p. 100.

so had birds, animals and trees. All seemed to be instinct with spiritual life and power.

I can still remember vividly a delusion which attacked me when sawing firewood in the woodshed of my home during recovery from a severe attack of depression. It seemed to me that I was cutting up the god Pan, who could eventually wreak a terrible vengeance upon me for my impiety. The wood appeared to take on strange shapes as of satyrs and fauns, and sometimes of snakes and other horrors. What connection there may be between Pan and snakes I do not know, unless it is the association of Pan with the Christian devil and hence with the Serpent in the Garden of Eden. But according to Sir James Frazer, Pan, like other goat-gods such as Dionysus, as well as Silenus and the satyrs, is undoubtedly a woodland deity, and he was called by the Arcadians Lord of the Wood.*

As far as I know I had at that time no knowledge of any association between Pan and wood, though it is of course difficult to be sure. But that does not affect the basic argument that primitive feelings have worn as it were deep grooves in the Unconscious, which manifest themselves plainly during periods of insanity or abnormality. As well as the anthropomorphic impulses I have described, I experienced other feelings which appear equally to be of primitive origin.

One of the most widespread of savage beliefs is that in sympathetic magic or "mana", to use the term discovered by Codrington in his study of the Melanesians. Mana is conceived as an abstract force pervading the whole universe, the motive-power of all things, strengthening their mechanical action without destroying it. By using this force, the savage believes it possible to influence the course of nature to an almost unlimited extent, without the intervention of any spiritual or personal agency. He feels that it is possible to attune himself so delicately to the harmony of the world that a touch of his hand or a turn of his head may send a thrill vibrating through the universal framework of things. Thus

* "The Golden Bough", Chap. III, Section 10.

he can attain to the divine powers so frequently attributed to man-gods in primitive societies.*

I can testify from experience that these are the actual sensations accompanying the delusions of power so common in asylums. The sense of being intimately in tune with the ultimate stuff of the universe can become so overwhelming that those affected naturally proclaim themselves to be Jesus Christ, or Almighty God, or whatever deity they have been taught to look on as the source of all power. In my own case I was fully convinced of my supernatural powers, and attempted to test them in various ways, mainly by somewhat childish experiments in sympathetic magic reminiscent of the instances in the *Golden Bough*. For example, I made life-sized dolls to represent a doctor I disliked and endeavoured to use them to bewitch him in various ways. Again, during a period of depression I evolved a complicated series of superstitions based to some extent on the principles of mana, and I was convinced that only the strictest adherence to the resulting rituals enabled me to survive.

If abnormal mental states thus reveal primitive ideas beneath the surface of ordinary consciousness, it is surely not unreasonable to suppose that they must also give some indication of the primitive feelings bound up with those ideas, which may in fact have given rise to them. In other words, the sensations which accompany some forms of insanity may well be a genuine return, though perhaps in a distorted form, to earlier types of consciousness. The lunatic may really feel something of what his remote ancestors felt as they surveyed their world. This would include the consciousness appropriate to animals, and may indeed have something to do with the type of delusion in which the patient imagines himself to be an animal. I have noticed a marked atavistic tendency of this kind in myself, particularly during periods of extreme manic excitement. The sensation is difficult to analyse, but its chief characteristic is a vastly increased suppleness which to me seems reminiscent of the cat tribe.

* Cf. Frazer, op. cit., Chap. I, Section 2.

The words "instinctive" or "instinct" are today out of favour with psychologists, as not being susceptible of clear definition. None the less, primitive or atavistic sensations of this kind can reasonably be classified as instinctive as opposed to rational, in the sense in which the terms are used in common speech. Perhaps the greatest prophet of instinct as a means for the understanding of life was Henri Bergson. In his principal work, *Creative Evolution*, he suggests that if instinct were only articulate, if we could ask it and it could reply, it would give up to us the most intimate secrets of the universe. Many instinctive forms of consciousness have been produced on other lines of evolution than that which ends in man. If only those other forms of consciousness could be brought together and amalgamated with intellect, the completed result might be a consciousness as wide as life itself. Such a consciousness, says Bergson in an unforgettable passage, "turning around suddenly against the push of life which it feels behind, would have a vision of life complete— would it not?—even though the vision were fleeting".*

To suggest that the abnormal consciousness of insanity may in some degree be of this nature will perhaps seem a large claim. Bergson's view of the importance of instinct is by no means universally accepted, and there are many thinkers who, like Bertrand Russell, exalt reason, intellect and logic above intuition or instinct as sources of truth. But even Russell admits that intuitive apprehension, views based on instinctive feelings about the world, may have a certain validity, and he shows how such feelings form the real basis of the systems of mystical metaphysicians from Parmenides and Plato to Hegel.†

One of the most striking features of the views which impelled themselves upon me in the course of my illness is their similarity to those professed by mystics of all ages and peoples. In later chapters I shall give more precise details of the analogies between my experience of a recognised form of

* Bergson, "Creative Evolution", Introduction, p. xii.
† Bertrand Russell, "Mysticism and Logic and other Essays".

insanity and mystical or religious experiences of various kinds, as well as the differences which seem to distinguish them. At this point I only want to show that the similarity irresistibly suggests a common origin.

The mystic insight seems generally to begin with a sense of a mystery unveiled, of a hidden wisdom now suddenly become certain beyond the possibility of a doubt. Its second characteristic is a belief in the unity of all things, in that reconciliation of opposites mentioned by James in connection with the anaesthetic revelation. Other features closely related to these two are a tendency to deny the reality of Time and also to believe that all evil is mere appearance.* All these features were strongly marked in the manic phases of my illness, while in the opposite or depressive phases they were to some extent reversed. The most marked was the sense of the unity of all things, including myself as part of the whole, coupled with an inner certainty that good and evil, if not identical, would at any rate ultimately be reconciled.

This sense of oneness has never really left me. The attempt to analyse it, to trace it to its source, to grasp its meaning, is the underlying motive of this book. In admitting this, I know that I am laying all that I write open to the criticism that is, in the useful term of the psychologists, a mere "rationalisation". It can be said that I am simply finding reasons for what I believe, or what I want to believe.

Yet I am at any rate in good company; for the same objection can be raised against all those, including some of the greatest thinkers who have ever lived, who have been influenced by the mystical intuition. Plato, Spinoza, Regel, Emerson, poets such as Blake, Shelley, Wordsworth and, above all, Goethe; all trace the deepest springs of their thought to mysticism in one form or another. Even science seems to bear its debt to mysticism; Mr Will Spens in his "Belief and Practice" argues forcibly that the appeal to in-

* Cf. Bertrand Russell, op. cit., pp. 8–11.
N.B. This is not always the case, sometimes in manic phases I have a strong consciousness of evil, but I always feel that an opposition is necessary (cf. Chap. IV).

tuition in the development of doctrine from mystical religious experience is justified by the proved success of the same appeal to intuition in the development of scientific doctrine from scientific data.

It is, I think, arguable that "rationalisation" is one of the principal methods by which the human mind works, and one productive of results if logically and conscientiously pursued. In other words there is little objection to intuitively or instinctively feeling the truth of a theory or system of thought and then setting out to prove it, provided that facts are not distorted to fit the theory. The objection becomes even less valid if the original springs are frankly admitted. And in my own case I can perhaps claim that frankness could go no further than to show how my ideas, for what they are worth, are derived from a period of what is technically known as insanity.

3. *Origins of Mystical Intuition*

What is the origin of the fundamental mystic sense of unity with the all? To answer that question with any degree of certainty would probably be to find the secret of life. Perhaps, as Bergson suggests, the instincts would tell us if we could ask them. Psychology may hold that key, but of all the sciences it is the least developed, and has the smallest common denominator of doctrine.

The Freudian explanation is typical of the school. Freud traces the sense to the original inability of the infant to distinguish between himself and external objects.* Thus the ego originally includes everything; only little by little does it detach the external world from itself. That original feeling is not only far more extensive than the shrunken, limited ego-feeling of the adult human being; it embraces the whole universe, and also includes a sense of unlimited power. In the womb, after all, all wishes are automatically fulfilled, and the child must feel itself more at one with the universe than it ever does in later life. Thus when a friend adduces the

* Cf. "Civilisation and its Discontents".

mystic feeling, described as "limitless, unbounded, something 'oceanic'," in support of his own religious beliefs, Freud explains this away in conformity with his general theory, as a manifestation of the infanticism from which he maintains all religion to be derived.

I suppose the fact that I experienced this sense of oneness most strongly during a period of insanity, which is generally recognised as involving a measure of regression to the infantile, goes to support the Freudian view. As we have seen, however, my abnormal state seems also to have consisted in regression to the primitive in the manner emphasised by Jung. And the particular sense of oneness can, I think, be shown to have a primitive derivation as well as an infantile one.

I have already touched on the two great primitive trends revealed by anthropology; the anthropomorphic view of the world as ruled by personal spiritual forces and the magical view of it as pervaded and controlled by the impersonal mystical force of "mana", with which man can be intimately in touch. These trends are clearly distinguished by Frazer, who sees in sympathetic magic a germ of the modern notion of natural law, or the view of nature as a series of events occurring in an invariable order without the intervention of personal agency; alchemy, as he says, leads to chemistry.*

It is not difficult to see how the anthropomorphic view arose. The savage, ignorant of the nature of the phenomena which surround him, would naturally tend to attribute them to the capricious will of beings like himself, and to make gods in his own image alternatively generous and benevolent or vindictive and passionate as he is himself. This is a simple process of analogy, though I shall later argue that it also has a deeper ground. No such logical process, however, can be traced in the origin of magic. Frazer associates magic with a feeling of attunement to the harmony of the world, as we have seen, and asserts that there is hardly a savage who does not fancy himself possessed of this power of influencing the

* "The Golden Bough", Chap. I, Section 2.

course of nature. Truly the most reasonable explanation of a view so manifestly in opposition to the actual facts of primitive life, "nasty, brutish and short", surrounded by innumerable dangers, is that it really corresponds to primitive feelings. In other words, primitive man experiences the Universe as something so intimately and vitally connected with him that he is convinced of his ability to influence it. This may be, indeed, some compensation for the brevity and "brutishness" of his life.

According to the great anthropologist R. R. Marett, savages are distinguished from civilised man above all by a greater "sense of the altogether". Of the two main methods by which the human mind functions, reflection or "discursive apprehension" on the one hand, and intuition or "massive apprehension" on the other, the primitive mind relies chiefly on intuition. It tends to grasp things wholesale instead of bit by bit. The savage, too, has a greater sense of sympathy and communion with others than has civilised man, a sense which runs right through his religious and magical beliefs,* and extends, too, to his relations with animals and the whole world of nature.

The fact that both these features, the intuitive or "synthetic" mode of thought as opposed to the analytical methods of civilised man, and the sense of communion with others and with nature, are equally characteristic of the mystical insight, can scarcely be fortuitous. It is a reasonable assumption that they can be traced to the same origins in primitive being, that they are in fact a regression to the primitive in the same way as are the abnormal experiences of which I am writing.

There is of course no contradiction between this view and the Freudian theory of infantile origin set out above. Not only the psycho-analytical schools, but the majority of psychologists outside them, are agreed in recognising the analogies between the development of the individual and that of the race—ontogenesis and phylogenesis. Just as in the

* Cf. Marett's article on "Psychology and Anthropology", in "Psychology and the Sciences", edited by William Brown.

physical sphere the human embryo compasses untold centuries of development into a few months, starting as a speck of protoplasm and climbing the ladder from invertebrate to vertebrate, doubtful at one moment whether to become a bird or a fish, before finally emerging as a mammal, so in the mental sphere the soul of the child seems to follow the path traced by his ancestors. He starts as a purely instinctive creature of a few urgent impulses and needs, with their corresponding sensations, and gradually puts on, partly as a result of environment and partly of development, the complicated psychological apparatus of modern civilised man.

Supposing we go the whole way with Freud and admit that the mystical intuition reaches back to buried memories of the time when we could not distinguish between ourselves and the cosmos, when all our wants were instantly and automatically supplied as are those of the foetus in the womb. The fact that this intuition is stronger in primitive than in civilised man would then be due presumably to being closer to this primal state, to having a less complicated psychical evolution separating the infant from the adult savage. Would this admission be tantamount to denying all validity to the intuition, or even to diminishing its importance?

"Except ye become as a little child ye shall in no wise enter into the Kingdom of Heaven." In tracing manifestations of mysticism and religion to infantile origins, does Freud go any further than Jesus Christ went nearly two thousand years ago? In deriving the idea of God from the adult's yearning for the parental care and protection he enjoyed in childhood, as Freud did in *The Future of an Illusion*, he merely underlines the psychological truth of Our Lord's favourite metaphor of the Fatherhood of God.

Perhaps the real illusion is that of those psychologists who imagine that when they have traced any particular religious manifestation or belief to "natural" psychological causes they have disproved and disposed of it for good. After all, if we find that God works in accordance with law in the physical world, we may surely expect to find a similar state of affairs in the mental world.

Any true view of life must take it as a whole. The parental relation is one of the most fundamental features of life. So is the fact that we all develop as individuals from an original state of non-individuality, when we were one with our parents and through them with life as a whole. Bergson has a conception which he calls the "continuity of genetic energy".* He compares life to a current passing from germ to germ through the medium of the developed organism. "It is as though the organism itself were only an excrescence, a bud caused to sprout by the former germ endeavouring to continue itself as a new germ." We are as it were off-shoots of an eternal Tree of Life, and if the psychologists tell us that our ideas of a future Heaven and a Paradise lost in the past are regressive yearnings for the peace of the womb, what is that but to say that a part of our nature harks back to that unity with the cell from which we developed?

The nearer the organism is to the germ-cell, the conductor of the current of life, the purer its impulses are likely to be. If Freud, referring to infantile sexual manifestations, calls a small child "a polymorphous pervert", it does not make it any the less innocent, with the innocence of life itself. Here are the primal instincts and impulses, the very stuff of existence, unadulterated and undistorted by the complications of later development. That the abnormal conditions through which I have passed show these instincts and impulses similarly undistorted, and illustrated with the developed fantasies of an adult mind, is my main justification for writing this book. In later chapters, therefore, I shall endeavour to give a more detailed picture of my condition, and in particular of the strange phantasies to which it gave rise.

* "Creative Evolution", p. 28.

CHAPTER II

UNIVERSE OF BLISS

1. *The Great Divide*

THE MENTAL disease to which I am subject is, as I have said, known as manic-depression, or, more accurately, as Manic-depressive Psychosis. As its name implies, it consists typically of alternating phases or states of mania on the one hand and depression on the other. The manic state is one of elation, of pleasurable excitement sometimes attaining to an extreme pitch of ecstasy; the depressive state is its precise opposite, one of misery, dejection, and at times of appalling horror. These states are generally, as in my own case, interspersed by periods of more or less complete normality.

For the benefit of any serious students of psychology and members of the medical profession who may read this book, I give below in tabular form the principal phases of my illness with the relevant dates. I was born in 1900, so that my age at the time of the attacks is easy to calculate.

Manic	Depressive
May 1936–Nov. 1936	Sept. 1935–March 1936
Nov. 1938–April 1939	Dec. 1936–Aug. 1937
Oct. 1944–March 1945	May 1939–Aug. 1940
Feb. 1947–April 1947	⎰Occasional minor depressive
Aug. 1947–Oct. 1947	⎱fits, but nothing serious or
Oct. 1949–April 1950	"abnormal"

In some degree, of course, this dualism is an everyday experience. We all know the type of individual who is "up in the air" at one time and "down in the dumps" at another. Psychologists call this kind of temperament "cyclothymic"; it is quite common, and only when there is serious nervous disturbance does it lead to true manic-depressive psychosis. When elated, either for genuine reasons to be found in external circumstances, or sometimes for no apparent reason at all, the subject sees the world through rose-coloured spectacles. He feels particularly fit; his reactions to his environment are rapid and well-defined; he has an inner certainty that he will succeed in any plans he may have formed in embryo in his mind; the world, in fact, is his oyster. When depressed, on the other hand, he feels more or less ill; he looks on the black side of everything; he is convinced he will fail in anything he undertakes; he is uncertain and doubtful, particularly about himself; he cannot concentrate properly; his reactions are slow, though often his mind is revolving very rapidly about his own troubles and fears.

When the nervous system is thoroughly deranged, the two contrasting states of mind can be almost infinitely intensified. It sometimes seems to me as though my condition had been specially devised by Providence to illustrate the Christian concepts of Heaven and Hell. Certainly it has shown me that within my own soul there are possibilities of an inner peace and happiness beyond description, as well as of inconceivable depths of terror and despair. Normal life and consciousness of "reality" appear to me rather like motion along a narrow strip of table-land at the top of a Great Divide separating two distinct universes from each other. On the one hand the slope is green and fertile, leading to a lovely landscape where love, joy and the infinite beauties of nature and of dreams await the traveller; on the other a barren, rocky declivity, where lurk endless horrors of distorted imagination, descends to the bottomless pit.

In the condition of manic-depression, this table-land is so narrow that it is exceedingly difficult to keep on it. One begins to slip; the world about one changes imperceptibly. For a time it is possible to keep some sort of grip on reality. But once one is really over the edge, once the grip of reality is lost, the forces of the Unconscious take charge, and then begins what appears to be an unending voyage into the universe of bliss or the universe of horror as the case may be, a voyage over which one has oneself no control whatever. The purpose of this and the following chapter is to describe as accurately as possible these two universes, and the states of consciousness associated with them.

2. *Geography of Sensation*

All that follows in this chapter, describing the manic state, was actually written (subject to minor revisions) while in that state. I am at the moment in a typical state of hypo-mania, and am a patient in a Mental Hospital. One result of my condition is that I am writing with far greater ease than in normal circumstances. Usually I am a very slow-brained writer, whereas now my pen can scarcely keep up with the rapid flow of ideas. It is thus obviously a good opportunity to describe as it were at first hand the symptoms and sensations of the manic state.

First and foremost comes a general sense of intense well-being. I know of course that this sense is illusory and transient, and that my behaviour while it persists is so abnormal that I have to be confined, so that a good deal of the gilt is taken off the gingerbread. It is only when I have been free in the manic state that the ecstatic sensations accompanying it have their full effect, but they are apt to produce dire results in the real world, as will be seen. Although, however, the restrictions of confinement are apt at times to produce extreme irritation and even paroxysms of anger, the general sense of well-being, the pleasurable and sometimes ecstatic feeling-tone, remains as a sort of permanent background of all experience during the manic period.

Closely allied with this permanent background is the second main feature of the manic state, which has been well described, notably by Henderson and Gillespie, as a "heightened sense of reality".* This phenomenon gave rise to some very interesting observations and suggestions in the Bampton Lectures by Professor L. W. Grensted, D.D., of Oriel College, Oxford.† He relates it to the similar states of consciousness described by various mystics, notably St Theresa.

* Grensted, "Psychology and God", pp. 221 ff.
† "Textbook of Psychiatry", by Henderson and Gillespie, pp. 543 ff.

If I am to judge by my own experience, this "heightened sense of reality" consists of a considerable number of related sensations, the net result of which is that the outer world makes a much more vivid and intense impression on me than usual. I will try to set them down systematically, starting with what I can actually observe in myself at the present moment.

I. *Intensified Visual Impressions.*

The first thing I note is the peculiar appearances of the lights—the ordinary electric lights in the ward. They are not exactly brighter, but deeper, more intense, perhaps a trifle more ruddy than usual. Moreover, if I relax the focusing of my eyes, which I can do very much more easily than in normal circumstances, a bright starlike phenomenon emanates from the lights, ultimately forming a maze of iridescent patterns of all colours of the rainbow, which remind me vaguely of the Aurora Borealis.*

There are a good many people in the ward, and their faces make a peculiarly intense impression on me. I will not say that they have exactly a halo round them, though I have often had that impression in more acute phases of mania. At present it is rather that faces seem to glow with a sort of inner light which shows up the characteristic lines extremely vividly. Thus, although I am the most hopeless draughtsman as a rule, in this state I can draw quite recognisable likenesses. This phenomenon is not confined to faces; it applies to the human body as a whole, and to a rather lesser degree to other objects such as trees, clouds, flowers and so on. Coloured objects make a particularly vivid impression, possibly in view of the associations they arouse (see below) and, curiously enough, so do large vehicles, particularly steamrollers, railway engines and trains. Perhaps the associations of childhood are involved here. Connected with these vivid impressions is a rather curious feeling behind the eyeballs, rather as though a vast electric motor were pulsing away there.

* I find that this is to a certain extent possible in normal circumstances, but the phenomenon is far more intense in mania.

II. *Other Sense-impressions.*

All my other senses seem more acute than usual. Certainly my sense of touch is heightened; my fingers are much more sensitive and neat. Although generally a clumsy person with an execrable handwriting I can write much more neatly than usual; I can print, draw, embellish and carry out all sorts of little manual operations, such as pasting up scrap-books and the like, which would normally drive me to distraction. I also note a peculiar tingling in my finger-tips.

My hearing appears to be more sensitive, and I am able to take in without disturbance or distraction many different sound-impressions at the same time. Thus, although busily engaged in writing this in a crowded ward with people walking up and down and the most diverse sounds all around me, from the cries of gulls outside to the laughter and chatter of my fellow-patients, I am fully alive to what is going on and yet find no difficulty in concentrating on my work. At times I have known sounds make a tremendous effect upon me, almost as though I were in a gallery with supernatural powers of resonance. At such times my own very ordinary bass voice appears to be as powerful as that of Chaliapin's at least; it is as though passages in my chest which are normally clogged were opened up, and my chest actually seems to set up abnormal vibrations.

At the moment my sense of smell seems more or less normal, and so does my sense of taste. In slightly more acute phases of mania, however, both these senses are well above par. Even now I have no doubt that if I were to be allowed to walk about freely in a flower garden I should appreciate the scents far more than usual; and I have often in manic states eaten ordinary cabbage leaves or new Brussels sprouts picked straight off the plants with such relish that they appeared to me the greatest delicacies—a kind of manna from Heaven. Even common grass tastes excellent, while real delicacies like strawberries or raspberries give ecstatic sensations appropriate to a veritable food of the gods.

III. *Abnormal Association of Ideas.*

Some other abnormal features in my condition can I think be directly related to the intensified sense-impressions mentioned above, and so can properly be classified under "heightened sense of reality". One of these is extreme rapidity of association of ideas. Since it is largely through the association of ideas that we take in the sense-impressions of the world around us, it would seem to be quite logical that intensified sense-impressions should be connected with a freer functioning of that particular faculty. Let me try to give an example.

As I sit here, looking out of the window of the ward, I see flocks of seagulls who have been driven inland by the extreme cold. The mere sight of these seagulls sets up immediately and virtually simultaneously in my mind the following trains of thoughts:—

1. A pond called Seagull's Spring near my home.
2. Mermaids, i.e. "Sea girls", sirens, Lorelei, Mother Seager's syrup, syrup of figs, the blasted fig-tree in the Gospels, Professor Joad who could not accept Jesus as the supremely perfect Man owing to particular incident.* Here the chain stops as I cannot remember the exact title of Joad's book, which was a confession of the failure of his agnosticism.
3. The Mental Hospital where I spent nearly a year during my worst attack of suicidal depression. The weather that winter was also very cold, and quantities of seagulls came into the courts of the hospital. At that time I was suffering from the delusion that I was a supremely evil person who had sold his soul to Satan, and the gulls terrified me for two reasons: firstly because I thought of myself as a sort of super-gull who had been "gulled" into selling his soul; and secondly because I thought I was responsible for all the death and evil in the world and that the spirits of all the lost seamen since

* Professor Joad, "God and Evil".

the world began were in those gulls calling for vengeance on me.

It is interesting to note that both in manic and in depressive periods of sufficient intensity animistic conceptions of this kind impel themselves forcibly upon me; I cannot avoid seeing spirits in everything.

4. Gulls equals girls, lovely girls, lovelies, film-stars, countless stars in the infinite wastes of space, query: is space really infinite? According to Einstein it is not; it is a sort of finite infinity best represented by a multi-dimensional sphere which it is theoretically possible to circumnavigate. Einstein has always had a peculiar fascination for me, but it is only in manic periods that I imagine that I can really understand him. No doubt it is pure delusion. My mind is filled with fantastic ideas revolving about Time and its associations, and in particular about the Wellsian concept of a Time Machine. Time seems to be as it were fluid and relative so that it must be possible to move about in it. The "space-time continuum" has a peculiarly vivid reality for me; I actually see it as a kind of endless band. Einstein's principle that all in the continuum must be relative to an observer situated at a given place and proceeding at a given speed in a given direction fits in very well, since it emphasises the essential connection between the human factor and the physical world, life and matter. On occasion I have had actual visions of a Time Machine, a horrible mechanism which would only work by utilising the psychic energy and contacts of a live human being, who in the process was put through infinite tortures. I was convinced that evil men were making or could in the course of time make such a machine. I can see it now as I saw it first, reflected as an "illusion" from the wall of my room, distorting the face and body of its victim in the most horrible manner conceivable. It was surmounted by a huge clock.

That will serve, I think, as a fair example of the associations and trains of thought aroused by the sight of those seagulls. It is quite reasonable that objects which can through the psycho-physical mechanism of the human body awaken such numerous and vivid associations should also make intense impressions on the retina.

Another good example of the arousing of associations by objects in the outer world is the effect of colours. The windows of my side-room look out on to a road much frequented by the female patients of the Hospital. They affect rather gay attire, and the colours are sometimes a little overpowering. During the last few days those colours have seemed to be threatening me in an extraordinary way, perhaps because there was an underlying possibility of a swift change from mania to depression. At one time green and red predominated. There was a time when I was terrified of green, because it was the signal to go, and the only place I thought I could be going to was Hell. However I eventually got out of Hell and at present green has no terrors for me. It is my wife's favourite colour—she does not think it unlucky; and it stands for grass and growth.

In combination with red, however, it does not seem so favourable. Red is the Devil's colour, and perhaps I am not quite safe from him yet. Red also means stop, and I don't in the least want to stop here for ever. However, with a certain amount of effort, concentration and prayer, I conquered the red with the help of the green and felt safe.

The next day the colours had suffered a kaleidoscopic change. Gone were the reds and the greens; there were nothing but blues, blacks and greys, with an occasional purple. The sky, which had been bright and clear, was overcast; it was raining. This new combination of colours constituted a new threat, with which I had to deal.

Blue was the heavenly colour; I was in Heaven, so that blue was appropriate and could be regarded as on my side. Black, on the other hand, was another of the Devil's colours. Was he going to get me after all? What had grey to say about it? At night all cats are grey, so perhaps grey was a feline colour. I like the cat tribe, particularly when in the manic state. They are, I know, slightly Satanic, but it is the kind of Satanism I prefer; it reminds me of a favourite delusion—that I am Satan, the Servant of All, the Scientific Snake who told the truth in the Garden of Eden (as Bernard Shaw pointed out in *Man and Superman*). So I need not fear the Devil or his sable colour. As for the purple, well in those circumstances I could reasonably look upon it as the imperial purple, a sign that I was Emperor of colours, if of nothing else. I asked the spirit of Julius Caesar by the simple process of tossing a coin with the image and superscription of his successor, King George. Julius was good enough to give me confirmation. The coin fell heads. Upon this I took a sheet of lavatory paper and printed in large letters

I HAVE MADE A CORNER IN COLOURS 8.3.47.

This document I showed with pride to the doctor when he came to see me on his rounds. Greatly to his credit he took me very seriously indeed. After all, an Emperor of Colours should be treated with respect!

With rapid association of ideas is involved abnormal suggestibility. I am so sensitive to the manifold suggestions conveyed by my environment that I seem to be in a perpetual state of what the Oxford Groupists call "guidance". I can look at nothing without receiving some idea from it leading to an impulse to action. This works in curious ways. For example, the sight of the inkpot in front of me does not suggest that I should go on dipping my pen in it and writing, but rather that I should go to the lavatory. The suggestion worked via the letters of the word "inkpot". I saw them visually in front of me in capitals INK POT, which in its turn suggested the lavatory.

That concludes, I think, the list of sensations and reactions which can properly be classified under "heightened sense of reality". I come now to the third main feature of the manic state. It is difficult to know just how to designate it, though it is obviously closely allied with the first two features. Perhaps it can best be described as a "breach in the barriers of individuality". What Professor Grensted has called, if I remember rightly, the "sense of estrangement, fencing in a narrowly limited ego" disappears altogether. The shell which surrounds the ego and so often gets harder with the years is pierced. The experience partakes of the nature of the goodfellowship produced by alcohol; it also constitutes in some degree a regression to a childish faith and confidence in the benevolence, the "akinness" of the surrounding world. The best description I know of it is in some lines of Walt Whitman's:—

> "Swiftly arose and spread around me the peace
>   and knowledge that pass all the argument of the earth,
> And I know that the hand of God is the promise of my own,
> And I know that the spirit of God is the brother of my own,
> And that all the men ever born are also my brothers,
>   and the women my sisters and lovers,
> And that a kelson of the creation is love."

It is actually a sense of communion, in the first place with God, and in the second place with all mankind, indeed with all creation. It is obviously related to the mystic sense of unity with the All, to which reference was made in Chapter I; in fact it is probably the same sense.

A feeling of intimate personal relationship with God is perhaps its paramount feature. The sun is shining on the paper as I write, and it suggests to me at once that the *Sun* of Righteousness, which is also the Son of God, is watching and helping me. The sun suggests, as it has in fact often suggested to me before when I was in a manic phase, an intense sense of the immediate presence of God, in the person of Jesus. I feel that I talk to Him and He talks to me without the slightest difficulty. St Theresa describes a similar state of mind in "The Interior Castle"; she even admits that she ventures on occasion to argue with God. I am an argumentative person, and I fear I sometimes do the same. In fact I have at the back of my mind the idea that the Almighty prefers people now and then to argue and even wrestle with Him, like Jacob in the

Old Testament,* to being surrounded with Yes-men like a dictator.

The association of God with the sun is of course an ancient image, and the strength with which it forces itself upon my consciousness might seem to bear out Jung's theories of a "Collective Unconscious". The moon has almost equally powerful associations, but here there is a strong suggestion that a female power is involved, which generally appears to me as Diana, Goddess of the Ephesians, or Ashtaroth, consort of Baal. In the state of consciousness I am trying to describe it seems quite plain that there is no ultimate antagonism between the Christian God and heathen gods and goddesses, all of whom seem vividly real to me. The All is utterly reconciled, as it were, and in particular the antithesis God–Nature, or Spirit–Flesh, which has played so large a part in the Christian and many other religions.† This passing beyond antithesis, this resolution of the opposites, is obviously linked with the sense of communion, and I shall have more to say about it later.

As Whitman's poem shows, the sense of communion extends to all mankind, dead, living and to be born. That is perhaps why mania always brings me an inner certainty that the dead are really alive and that I can commune with them at will. This seems to be quite common among manic-depressive patients; only the other day one said to me that he could converse with "any old spirit". I hold imaginary conversations—which appear absolutely real to me—with all my favourite historical characters, notably anima-figures (in Jung's sense) like Cleopatra and Mary Magdalene. These figures actually appear to me in visions, and so do my own ancestors, in whom I take far more interest when in the manic state than at any other time. Close relations and friends who have died seem of course particularly near.

At times this system of ideas attains such force that a sort of resurrection by reincarnation appears to be happening all

* Genesis 32, 24.
† Cf. the experiences of William James under nitrous oxide, Chap. I.

around me. To meet a person and say a few words to him or her is quite sufficient to awaken in me a suggestion amounting to a certainty that such and such a spirit is talking to me. Only a few minutes ago, for example, I was in the ward talking to a new patient, an American citizen. I immediately associated him with Abe Lincoln and asked him if he was Abe come back to life again. His reply was: "Waal, I could be; in fact I have a hunch that I am". In the ward I have also Voltaire, Frederick the Great, Julius Caesar, Goethe, Thomas Hardy, Plato, Nietzsche and St Paul, not to mention some of my own ancestors, relations and friends.

I am not going to suggest that this is anything but a delusionary system of ideas, real though it appears to me. Certainly Abraham Lincoln does not appear to know as much about the Civil War as I do; I have just been trying him out. No doubt the whole concept is merely a rationalisation of the breaking-down of barriers, the sense of intimate communion to which I have referred, and strongly influenced by delusions of grandeur; it will be noted that my resurrected characters are mostly V.I.P's. But that does not detract from the importance of the sense of communion itself.

Although this sense is of course purely subjective, I have on occasion noticed a curious sympathy between my own mind and those of others in an excited mental state. This may largely be due to vanity or abnormal suggestibility; it is remarkable how often my fellow-patients (like Abe) agree with my delusions about them, but no doubt they like the idea of being V.I.P's come to life. There have been times, however, when other patients have said things to me without any prompting which corresponded in a very remarkable way with what was in my own mind at the time, as though some sort of telepathy was involved. One of the best instances which occurs to me was during my last manic period. I was overwhelmed at the time with delusions of grandeur, and dreamt one night that I had won a great prize for which the whole world had competed. When I woke up, St Paul's words were running in my head: "They that run in a race run all, but one receiveth the prize", and a flight of ideas on these lines took as it were possession of me. Almost the first patient I met that morning was another manic-depressive who said to me: "You have won the great prize, you know, what are you going to do with it?" My memory of the incident is quite clear, and I am quite certain that I made no suggestion to the patient in question; in fact he made the remark before I had even spoken to him. That telepathy is possible and works through the Unconscious is increasingly recognised by psychologists, so a tendency towards telepathic communion between those who owing to abnormal mental conditions are under the dominion of the Unconscious is presumably to be expected.* Whether any experiments with mental patients have been conducted on these lines I do not know, but it might be a fruitful field. I would emphasise that the instance I have quoted is only one among many. The remark of my fellow patient did not surprise me in the least, though the first time I had an experience of the kind it produced extreme excitement, since it seemed to confirm my ideas.

The sense of communion extends to all fellow-creatures with whom I come into contact; it is not merely ideal or imaginative but has a practical effect on my conduct. Thus when in the manic state I have no objection to being more or less herded together—as is inevitable in public Mental Hospitals—with men of all classes and conditions. Class barriers cease to have any existence or meaning. Sometimes, it is true, I get cross with one or the other of my fellow-patients, but I find no difficulty in making up the quarrel almost at once. I seem to be filled with a sense of universal benevolence and constantly bear in mind the text "Love your enemies". I take particular pleasure in actual physical contact with my fellows, such as a sentimental holding of hands. This attitude of mind has been noted by psychiatrists in connection with manic-depressive patients, though I cannot at the moment remember the instances.

William James in *Varieties of Religious Experience* calls

* Cf. in particular Hans Driesch, "The Crisis in Psychology".

this sense "the inhibition of instinctive repugnance", and maintains that if it could only become widespread in humanity it would alter the whole basis of human relations. It is not inconceivable, he suggests, that the precept "Love your enemies" could become a reality. The fact that the possibility is rooted in certain instincts is shown in particular by the experience of saints who have not only shown love towards enemies, but to those who are personally loathsome, and he instances particularly in this connection the action of St Francis in kissing the sores of lepers.

In the manic state action of this kind is in no way repugnant to me; in fact my impulses are undoubtedly in this direction. In the course of my illness I have been brought into contact with mental cases whom I should normally regard with extreme repulsion, but I actually like being with them and have felt impelled to do them little services, or to offer to help the attendants to handle them.

The inhibition of the sense of repulsion extends to all objects which would normally provoke repulsion, and constitutes in fact the fourth peculiar and distinctive feature of the manic state. Like all these features it is precisely the opposite of what occurs in the depressive state, and it can best be described by emphasising the contrast.

This contrast has just been brought forcibly to my mind by the fact that I had to go to the lavatory, and when I returned brought back the association or suggestion of Hell. This association is one I have had on innumerable occasions since it first appeared when I was suffering from the intense terror of eternal punishment which will be described in the next chapter. I saw Hell, with a sort of hallucinatory vividness, as a universal lavatory where evil men such as I felt I was disappeared for ever. All medical men with experience of mental institutions know that the association is a common one. It is also a not uncommon delusion among the insane that in the act of excretion they are actually getting rid of a person or persons they dislike. When I was last here, about two years ago, a certain patient kept repeating, every time he went to the lavatory, that he was excreting (he used a shorter word) Hitler into Hell. Since in periods of extreme depression I looked upon myself as the person to be got rid of and had an intense repulsion towards myself, there was a certain logic in my repulsion to excretion.

There seems to me, however, to be very much more in this whole question than the facile logic of insane conditions, and readers will, I hope, forgive me if I deal with it at some length.

When in a depressive period I have an intense sense of repulsion to lavatories, excreta, urine, or anything associated with them. This repulsion extends to all kinds of dirt. I loathe going to the lavatory, using a chamber-pot, or touching anything in the least bit dirty. With this repulsion is associated extreme terror, in my case terror of eternal punishment in Hell. It is also associated with repulsion to fellow-creatures, repulsion to self, repulsion in fact to the whole universe. Finally it is associated with a sense of intense guilt.

In the manic phase repulsion gives place to attraction. I have no repulsion to excreta, urine and so on. I have no distaste for dirt. I do not care in the least whether I am washed or not, whereas I am terrified of the slightest speck of dirt and continually wash my hands like Lady Macbeth when in a state of depression. At the same time I feel a mystic sense of unity with all fellow-creatures and the Universe as a whole; I am at peace with myself; and I have no sense of guilt whatsoever.

This set of associations must, it seems to me, represent something quite fundamental, particularly when it is considered in connection with religious experience like that of St Francis with his lepers. When in a state of acute mania it would give me the greatest pleasure to do the same. A good many well-known saints and mystics have acted in a similar manner.

I sincerely hope no one will misunderstand me. I am very far indeed from being a saint or claiming to be one, as everybody who knows me will admit. But there are undoubtedly parallels between the mental and physical condition of the mystics at certain times in their lives and that of ordinary people suffering from mental abnormalities. Even Baron von Hügel, who puts mystics, and particularly his favourite Catherine of Genoa, on a very high pedestal indeed, admits this; and modern psychology takes it for granted.

There is surely no reason to doubt that the state of attraction towards dirt and excreta found in mania must be in some way analogous to the same state when experienced by saints, anchorites, hermits, etc. Now not only do the saints commonly recognised as mystics seem for the most part to have experienced something of the kind, but we have here an intelligible and reasonable explanation of the otherwise incomprehensible and absurd behaviour of a large class of persons thrown up by the Christian Church in the fourth and fifth centuries A.D. I refer to the anchorites and hermits of the Desert and in particular to people like St Simon Stylites. St Simon spent about twenty years on a pillar in the desert wallowing in his own excrement. At that time he was regarded as a most holy person, presumably because he was supposed to be mortifying his flesh. I suggest, with all due respect, that St Simon was rather a fraud. He stayed on his pillar in his own filth because he liked it; in fact I can conceive of doing the same thing myself if that particular state of mind were to last twenty years with me.

Now here I have no choice but to continue the argument on a personal note. It is, as I have explained, an invariable rule that this state of attraction to dirt is associated with an intense sense of intimate relationship with God; indeed with a feeling of being virtually in the Kingdom of Heaven. No doubt St Simon Stylites felt much the same, as did other saints and mystics who had the same experience. Conversely, abnormal repulsion to dirt is associated in my case with the feeling of being infinitely far from God; indeed of being actually in Hell. It would in fact seem that the old adage "Cleanliness is next to Godliness" should be reversed to make it conform to psychological truth.

In another sense, however, it is profoundly true. Lady

Macbeth is typical. The sense of guilt has from time imme-
morial been associated with a desire to be "clean". This association of the moral and the physical is, I believe, no super-
ficial analogy. It goes back to deep and obscure processes of
the Unconscious and is intimately related to the sense of
repulsion towards excreta, dirt and in fact all things which
normally arouse that sense. From my own experience I can
certainly say that the "guilt complex" or sense of sin that
plays such an enormous part in both psychology and religion
is very closely bound up with this whole question of repulsion
and attraction. We are, in fact, getting near to the very
foundations of the human soul.*

Equally near to those foundations, I believe, lies the whole
domain of sex. Again judging from my own experience, the
sexual symptoms of the manic state seem to be the most
powerful and important of all.

The fifth peculiarity of my condition lies in a release of
moral tension, particularly in the sexual sphere. The normal
inhibitions disappear, and sexual activity, instead of being
placed, as in our Western Christian civilisation, in opposition
to religion, becomes associated with it.†

This release of the underlying sexual tension, which for
Freudians constitutes the motive-power of all human achievement, seems to me to be the primary and governing factor of
all the ecstacies and many other experiences of the manic
state. This was very clearly illustrated by the course of my
first really intense manic period, the first time my mind really
slipped over the edge of the plateau of "reality" and pene-
trated into the infinite regions beyond. It is perhaps worth
while giving a detailed account of it here.

It began in the autumn of 1938, when I was just 38 years of
age. For some years I had suffered from bouts of nervous de-

---

* Cf. the Freudian stress on the importance and dangers of "house-
training".

† This association is well known. See Henderson and Gillespie's
"Textbook of Psychiatry", p. 233, for the case of a healthy girl combin-
ing shamelessly erotic behaviour with a pronounced religious trend in
her talk.

pression, and I had had one attack of elation. None of these had been really serious, however; at any rate I had not had to be confined in a Mental Hospital or Asylum. I had been free of trouble for rather more than a year and had settled down in a congenial job.

The first symptoms appeared on Armistice Sunday. I had attended the service which commemorates the gallant dead of the "War to end Wars". It always has an emotional effect upon me, partly because my work has had a good deal to do with the tragic aftermath of that war in Europe. Suddenly I seemed to see like a flash that the sacrifice of those millions of lives had not been in vain, that it was part of a great pattern, the pattern of Divine Purpose. I felt, too, an inner conviction that I had something to do with that purpose; it seemed that some sort of revelation was being made to me, though at the time I had no clear ideas about what it was. The whole aspect of the world about me began to change, and I had the excited shivers in the spinal column and tingling of the nerves that always herald my manic phases.

That night I had a vision. It was the only pure hallucination I have ever experienced; though I have had many other visions, they have always taken the form of what are technically known as "illusions". I woke up about five o'clock to find a strange, rather unearthly light in the room. As my natural drowsiness wore off, the excited feelings of the day before returned and grew more intense. The light grew brighter; I began, I remember, to inhale deep gulps of air, which eased the tension in some way. Then suddenly the vision burst upon me.

How shall I describe it? It was perfectly simple. The great male and female organs of love hung there in mid-air; they seemed infinitely far away from me and infinitely near at the same time. I can see them now, pulsing rhythmically in a circular clockwise motion, each revolution taking approximately the time of a human pulse or heartbeat, as though the vision was associated in some way with the circulation of the blood. I was not sexually excited; from the first the experience seemed to me to be holy. What I saw was the Power of Love—the name came to me at once—the Power that I knew somehow to have made all universes, past, present and to come, to be utterly infinite, an infinity of infinities, to have conquered the Power of Hate, its opposite, and thus created the sun, the stars, the moon, the planets, the earth, light, life, joy and peace, never-ending.

One of the first associations which came to my mind was with the closing lines of Goethe's *Faust*:—

> "Alles Vergängliche ist nur ein Gleichnis,
> Das Unzulängliche, hier wirds Ereignis,
> Das Unbeschreibliche, hier wird's getan,
> Das ewig-Weibliche zieht uns heran."

Surely I must have seen the eternal dance of Love that was Goethe's great vision? The Eternal Feminine draws us ever on, but at the last, and beyond Time and Space, the opposites are reconciled, the Eternal Masculine and Feminine are united and there is peace.

In that peace I felt utterly and completely forgiven, relieved from all burden of sin. The whole of infinity seemed to open up before me, and during the weeks and months which followed I passed through experiences which are virtually indescribable. The complete transformation . of "reality" transported me as it were into the Kingdom of Heaven. The ordinary beauties of nature, particularly, I remember, the skies at sunrise and sunset, took on a transcendental loveliness beyond belief. Every morning, quite contrary to my usual sluggish habits, I jumped up to look at them, and when possible went out to drink in, in a sort of ecstasy, the freshness of the morning air.

The phenomenon is well known, of course, and is technically known as "photism". A good example is the following extract from the diary of a University professor describing the morning he realised he had fallen in love:—"It was as if it were the first time I saw real sunshine, everything I had seen before being pale and lifeless compared to that sunshine. I thought I discovered the real life and beauty of the varied colours of the fields and meadows and mountain-slopes as they had never been discovered before."*

In a way I had fallen in love too—with the whole Universe. Everything felt akin. I was joined to Creation, no longer shut away in my little shell. And my vision of the Power of Love was the key to it all.

In sober fact I was in a state of acute mania, and had to go for the first time to a regular Mental Hospital. I did not stay more than a few days, however, as I was only a voluntary patient, and was thus able to insist on leaving much too soon, though I did make a temporarily successful effort to pull myself together and appear sane enough to leave. I spent the next couple of months at home in a state of elation which would probably be classified as mild hypo-mania, enjoying the marvels of the new world which had appeared to me and day-dreaming in the wildest manner of the future. Finally I was carried away in a disastrous but revealing climax which put an end to the manic period.

The release of sexual tension symbolised in my vision was quite clearly at the root of the whole experience. During my previous periods of depression I had suffered from an acute sense of guilt, centred chiefly round my very real sexual sins. That burden was completely lifted. I was sure of forgiveness. Moreover the meaning of my vision seemed to be that the love of the flesh and the love of the spirit, eros and agape, were really one, so that the impulses of sex were not sinful but rather the holy fount of life itself. The intense opposition set up in the human psyche by the contrary conviction of the early Christians, which culminated in St Augustine's doctrine of the Two Loves and the Two Cities, thus disappeared completely in my case, and the amazing sense of relief and release produced by its disappearance is perhaps a measure of the extent to which it still controls our Unconscious minds today.

As I said earlier, the result was that the antagonism between sex and religion which is normal in Western Christianity, was turned into an alliance in my mind. Both factors

* Quoted by Leuba, "Psychology of Religious Mysticism", p. 256.

were thus greatly strengthened. Religious feelings and emotions eventually combined with sexual impulses to cause me to give away some three hundred pounds, which I could ill afford, to ladies of easy virtue. As long as I stayed 'at home all was well. I felt myself to be in a state of "guidance", but I allowed myself to be "guided" by my wife and led a quiet life, with my elation and excitement in the realm of the imagination. Eventually, however, I went to London, where disaster overtook me.

The first time I was accosted was somewhere in Bond Street. It did not for a moment occur to me to pass on; I should have felt that to be a wicked action. It was a call. Somebody wanted me and I could not refuse. She was not in the least attractive but I felt that I loved her and wanted to help her. Strangely enough she had a Bible in her room, and we read it together. I gave her five pounds.

It seemed to me that I had found a mission. I could and must serve these women—any harlot who called; it would certainly not be right to exercise any choice. Those I met soon found the trick to get my money; all they had to do was to pretend that they wanted to leave the life of the streets, but needed money to pay their debts and so on. I gave money away until my bank warned me about my overdraft, but I was convinced that God would give me money to carry on the good work, and approached the Christian Science Church in Curzon Street with a request for money for a particular girl in whom I was interested. Very naturally they refused, but I was so filled with righteous indignation that I pulled down in maniacal frenzy everything I could reach, with the idea of making myself a martyr, and thus showing up the meanness and hypocrisy of churches in general. The police came along in due course; I naturally waited defiantly for them; and the next day I went before a magistrate, who remanded me for a week's observation in Brixton. I spent the week in a state of more or less acute mania, but the attack subsided quickly and after a further fortnight in hospital under observation I was discharged as cured.

One of the most interesting features of this experience is the light it throws on the nature of the sexual urge in mania. This urge is almost entirely impersonal. The question of selecting an attractive girl, which normally plays a large part in sexual adventures, did not trouble me in the least. I was quite content to leave it to chance. Moreover it would be quite wrong to dismiss the whole episode as just a matter of unbridled "lust". Lust is something very different. In the first place lust is an urge which does not concern itself in the least with the welfare of its object, whereas I was very genuinely concerned with the welfare of the ladies in question, as is shown by the money I spent. Secondly, lust is to a considerable extent a matter of mere refinement or novelty of sensation. It is strictly true to say, I think, that the urge and its satisfaction in the cases of which I am writing, in spite of the relative unattractiveness of some of the ladies, was sentimentally, psychologically and physically like the process in a case of genuine love. Like Whitman, I really did feel all women to be "my sisters and lovers", particularly perhaps those of the unfortunate class with which I was concerned. Normally that class has not attracted me at all.

Later on, I hope to be able to show that this is not without meaning. There was from the outset of the episode no doubt whatever in my mind that it was women of the harlot class to whom I had to go. This seemed to me to have a religious significance, and all the emotions concerned were bound up with religion. I associated this at the time with the recorded kindness of Our Lord towards "sinners", or women of this particular class, but flights of ideas in subsequent manic periods have shown me that the state of mind has much more ancient associations. It was in fact, I believe, a regression to very ancient forms or orgiastic religion with which harlots, and ritual or religious prostitutes in particular, have been connected. In those forms of religion, as in my own case, sexual release and a sense of unity with God and the Universe were achieved at the same time.

The release of sexual tension so clearly brought out in this manic period brings with it freedom from other moral tensions. It is probably impossible to appreciate the intensity of the strain imposed by the inhibitions in modern civilisation unless one has experienced their removal. The burden of conscience, of the "super-ego" of Freudian theory, is enormous. In mania it is lifted as it were by magic. And the lifting of the burden opens the gate into the Infinite, or so it seems.

I do not mean to say that I feel myself entitled to commit all the sins in the calendar, or that I do not realise that there are such things as sins. It is rather that the sense of guidance brings with it the conviction that I am being helped to avoid them. If the Power of Love is in control, so I feel in this state of mind, I cannot surely do evil to others, which is the real essence of sin. The same feeling has inspired many mystics; it has appeared again and again in religion; and it is behind the Oxford Group today. The so-called pantheistical mystics of the thirteenth century pushed it to extremes. Man can rise to union with God, they maintained, by effort and prayer. As soon as he reaches this state of union he attains a glorious freedom. He may then reject all externals and follow the promptings of the Spirit within him. Desire and duty, I want and I ought, the impulses of the Unconscious and the commands of conscience are brought together. That marriage, and the ineffable sense of relief and relaxation that goes with it, is a psychological paradise towards which some of the deepest yearnings of mankind are directed.

I come now to the sixth main feature in my catalogue of abnormal conditions. It consists in the delusions of grandeur and power which are perhaps the most typical feature of manic-depressive insanity. They are closely connected with the first feature, the "elation" or sense of well-being which is a background to the whole state.

This elation is according to Henderson and Gillespie * "the mood appropriate to the fulfilment of a wish". It seems to me that all my wishes are coming true, that all my ambi-

* Op. cit., p. 223.

tions, in work and in play, political, financial, personal, are going to be realised, that vital secrets of the Universe are being revealed to me and so on. This applies not only to normal wishes and ambitions but to wholly abnormal and unreasonable ones. Since I am presumably a very ordinary human personality, I assume these wishes and desires, so all-embracing in their nature that their catalogue would itself fill a book, are in fact natural instinctive trends common to all human creatures. I must assume that the human psyche, indeed, desires infinite expansion, the expansion in fact of a God.

There is a passage from Amiel's *Journal Intime* which I think I can quote from memory.* It expresses the precise sensations I am trying to convey:—

"Moments divine, ecstatic hours; in which our thought flies from world to world, pierces the great enigma, breathes with a respiration broad, tranquil and deep as the respiration of an ocean, serene and limitless as the blue firmament; . . . instants of irresistible intuition in which one feels oneself great as the Universe, and calm as a god. . . . What hours, what memories! The vestiges they leave behind are enough to fill us with belief and enthusiasm, as if they were visits of the Holy Ghost."

I feel so close to God, so inspired by His Spirit that in a sense I am God. I see the future, plan the Universe, save mankind; I am utterly and completely immortal; I am even male and female. The whole Universe, animate and in-animate, past, present and future, is within me. All nature and life, all spirits, are co-operating and connected with me; all things are possible. I am in a sense identical with all spirits from God to Satan. I reconcile Good and Evil and create light, darkness, worlds, universes.

Of course it is all a dream, a vision, pure imagination if there is such a thing. I know perfectly well that in fact I have no power, that I am of no particular importance and have made rather a mess of my life. I am a very ordinary man and

* Subsequently verified and corrected.

a miserable sinner; and I can truthfully say that never in the midst of the wildest flights of grandiose ideas have I ever allowed myself to forget that. Moreover, psychologically speaking, I know that my delusions of grandeur are merely compensation for the failures and frustrations of my real life. In particular, in my sane periods, the sense of identity with God seems to me an appalling blasphemy. Yet it is absolutely overwhelming, however much I struggle against it and endeavour to rationalise it on orthodox Christian lines as a vision vouchsafed by God. The fact that it is not only a common feature of insane conditions but also an experience of many of the mystics seems to show that the instinctive drive to power and the experience of the Immanent God are more closely related than is generally realised.

As the seventh and last main feature, I would list a sense of ineffable revelation which persists in varying degrees throughout the state and seems to be intimately linked with the delusions of power. It seems to me as though all truth, all the secrets of the Universe were being revealed, as though I had some clue, some Open-Sesame to creation.

I dealt to some extent in Chapter I with the question whether the strange flashes of insight—delusions if you prefer to call them so—which accompany abnormal mental states can be said to have real meaning, and I shall return to the subject later.

There is no doubt that this ineffable revelation—the term is not mine, it is used by Leuba and I think also William James—very largely baffles expression. It occurs in many trance states, notably the nitrous-oxide trance referred to in Chapter I, and in mystical experiences as well as in insanity. The mystic St Francis Xavier described it as follows:— "It seemed to me that a veil was lifted up before the eyes of the spirit, and that all the truths of human sciences, even those that I had not studied, became manifest to me by an infused knowledge, as was the case with Solomon. This state of intuition lasted about twenty-four hours, and then, as if the veil had fallen again, I found myself as ignorant as before." *

Such a lifting of the veil has accompanied every manic period I have had. It seems to me to have some relation to the heightened sense of reality, and in particular to the rapid association of ideas connected with this sense. In the manic state I appear, at any rate to myself, to have a peculiar faculty for seeing things whole instead of bit by bit, to possess the intuitive faculty which R. R. Marett noted in primitive savages (see Chap. I). Suddenly, or it may be gradually, I seem to see a vast chain of associations, often extending into departments of thought not normally connected at all. I am not referring here to purely fortuitous irrational associations such as those given earlier in this chapter, but to associations which have or seem to have a deep meaning, though admittedly in my sane periods I find it extraordinarily difficult to express that meaning intelligibly. For example, in a recent manic period it seemed to me possible to classify the whole of creation under "positive" and "negative" on the analogy of electricity, and I had a whole series of visions in connection with this, which still seem to have a meaning and are the basis of Chapters IV, V and VI. The sight of some ordinary object, say the straight Roman road I crossed on the way to this hospital, awakened a splendid and exciting vision of the procession of the Roman legions across the pages of history. Thoughts and impressions, in fact, do not appear in isolation as they so often do in ordinary life; they seem linked up with a whole.

In my own case this process is always marked by the creepy or shivery feeling in the spinal column to which reference has been made. This is of course a normal accompaniment of nervous excitement, and no doubt indicates the exciting nature of the thought-process in mania, particularly when the sense of ineffable revelation is marked. A curious feature about it is that it seems to indicate with some precision the linking-up of tracts of associations in the psycho-

* Quoted by Poulain, "Graces of Interior Prayer", p. 279.

physical mechanism. It is almost as though it were evidence in favour of the old concept of psycho-physical parallelism, now virtually abandoned, which regarded the nervous system as a kind of telephone system with the nerves as lines and the ganglia as vast telephone exchanges, through which the whole process of thought as well as of reaction to environment was worked. I have noticed again and again that when thinking or writing in a state of mania, every time unusual connections between departments of thought or tracts or associations occur to me I get this sensation in direct proportion to the importance and extent of the departments or tracts thus connected. As every writer knows, it is nearly always such connections and associations that cause difficulty and hesitation in thought. As I sit here in the ward writing, I know that if I get a shiver in my back after puzzling about something for a minute or so, it means that the connection has been established. And if the shiver is really intense, it indicates that the line of thought leads to a large tract of related associations, as though the link or contact involved the passing of an electric current proportionate to the extent of the associations and the shiver was an ammeter to measure the current. Now and then, when it really appears as though some vital missing link had been revealed to me, I get an additional feeling as though something had clicked or fallen into place in my head, rather as a combination lock is said by detective-story writers sometimes to click when the combination is dialled. This feeling is neither purely physical nor purely psychological, but a sort of combination between the two.

I am reminded in this connection of the observations of Koehler in his work on the *Mentality of Apes*, which is the basis of the modern theories of Gestalt Psychology. Koehler notes that the moment when anthropoids, animals or children hit on the solution of some problem is marked by "a kind of jerk".* The pattern or "Gestalt" has fallen into place in their minds and they straightway go ahead and perform the

* Koehler, "Mentality of Apes", p. 17.

necessary physical actions, for example to reach the food or whatever their objective may be.

It is probable that in the ineffable revelation, whether of mania or of trance, processes of this kind take place on a very large scale in the mind. Patterns of thought are completed much more easily than usual. The whole pattern of one's life, in fact, seems to fall into place and make sense, though unfortunately, as far as this life in the real world is concerned, much of what has appeared so clear turns out to be illusion. For my own part I am always impelled to rationalise this with the idea of an infinite life beyond Time and Space in which all things are possible and indeed all patterns are completed. If the ineffable revelation is, as it appears to be, a sort of grasp of the whole, a passing beyond the antitheses, an interpenetration of the innumerable watertight compartments of life and experience, this must surely be so in some degree.

3 Recapitulation.

I have endeavoured to describe above the main characteristic features of the manic state They are, to recapitulate:—(1) Intense sense of well-being, (2) heightened sense of reality, (3) breach in the barriers of individuality, (4) inhibition of sense of repulsion, (5) release of sexual and moral tension, (6) delusions of grandeur and power, (7) sense of ineffable revelation. In addition to these, a number of minor symptoms and sensations are not without significance. Some of these are particularly associated with one or other of the main features.

In connection with the delusions of grandeur and drive for power should be noted the peculiar sensation already mentioned in Chapter I as reminiscent of the cat tribe. I first noted it in the padded cell at Brixton while in a state of acute mania. I saw a series of visions which impelled on my consciousness a strong sense of destiny and leadership. I imagined myself a sort of lion destined to conquer the world, and in conformity with this delusion paced interminably round and round my cell on the balls of my feet with a sense of extra-ordinary muscular looseness or suppleness.

In Harold Nicolson's book *The Congress of Vienna* there is a remarkable description of Napoleon's manner towards the sovereigns of Europe assembled at Dresden just before the ill-fated Moscow campaign, which irresistibly suggests my own sensations. Apparently there was a great difference between Napoleon's histrionic military manner, with his rapid walk, occasional pauses, hat on thigh, and hand thrust deep into his waistcoat, and his manner at courts. On the latter occasions he would walk in a fashion that can only be described as sinister, on the balls of his feet. It gave the impression to observers of a lion entering the arena, slowly, cautiously, on padded feet.

There is, I may perhaps say, no question of my having got the original idea from reading Nicolson; I have only just read the book. Perhaps it is only natural that the sensations and impulses associated with real power should be akin to those of delusions of power and this merely goes to support the widely held view that the power-seeking Napoleonic type has a psychological mechanism similar to that of paranoiacs and other sufferers from delusions of grandeur. But the parallel struck me very forcibly. There may be deeper reasons than is generally thought why the great beasts of prey of the cat tribe are traditional symbols of power. The only other association of that particular sensation which comes to my mind is the rather incongruous one of jazz music. In the manic state this sometimes gives rise to similar sensations, though in this case my movements tend to be rather faster and the phantasy is not so much one of being a lion or tiger as a savage dancing a war-dance.

Another symptom is the ability to see visions in the form of illusions, that is to say distortion of visual images. This power is proportionate to the acuteness of the mania. At the present time I am seeing no visions. In periods of acute mania they can appear almost like a continuous cinema performance, particularly if there are any complicated and variable light-patterns with which my optical mechanism can play the necessary tricks. These visions generally appear on the walls of my room, if these are shiny enough to reflect light. They are infinitely varied, and bear a close relation to the processes of thought passing in my mind at the time. They are obvious products of the Unconscious, which in this state is of course largely in control of my mind. It is quite impossible to give a catalogue of them, though some will be mentioned in due course. Ancestors, historical characters and friends, both dead and alive have appeared to me in this way; I have seen future historical events such as, for example, the trial of Joseph Stalin after World War III (which may, of course, be wishful thinking); there have been visions of Heaven—and Hell—of gods and goddesses and devils, and so on.

The technique of seeing these illusions is a sort of relaxation of the focusing of my eyes. This seems to be connected with the fact that although I am normally astigmatic and have great difficulty in reading without spectacles, during a manic period I can readily manage without them, while in acute mania they are totally unnecessary and of no help whatever. I have asked both oculists and psychiatrists if they knew of any possible explanation, but without result. Recently my oculist, Dr Martin-Jones, of Salisbury, suggested a possible explanation, which seems to be of some considerable significance. My need of spectacles, he said, though partly astigmatic, was really a perfectly normal phenomenon of age. It was a question of focusing and adjustment. With advancing years the muscles concerned become less and less able to make the very considerable adjustments which are possible in youth. Their elasticity diminishes; they are more stretched and tense. Presumably in mania some sort of relaxation of tension takes place, which enables the muscles to function more freely and thus more effectively. It occurred to me at once that there might be some connection between this phenomenon and the Freudian concept of regression. If mania is a regression or return to a childish or adolescent phase of mental development, may it not involve some concomitant physical changes in the same direction? I put this to Dr Martin-Jones, who said he saw no reason why this should not be so, though he had no specialised psychological knowledge. I cannot help feeling that there is a field here for experiment. If mental regression really does involve physical regression, even in a slight degree, to a more youthful bodily state, this would seem not only to reinforce the evidence for the intimate connection of mind and body, but also might have implications for the treatment of conditions in which age plays a part.

I feel sure that some sort of relaxation of normal nervous tension is involved. It may be of interest that it affects the normal co-ordination of hand and eye. I am a keen tennis player and have often had opportunities of playing while in a state of mania. I find it practically impossible to hit the ball at all; my racket comes forward far too late. As my mental state improves, so does my timing, and it is clear that con-centration is involved, a concentration affecting the whole body. By making a terrific effort of concentration I have been able to get back normal co-ordination of hand and eye, but it takes a day or two to do so. At the same time the power to see visions disappears and the need for spectacles returns.

With visions are associated dreams. When in a state of acute mania it is not always easy to separate the two. There is a very close correlation between dreams and waking thoughts and imaginings. I wake up and my mind carries on the same train of thought which has been begun in a dream. I go to sleep and go on dreaming about the subjects I have been thinking about. This is presumably to be ex-pected, since both dreams and the visions and trains of thought in mania are governed by the Unconscious.

It is of course this control by the Unconscious which pro-duces the "irrationality" of the manic state and renders it necessary for the sufferer to be confined. The great emo-tional forces, whose power seems to be almost unlimited, have charge of the personality. Reason, to use the Platonic metaphor, no longer controls the chariot; the horses of passion and instinct have run away. The immense enjoyment that they have in doing so governs one's whole being. All brakes or clogs or checks on the whole functioning of the psycho-physical mechanism are removed; the channels of instinct are freed; the libido can flow where it will.

That is, I suppose, the reason for the intense sense of well-being, which is physical as well as mental, and not wholly illusory. My digestive system functions particularly well, without the slightest trace of constipation or diarrhoea, and I have an inordinate appetite. Metabolism is rapid. I can stand cold without difficulty or discomfort; an inner warmth seems to pervade me. I can, for example, walk about naked out of doors on quite cold nights—to throw off my clothes is incidentally a strong impulse and presumably symbolises the freedom from restraint which is a feature of the whole condition. My skin seems peculiarly resistant; I have walked barefooted on stony and thorny ground, squeezed myself naked through furze fences and so on without suffering discomfort. Perhaps this is akin to the strange feats of fire walkers or dancing Dervishes. It certainly seems to show the influence of mind over matter. I fear nothing—freedom from fear is another notable symptom—so nothing seems to hurt me.

That concludes, I think, this rather overlong catalogue of the features and symptoms of the manic state as I have experienced it. It may sound a delightful condition. Perhaps it would be if it were not such a nuisance to others and did not so easily change into its opposite. I have described the heights of mental abnormality, with their ecstasies and their beatitudes, to the best of my ability. In the next chapter we shall take a voyage into the depths.

CHAPTER III

UNIVERSE OF HORROR

1. *Twilight*

THE FOLLOWING account of the deep caverns of the soul to which the depressive phase of manic depression leads is being written while I seem to be on the threshold of the phase. My last manic attack ended about four months ago. It was rapidly and effectively cured by electrical convulsion therapy, the first time this has been tried on me.

There is no doubt in my mind that the convulsion therapy has effected a more radical cure of my elation than I have experienced for several years. The only trouble is that it may have pushed me over into the reverse phase.* It will be seen by reference to the table at the beginning of the last chapter that I have not had a serious depressive attack since 1940. I have had tendencies to depression on occasion, but I have succeeded in conquering them, mainly by hanging on like grim death to the consciousness of relationship with God which came to me in my manic phases. Now, however, that sense is becoming increasingly difficult to recapture. It is as though the shock or convulsion turned a great switch in my system, putting out the light, mad though it was, and plunging me into what the mystics, notably St Theresa, call the Dark Night of the Soul. Or rather, at the moment I am in a sort of twilight, more like what St Theresa calls a "State of Dryness", which may change into the night of horror that I know so well.

The features of the depressive state are precisely the reverse of those of the manic. Instead of the sense of well-being

---

* It did not. I soon got back to normal without treatment. For detailed description of the effects of convulsion therapy, see Appendix B.

I feel miserable and ill; instead of a heightened sense of reality
I seem

> " . . . to move among a world of ghosts
> And feel myself the shadow of a dream." *

This feeling is closely linked with a sort of strengthening of the
barriers of individuality, a hardening of the shell of the ego. I
seem shut into myself, withdrawn from real contact with the
outer world as also from contact with God; the sun does not
really shine, the trees and fields are not really green; I am
shut in with my thoughts, always of a depressing and melan-
choly nature.

This sense of isolation, of being cut off from God, one's fellows and the world, seems to me to be the paramount feature
underlying the whole state and I shall be describing in due
course the lengths to which my mind can carry it. It is a sense
which appears at the root of several psychoses; Janet has
called it the "maladie de l'isolement".† Just as its opposite,
the breach in the barriers of individuality, seemed connected
with the inhibition of the sense of repulsion, so this state involves a heightened sense of repulsion and horror of dirt and
repulsive objects carried to absurd lengths. To give a homely
if somewhat coarse instance, I have at times felt impelled to
use up to twenty pieces of toilet-paper.

Moral tension returns in full force. I am haunted by a
sense of guilt; my conscience gives me no rest, even when
there do not seem to be any particularly grievous sins upon it.
Whatever I am doing I feel I ought to be doing something
else. I worry perpetually about my past sins and failures; not
for a moment can I forget the mess I seem to have made of
my life. However I may pray for and think of forgiveness,
no forgiveness comes. Eventually the terrors of Hell approach.

This state is so exactly what is described by the mystics
that I will give two quotations. The French mystic Madame
Guyon writes: "everything seemed to me full of faults; my
charities, my alms, my prayers, my penances; one and all

---

* Tennyson, "The Princess".
† P. Janet, "Les Obsessions et la Psycasthénie", Vol. I, p. 308.

they rose against me. Either by you, O my God, or by myself, or by all creatures, I felt myself universally condemned." * St Theresa goes further: "All the favours ever granted me were swept out of my memory. My mind was so greatly obscured that I stumbled from doubt to doubt, from fear to fear. I believed myself so wicked that I regarded my sins as the cause of all the evils, and all the wickedness that afflicted the world."†

St Theresa's description gives exactly what happens in my mind as depression progresses. She writes of her mind being "obscured". That is what is happening to my mind at the very moment I am writing. Instead of the light of ineffable revelation I seem to be in perpetual fog and darkness. I cannot get my mind to work; instead of associations "clicking into place" everything is an inextricable jumble; instead of seeming to grasp a whole, it seems to remain tied to the actual consciousness of the moment. The whole world of my thought is hopelessly divided into incomprehensible watertight compartments. I could not feel more ignorant, undecided, or inefficient. It is appallingly difficult to concentrate, and writing is pain and grief to me.

As for wickedness, although my mind has not reached the stage of regarding myself as the most wicked person in the world and responsible for all the sin and evil afflicting mankind, I know too well that it can do so. That appalling self-centredness is the reverse of the delusions of gradneur and power. It leads to the uttermost depths.

2. *The Horrific Vision*

The best way to give an idea of what happens to the mind in the extremes of depression is to describe in some detail my last attack, which came early in 1939, shortly after the episode which took me to Brixton.

Twice before I had suffered from serious depression, with

* Quoted by Leuba, op. cit., p. 82.
† Quoted ibid., p. 107.

acute insomnia and impulses to suicide. Prolonged rest under drugs in an excellent nursing-home had effected a cure in each case. I could, however, no longer afford the fees at the nursing-home, and so had to go on this occasion to a private Mental Hospital.

In Chapter II wrote of a metaphorical table-land, off which the manic-depressive slips in one direction or another, until the last grips on reality are lost and the Unconscious takes charge. Here I want to refer to a further factor, which is a little difficult to fit into the metaphor.

In my experience there seems to run through manic-depressive states a sort of dividing line between the earthly and the transcendental, or perhaps one might even say the phenomenal and the noumenal. In more ordinary medical parlance, there are states both of mania and depression which do not involve the illusions and hallucinations, the ecstasies and horrors, the overwhelming forces of the deep Unconscious, with its Heaven and Hell, its Gods and Goddesses, witches, warlocks and devils.

In my previous states of depression I had never really lost my grip of reality. I had begun to slip off the table-land down the slope to the left, but there was still as it were a ridge in front of me which might hold me up. I was utterly miserable and wanted to die, but my fears, troubles and worries were of normal human mischances which might happen to anybody. I feared poverty, failure in life, inability to educate my children, making my wife miserable, losing her, ending up in the gutter as the most revolting type of beggar and so on. My fears had in fact become so overpowering as to appear to me like certainties, but they were only earthly, human fears. Beyond the ridge bordering this ordinary universe of common human experience unending horrors awaited me. But I did not know; I had not crossed it, at any rate in that direction.

Had I had anything like the insight into my own mind that I have now attained, I should have known what to expect, for during the foregoing manic period I had crossed the ridge down the slope to the right of the plateau. I had experienced unearthly joys; I had imagined myself in Heaven; in the padded cell at Brixton I saw vision after vision, and though I rather doubt whether orthodox Roman Catholics would allow those visions the predicate "beatific", they were undoubtedly my particular form of the Vision Beautiful.

If you are a saint, you may, I suppose, aspire to see the Beatific Vision without experiencing its opposite, which I will call the Horrific Vision. You struggle and sacrifice and mortify your flesh; you pass through the "Cloud of Unknowing" and the Dark Night of the Soul when you feel, like St Theresa, that God has deserted you, but you need not necessarily go through the terrors of Hell. None the less, many famous religious leaders—Martin Luther and John Bunyan are notable cases in point—have experienced something of the kind, and for the ordinary sinner it is sound Catholic doctrine that Heaven without Purgatory is inconceivable.

Thus, since I had had experience of Heaven, it was only reasonable to expect that I should be shown Hell in due course. Let me try to summon up all my descriptive powers to give some idea of the pass to which conscience can bring a human soul, once it has slipped over the ridge to the left of the narrow plateau and lost its foothold on reality.

I lay in my bed in the ward of the Hospital dominated above all by an overpowering sense of fear. At first I did not know exactly what it was that I feared, except of course that my mind, which I strove as hard as I could to keep blank, would insist on working about the ordinary, human fears I have outlined above. Wisely, no attempt was made to get me up, and I lay as motionless as I could, covering my head as a rule with the bedclothes, partly to shut out the sights and sounds of the ward, and partly as a sort of instinctive reaction.

Dr W. H. R. Rivers in his suggestive work *Instinct and the Unconscious* has given one of the probable reasons for this attitude.* It was the reaction of the animal who under

* "Instinct and the Unconscious", pp. 61 ff.

the compulsion of the fear-emotion remains absolutely immobile, "paralysed by fear" as the popular locution has it. It does so, of course, because in the course of evolution immobility, "lying doggo", has proved a sound means of defence. The reaction is what Rivers calls an "all or nothing" reaction, because for gregarious animals it is abolutely essential that all the members of the group should remain equally immobile; if one moves, the whole purpose of the reaction is defeated.

About the second reason I am not so clear. I believe, however, that to cover oneself up with the bedclothes suggests, at any rate to some extent, the safety of the mother's womb, the ultimate refuge, according to good Freudian doctrine, towards which so much psychological striving is directed.

Anyway, there I lay for some days, only putting my head outside the clothes to eat my food, take my drugs, and for absolutely necessary purposes. Gradually, however, the sounds if not the sights of the ward forced themselves in on my consciousness.

In the bed opposite me there lay, also in a state of extreme misery and dejection, a patient named Bar——. He moaned unceasingly; I could not help hearing what he said. He only said two words, at least I never remember hearing him say anything else. Those words were, "no hope, no hope, no hope," ceaselessly repeated in a hollow moan. I soon learnt his name; it began with the fatal syllable Bar.

I was barred, my mind began to repeat to me, barred from hope, there was no hope for me. The obvious association soon followed. I do not know much Italian, but I had once made an attempt to read parts of Dante's *Inferno* in the original.

Lasciate ogni speranza voi ch'entrate.

So that was where I was going was it? No, I tried to argue with myself, it was impossible. There must be some hope, some escape from Hell. A Creator who condemned his creatures to eternal punishment, whatever their sins, would be a monster, and the God of Jesus was a God of love. This reasoning, I may say, represents a considered view that I have always held. It comforted me for a time.

There was a very charming Anglican parson in the ward, whom I will call G.G., as he may prefer me not to mention his name. On various occasions he had done me little kindnesses, and though I hardly talked to anybody, I did now and then talk to him. As the subject of Hell was getting on my mind, I broached it to him in an endeavour to get some reassurance.

G.G., however, was not impressed by my reasoning. He brought his little Bible along and produced texts to prove his thesis that an eternal Hell was a part of God's purpose and Word, and that Jesus Christ explicitly endorsed this view. "Everlasting fire prepared for the Devil and all his Angels", "and these shall go away into eternal punishment, but the righteous into eternal life", and so on. How could I argue away the plain meaning of the words concluding the great parable of the sheep and the goats?

I tried hard; G.G. did not defeat me in argument. But unfortunately the inner voice of conscience told me that he was right.

Forgiveness of sins, G.G.—a most human person—went on to explain, could be attained by those who truly repented. I need not, indeed I should not worry about my sins; all I had to do was to repent of them. This did not comfort me in the least. My reasoning went roughly like this.

First of all, I had by now become quite convinced that I was finished for good and all. There was no possible chance of my coming out of the Hospital alive. In fact though not actually dead, I was as good as dead. For some inscrutable reason, perhaps because I had committed "the unforgivable sin" or just because I was such an appalling sinner, the worst man who had ever existed, I had been chosen to go alive through the portals of Hell, in an ordinary English lunatic-asylum. Therefore it was obviously too late for repentance. It was, I knew, quite unsound theology to imagine that people got another chance after they were dead. Obviously when they saw what they were in for they would repent; anybody would. But they would be cast into outer darkness and the Lord would not bother about them any more, however much they wept and gnashed their teeth. I knew what I was in for; I had been before the Bar (Bar——); I had been told there was no hope of a reprieve; and that was the end of it.

All this I kept to myself, of course; I did not argue with G.G. about it. Nor did I tell the doctors. They were not particularly sympathetic and did not invite confidences; moreover I was quite astute enough to realise that to talk on these lines would be regarded as further proof of insanity; I might even be certified. As long as I was voluntary, there was perhaps just the faintest chance that I might get out and succeed in making away with myself.

My wife, who visited me nobly at least twice a week for the whole eleven months of my confinement, never could understand the logic of this attitude. She was the only person to whom I dared confide my horrors, and I tried hard to show my train of reasoning. Roughly it was that I was a sort of opposite of Jesus Christ. Satan's job had been to catch a man, get him to sell his soul to him completely and utterly, like Faust, and then take him down alive into the pit. That was a sort of necessary counterweight to the resurrection of Jesus and the elect. I was the man. But if I could only kill myself, it might blow up the whole Universe, but at least I would get out of eternal torture and achieve the oblivion and nothingness for which my soul craved. I did in fact make three attempts at suicide, the most serious of which was when I tore myself from my attendant and threw myself in front of a car, with my poor wife, who was visiting me, looking on.

Although my attempts at suicide failed, they had one satisfactory effect; the doctors increased my drugs. As long as I was able to attain unconsciousness at night (with the aid of three or four doses of paraldehyde), and to maintain a fairly soporific state during the day (with anything up to four tablets of allonal), I could just keep the horrors at bay. My whole conscious effort was now directed towards the aim of putting off the moment when I would disappear finally into Hell. I visualised this process as happening quite naturally. Some day, at some moment, the iron control I kept on my terrors would break. I should start shrieking in agony. Naturally the attendants would then shut me up in a side-room, probably in one of the worse wards. After that the process of torturing a human soul in the living flesh would just go on. I should shriek, but so do many lunatics; nobody would do anything for me; they would naturally think my pains were imaginary. But they would be real pains; anyway I knew that the philosophical distinction between real and imaginary was very difficult to make. It did not matter much when I "died" in the body. I might spend days, months, or years shrieking in my side-room before they buried me. For me, it would all be the same process of eternal, progressively increasing torture.

Progressively increasing, that was the appalling part of the picture. It seemed to me as I brooded on the problem, that the ancient prophets, thinkers and poets, including of course Dante, must be wrong in regarding Hell, eternal punishment, as something static. Nothing in the Universe seemed to be static; why should Hell be so? Nor, in fact, could Heaven be static either. It was borne in upon me that the creative process was all one, really. The vast evolutionary process, from the whirling spiral nebulae to man, superman, God, was a progressive movement forwards, or upwards, if you prefer it. But there must always be balance, otherwise nothing would work. So the progressive movement forwards or upwards must be compensated by a regressive movement backwards or downwards.

The progressive revolutionary movement upwards had its counterpart in the world or worlds outside space and time. This was "Heaven". The regressive movement backwards (I was not quite clear what it actually was in the physical world, but I knew it must exist somewhere) had its counterpart in Hell. In Heaven, the souls of the just, of the "elect", progressed towards increasing enjoyment, knowledge, power, love, life. In Hell, the souls of the unjust, Satan's elect—probably an approximately equal number to those of the just, in order to maintain balance—regressed down an equally infinite scale first of mental, then of physical torture. It was a remarkably logical picture, given the premises; I am sure it would have delighted Calvin to see his views so scientifically worked out.

About the time I had reached this point in my compulsive train of reasoning, possibly three months or so after my arrival in the Hospital, I was lying one afternoon—I can't remember when; it was after I had begun to get up after breakfast—in the company of an old patient. As if specially sent by the Powers of the Universe to confirm my train of thought, he began to recite, in a monotonous but rhythmic voice:—Opposites, opposites; down, up; backwards, forwards; clockwise, anti-clockwise; push, pull; hot, cold; black, white; earth, air; fire, water. I don't remember exactly how many opposites he mentioned, but that gives the general idea. Jung, incidentally, regards the 'opposites' as an important part of the Unconscious, and I have often heard mental patients refer to them in their delusionary or compulsive trains of thought.

Perhaps I might just remark here in parenthesis that gradually all the associations of my environment came to confirm the ideas which were being forced upon me. When the wireless happened to be on, it often seemed to be speaking to me; something would be said to confirm or increase my fears. This is of course a common delusion. The fact is that the whole mechanism of 'association', to which reference has been made in the previous chapter, automatically came to work in the same direction as my thoughts. Every word, almost every letter, of a newspaper I might chance to look at, would contain some dire message of evil.

To illustrate this, I will try to put myself back in the condition of mind I was in at that time, and then take the first suggestive association that comes to hand. In front of me is a pad of Basildon Bond writing-paper, blue. Looking at it with my eyes of eight years ago I see St Basil damning me (D) ON a blue bond. Blue stands for Heaven, which is *BL*asting me (i.e. yo*U*) *E*ternally. I hope this makes the associations clear. They are, of course, typical of certain types of mental disease.

In such a state of mind any normal behaviour becomes virtually impossible. Yet at about this time I began to lead a rather more normal life, getting up, as I said, after breakfast, playing croquet, billiards, badminton, and so on. This was partly due to my wife's persuasive efforts, partly to the efforts of the attendants, and most of all, I think, to the fact that even with the drugs I was taking I was no longer able to keep myself in a state of drowsiness. Bed, alone with my horrors, thus became intolerable, and occupation did keep my mind off them for the moment. Even though my incorrigible mind related everything, even billiards and croquet, to my terrible predicament, as long as I could get through the time somehow without losing control and thus starting my eternal punishment, that was something gained.

I used to concentrate on getting through the intervals between my wife's visits and seeing her again. As she left me, each time, I would tell her that she would not find me there when she came next time, and as the door shut behind her, something clanged in my soul and I felt sick to death. But I used to pull round and concentrate on being there for the next visit.

By this time, say four or five months after my arrival, I had evolved a definite technique to help me in this effort of getting through the days and nights. I had frankly admitted my position. God had turned His back on me and left me to Satan, but perhaps I could persuade Satan to put off the evil day a bit. That was all I asked for, and it seemed to me I stood a chance of getting some postponement if I could worship Satan really properly. So I evolved my own little rituals —they incidentally have little to do with genuine Satanism, which is obviously much more closely associated with my manic periods.

Every night I said the Lord's Prayer backwards, letter by

letter, smoking three ritual cigarettes as I did so. By that time the drug I had taken used to begin to work, and I always got to sleep before I had finished the prayer. Letter by letter, beginning with NEMA (AMEN), and continuing REVE DNA REVE ROF (for ever and ever), and so on, the Lord's Prayer is very complicated indeed. It probably takes about twenty minutes, and I cannot recall that I ever finished. I am sure Mr C. S. Lewis's Screwtape enjoyed the performance; it must have gratified him immensely; anyway neither he nor his master seemed to bear me any ill-will for not finishing.

This superstition was a great help. My mother is very superstitious; she has a horror of magpies, thirteen at a table, and so on. I evolved little superstitions which helped to build up my self-confidence. One was that if, as I left any room, I fixed my eyes on something red (Satan's colour), he would manage to get me back to that particular room or place again. I was thus certain to be preserved from eternal punishment until I went back to that room. This was the most reassuring of my superstitions, and I did not abandon it, nor for that matter did I dare to pray the right way round, till long after I had got back home again. There were many others; some depending on pure suggestion, like an idea I had that as long as I had a box of *dates*, I could be sure of having a *date* with my wife. Many were connected with my games. For example in billards God was represented by the plain ball and the devil by spot. In no game in which I was concerned, therefore, could I allow plain to win. As long as spot won the devil would save me. If spot looked like losing I would make some excuse and leave the game.

Further details would only be wearisome. I come now to the central feature of my whole experience. Somehow I want to find adequate words to describe the dawn of what I may call the Horrific Vision.

I am not quite sure when it began to break in upon me, but it was certainly within the first month or so, when I was still in bed. Thereafter it progressed *pari passu* with my ideas; it never left me for an instant.

A crumpled pillow is quite an ordinary everyday object, is it not? One looks at it and thinks no more about it? So is a washing-rag, or a towel tumbled on the floor, or the creases on the side of a bed. Yet they can suggest shapes of the utmost horror to the mind obsessed by fear. Gradually my eyes began to distinguish such shapes, until eventually, whichever way I turned, I could see nothing but devils waiting to torment me, devils which seemed infinitely more real than the material objects in which I saw them.

They had names, too. There was the god Baal, with a cruel mouth like a slit (a wrinkle in the side of a bed), waiting to devour me as a living sacrifice. There was Hecate, who used generally to appear in pillows, her shape was, I think, the most horrible of all. When I went out I saw devils by the hundred in trees and bushes, and especially in cut wood, generally in serpent form. Even now, I can still see them on occasion; the trick of illusion by which they appeared remains with me to some extent; and now that I am depressed again I cannot help wondering if they will reawaken the sense of utter terror that they did when they first appeared. I thought I had exorcised them, but now I am not so sure.

With these visions surrounding me it is not strange that the material world should seem less and less real. I felt myself to be gradually descending alive into the pit by a sort of metamorphosis of my surroundings. At times the whole universe seemed to be dissolving about me; moving cracks and fissures would appear in the walls and floors. This, incidentally, is a phenomenon which I have often noticed in the opposite state of acute mania, though it has then, of course, a totally different underlying feeling-tone. The climax of this sense of unreality was an extraordinary vision which is difficult to classify under the normal head of "illusion", though it was not a hallucination or apparition either. It seems to me to have interesting philosophical and psychological implications.

There was a series of sporting prints round the walls of the ward day-room. They were so placed that, if you sat in an arm-chair with your back to the large windows, and facing the prints, you could see, reflected in the picture-glass, the buildings of No. 9 ward, on the opposite side of the small lawn on to which the windows looked out.

I used generally to sit concentrating on a novel—that was another good way of keeping the horrors at bay—with my back to the windows; there seemed to be fewer devils in the ward than there were outside, somehow. Little by little, over a period of about a month or six weeks probably, the reflection of No. 9 ward was distorted. The chimneys left the vertical plane and moved round to the horizontal, eventually to forty or fifty degrees below the horizontal, while the reflection of the building itself became correspondingly curved, until the whole vertical structure formed a sort of inverted U. This puzzled me greatly; I don't think I was horrified at first. What could it mean? My vision was otherwise quite normal; I could play badminton, billiards, and so on. But whenever I sat in one of those chairs and looked at the prints, I could see this strange phenomenon.

Certainly I was bewitched. But that was no new discovery; it did not frighten me more than I was frightened in any case.

Then, suddenly, the answer came. Bishop Berkeley was right; the whole universe of space and time, of my own senses, was really an illusion. Or it was so for me, at any rate. There I was, shut in my own private universe, as it were, with no contact with real people at all, only with phantasmagoria who could at any moment turn into devils. I and all around me were utterly unreal. There in the reflection lay proof positive. My soul was finally turned into nothingness— except unending pain.

It was getting dark when this burst upon me. I shivered; my teeth were chattering with sheer terror. And then I saw a star.

My father used to talk to me a great deal about stars. He was fascinated, like Hardy's young astronomer in *Two on a Tower*, by the vast perspective of space and time which they open up to the human mind. And he fascinated me. When I saw that star it all came back to me, as though it was the first star I had seen since as a boy I stood with him on the terrace at home and watched the glory of Orion rising in the East. Probably, it flashed upon me, the light from that star had taken thousands of years to reach the earth. Perhaps it was a new star, a young star, as stars go. Long after the light in the solar system had gone out for good, that star might well be shining as brightly as ever. But my unending punishment would scarcely have begun. Perhaps I should have to endure it in that very star; perhaps the actual heat in the stars, the product, so I understood, of atomic energy, came from the burning of human souls. Perhaps the Universe could only work that way. Some had to be damned, that others might be saved. Many if not most great Christian thinkers had reasoned on such lines. Even the humane Baron von Hugel, in his great work on Mysticism, had attacked Origen and the great Greek Fathers for their noble attempt to prove that the Almighty Father would save all his children in the long run, that pain and punishment were only sent for the good of souls, as an earthly father punishes his children. What hope could there be for me? But with modern ideas of astronomical time, the prospect of eternal, progressively increasing punishment was so utterly appalling!

Not long before my attack, I had been reading James Joyce's *Portrait of the Artist as a Young Man*. The description it gives of a sermon preached by a Jesuit father on the meaning of damnation had made a great impression on me. As I sat there I could recall almost every word.

"For ever," says the preacher, "for all eternity. Try to imagine the awful meaning of this. You have often seen the sand on the seashore. . . . How many of those tiny grains go to make up the small handful which a child grasps in its play? Now imagine a mountain of that sand a million miles high . . . and a million miles broad. . . and a million miles in thickness; and imagine such an enormous mass of countless particles of sand multiplied as often as there are leaves in the forest, drops of water in the mighty ocean, feathers on birds, scabs on fish, hairs on animals, atoms in the vast expanse of air: and imagine that at the end of every million years a little bird came to that mountain and carried away in its beak a tiny grain of that sand. How many millions upon millions of centuries would pass before that bird had carried away even a square foot of that mountain; how many aeons upon aeons of ages before it had carried away all? Yet at the end of that immense stretch of time not even one instant of eternity can be said to have ended. At the end of all those billions and trillions of years eternity would have scarcely begun. And if that mountain rose again after it had all been carried away, and if the bird came again and carried it all away again, grain by grain: and if it so rose and sank as many times a there are stars in the sky, atoms in the air, drops of water in the sea, leaves on the trees, feathers upon birds, hairs upon animals, at the end of all these innumerable risings and sinkings, not one single instant of eternity could be said to have ended; even then at the end of such a period, after that aeon of time, the mere thought of which makes our very brain reel dizzily, eternity would scarcely have begun."

At that moment I had reached the extremity of fear. Paroxysms of terror overcame me, and I nearly jumped straight out of the window with the idea of killing myself with the broken glass. But the fit passed, and looking back I date my improvement and subsequent recovery from that moment. No imagination could produce a greater horror than that vision of infinitely increasing physical pain through astronomical time. My soul had plumbed the lowest depth.

There is little more to tell about that awful attack of depressive insanity. Although for months yet my mind went on revolving in the same channels of fear and despair, the weight of the anticipated horror and pain seemed to be lifted, to recede as it were. I was able to behave more normally, until in March 1940 my family took the risk of bringing me home, quite against the doctor's advice. It was a wise decision. I nearly shot myself once when I got at my guns at last; my toe was on the trigger and the muzzle in my mouth. But I did not pull it; somehow I wanted to live again. I have never suffered from serious depression since.

3. *Repulsion and Sin*

If I were asked to characterise in the briefest possible way, the whole experience of the depressive phase, I would describe it as a total reaction of repulsion between those fundamental poles of all being as we perceive it, which can be roughly and variously designated as the individual and the environment, the "I" and the "Not I", the ego and "the other", the perceiver and the perceived (including inner perceptions), or even as the soul and God. The basis of that repulsion seems to be fear, or "anxiety", to use the word generally employed to translate the Freudian concept of "Angst". And in the last analysis, as I have tried to show, the fear or anxiety seems to resolve itself at the climax into the fear of physical pain in the most terrifying form.

There is something quite logical about this. At the very beginning of the evolution of the nervous system, the essential foundation of all conscious life, this type of reaction, a total reaction to the environment, is all that is possible. The simplest forms of animal life, that is to say the simplest organisms with the power of motion, are merely aware of changes of a pleasant or unpleasant nature in their environment, and they move accordingly towards or away from the source. W. H. R. Rivers regards this as the origin of the protopathic sensibility of the nervous system, which has been proved (Head's experiment on sensory changes) to be crude and vague without the possibility of localisation.* He opposes to this the far more delicate epicritic sensibility, which appears to be of a wholly different kind and, in his own words, "enables the many forms of reaction which become possible when the exact nature of the stimulating object is recognised". Rivers associates the instincts with protopathic sensibility, centred in the thalamus, and intelligence with epicritic sensibility, which depends on the cortex. He points out

* W. H. R. Rivers, "Instinct and the Unconscious", pp. 23–4.

that the reactions to the instincts as so defined tend to have an "all or none" character,* corresponding to the crudeness of protopathic sensibility.

Certainly it seems to me that my reactions in the depressive phase are crude in this sense, or "total", the word I used above. There is little or no discrimination; everything is abhorrent to me, everything repels me, everything frightens me. My consciousness has as it were regressed to that earliest stage of the simple organism which, finding its environment unpleasant, wants to get away at all costs. I want to get away into the nothingness of annihilation, hence my suicidal impulses. Yet the unpleasantness of my situation thrusts itself upon my consciousness with all the intensity and with all the endless variety and refinement of torture made possible with the vast and intricate development of the nervous system in man. Infinite possibilities of horror and pain occur to me. If I have the slightest pain, that pain becomes in anticipation infinite and increasing, absorbing my whole consciousness. Every unpleasant reaction or thought is magnified to the limit.

Much the same is true, *mutatis mutandis*, of the manic phase. There is the same total reaction, of pleasure instead of pain, or "unpleasure". Instead of being repelled, with horror and fear, from my environment, I am attracted to it. I feel, as I have tried to explain, "at one" with the Universe.

Later on in this book, I propose to put forward some tentative and very speculative ideas to which reflection on the strange phenomenon of manic-depression has led me. At this point it will suffice to stress that there really does seem to be something fundamental about it, something at the very core of existence.

Attraction and repulsion, naturally opposing and mutually balancing, are at the root of the physical universe; gravitation, for example, is balanced by centrifugal force to hold the stars and planets on their courses in intelligible systems. I am not sufficiently versed in modern physics to discuss its effects

* Also see pp. 64 and 65, supra.

on the general picture, but I understand that the same principles still hold good. Similarly, in the psychological world, according to Freud all life is ruled by the pleasure–pain principle, which is merely a specific manifestation of attraction and repulsion. In the condition of manic-depression this principle is pushed to its most extreme limits. In biological existence the attraction of Eros is the prime condition of the renewal of life, while the repulsion of fear and pain (as danger-signals) as well as of disgust and anger, etc., are also necessary for survival. Finally, in almost all religions the Heaven–Hell concept plays a major part. And that concept —the pleasure–pain principle raised to the nth degree—is always associated with attraction to or oneness with the god or gods on the one hand, and repulsion towards or separation from them on the other. In close relation to this stands the moral law itself, indeed the whole concept of good and evil.

Although the entities, "I" and "Not-I", ego and "other", between which this attraction and repulsion takes place, may be described as the fundamental poles of being as we perceive it, the distinction between them is not easy to make. Psychological research has shown that it is a gradual growth, that the human infant, for example, finds it at first exceedingly difficult, and incidentally very unpleasant as well. As I have tried to explain, the process of repulsion between the two entities which takes place in the depressive phase leads to an increasingly sharp division; the ego becomes more and more isolated, while its pain and fear at this isolation grow correspondingly. Conversely in the manic phase the attraction between the ego and the outside world or "other" destroys these barriers and produces a sense of oneness coupled with intense joy, which is presumably a regression to the infantile state of consciousness before the differentiation took place. Except ye become as a new born infant, or, better still, a foetus in the womb, ye shall not enter into the Kingdom of Heaven.

In the Kingdom of Hell which depression reveals, the ego is not merely cut off; it is also increasingly restricted, until it seems to become an almost infinitesimal point of abject misery, disgust, pain and fear. It is very noticeable that the repulsion is not only felt for the outside world; it invades the personality in the form of intense disgust for oneself, horror of one's body, of seeing one's reflection in a mirror and so on. Clothes and personal property associated with oneself become objects of repulsion, whereas in the manic phase clothes and other property take on an extraordinarily attractive aspect; I have often felt them imbued with magical powers, filled with "mana" as it were. At the same time one takes a narcissistic delight in one's own body.

It is quite evident both from my own introspective experiences and from rational considerations that this phenomenon of attraction and repulsion between the ego and "the other" must be intimately linked with the attraction and repulsion in respect of excreta and other normally repulsive objects to which reference has been made. And it is, as we saw in that connection, closely bound up with the sense of sin.

This in depression is dominating and all-pervading, as I have tried to show. It can reach incredible extremes. Yet I have always found it difficult to give a rational answer to a question my wife often put to me during the course of my depression. How could I possibly imagine, she asked, that my sins were so appalling as to make me the unforgivable, uniquely evil creature I conceived myself to be? What were these sins, anyway?

As far as I can analyse it, the sense of sin from which I suffered was dominated by two factors. The first factor was a tremendous sense of repulsion towards and guilt in respect of the whole of consciousness associated with the manic period. It seemed to me that during that period I had been controlled by a "power of evil". I had "sold myself to Satan", who had "tempted me" with the lovely but wicked visions of mania, and I was now placed in irremediable opposition to the "power of good", or "God". The second factor was an overpowering sense of sexual sin.

Reason tells me that I am a very ordinary sinner, addicted

to those sins of the flesh, which, to the modern conscience at any rate, are by no means the most grievous. But if I may generalise from my own experience it seems quite certain that there is an aspect of the Unconscious which does not agree with the modern conscience. It is wholly on the side of the most ascetic early Christians, for example; it would unreservedly support St Augustine in building his City of God and City of this world on "pure" and "carnal" love respectively. The forces in control of my mind made my carnal sins loom mountainous and overwhelming; I scarcely worried or thought of any others. My consciousness, in fact, behaved in the most orthodox Freudian manner, practically equating "sins" with sexual sin. And on my sexual sins I brooded ceaselessly and in extreme detail, finally convincing myself that nobody had ever sinned as I had.

My fall, like that of Adam, was entirely sexual. I had strange fantasies, I remember, about the Garden of Eden, connected with a man called Adamson, who used to walk on occasion in the garden of my ward. There was a tree there which to me was the Tree of Knowledge. Adamson had a curious trick of grimacing with his false teeth, which made him look rather like pictures of primitive man. Undoubtedly he was Pithecanthropus Anthropus Adam come to life again. I did not see Eve.

Except in shapes of horror, women never appeared in my depressive phantasies. I was dominated by a sense of repulsion to women and all forms of sensuality, bound up with my sense of sin. It was as though the whole tide of Eros in my being was at the lowest ebb. This is a regular feature of my depressive periods; even in minor attacks I cannot even trouble to notice a pretty girl. At the same time I am practically impotent, and if I attempt sexual relations premature ejaculation makes them virtually impossible. Precisely the opposite conditions prevail in manic periods.

Everything, in fact, seems to suggest that the opposed states of manic-depression are closely related with or possibly caused by some fundamental opposition or process connected with sex. Eros is, after all, the life-principle of attraction, a point Freud is never tired of making. Just as Eros dominates the manic phase, producing the sense of joyful oneness with God, man and the world as well as more purely sexual manifestations, so an opposite principle of repulsion, an "Anteros", dominates the depressive phase, producing the isolation, the sense of carnal sin and the terror of which I have written. Freud in his later works postulates a "death instinct", which might be involved. Further speculation must however be left till later.

CHAPTER IV

FANTASIA OF OPPOSITES

1. *Repulsion and Attraction*

As I HAVE tried to depict it in the last two chapters, manic-depression is a condition with two aspects in some sort of fundamental opposition to one another. To my subjective consciousness it appears that these contrary aspects are due to the opposition of powerful forces within the whole complex of being as I perceive it. I have described them as forces of "attraction" and "repulsion"; at any rate they seem to be analogous in the psychological sphere to these physical forces.

It is worth noting in this connection that metaphors or similes relating to "force" and "power" seem peculiarly appropriate to abnormal mental conditions of this kind. Delusions concerning electricity are very common. August Strindberg, a typical manic-depressive, describes the sensations which accompany them as follows: "Then I feel, at first only faintly, something like an inrush of electric fluid. I look at my compass, but it shows no sign of wavering. It is not electricity, then. But the tension increases; my heart beats violently; I offer resistance, but as if by a flash of lightning my body is charged with a fluid which chokes me and depletes my blood."* In my own case, vast forces which I feel physically, seem in the manic state to be flowing through me, while in the depressive state I seem to be "hard", "solid", "non-porous", while forces acting from outside "repel" me.

As we have also seen, the experience of these forces of "attraction" and "repulsion" is not peculiar to manic-depression, or even to insane conditions; it is a common feature of mystic states and can be found in some degree in the ordi-

* Strindberg, "The Inferno", p. 92.

nary course of many "normal" lives. There are grounds for
thinking that there may be something fundamental about it;
I have suggested a possible biological derivation from the
most primitive type of "protopathic" reaction to the environment, and it can be traced in the infancy of the individual as well as in that of the race.

It is interesting that Leuba, whose *Psychology of Religious
Mysticism* is probably the most thorough study of the
subject in connection with the abnormal mental states with
which I am specially dealing, is also of the opinion that an
opposition basic to human nature is in question. He classi-
fies the tendencies and habits of man into two main groups.
In the one he places fear and the various expressions of
aggression and aversion; everything in fact that divides, that
enhances the self-conscious separation of the individual from
the rest of the world, the ego from "the other". The other
group includes all tendencies that unite, notably curiosity
and the expressions of liking and affection. He derives these
tendencies on the one hand from the conflict-instincts with
which animal life appears to have begun, and on the other
from the parental instincts in the animal family as "the
cradle of the co-operative method of life". The roots out of
which this antithesis has developed, he maintains, "pene-
trate so deep into human nature that their growth may be
traced in other directions, particularly in the processes of
thought. Consider the man of science and the philosopher;
they do their work by alternating analysis and synthesis;
they cannot do it by one of them alone. . . . Completed
thinking implies these two movements: sundering and
uniting."*

It seems quite clear that Leuba's concepts are the same as
those I have endeavoured to convey. The movement towards unity, synthesis, merging, the tendency to diminish the
barriers surrounding the individual, which Leuba places at
the root of the mystical experience, is the same force of
"attraction" which dominates me in the manic state; where-

* Leuba, "Psychology of Religious Mysticism", pp. 6 and 7.

as in the ego-isolated state of depression the converse sundering movement or force of "repulsion" holds sway.

In view of the peculiar series of phantasies I shall shortly describe, it is noteworthy that Leuba also relates the movement towards unity with ancient forms of orgiastic religion such as the Dionysian and Bacchanalian celebrations, the Babylonian and Syrian fertility rites against which the Jewish prophets reacted so strongly, and similar orgiastic communal practices of modern primitives, as described by Frazer and others.* He is at pains to trace sexual manifestations in the ecstasies of the mystics. In this connection my suggestion will be recalled that the basic opposition we are considering must be closely connected with the whole domain of sex.

2. *"Positive" and "Negative"*

I am now going to try to give a coherent account of a series of phantasies or flights of ideas, based on these fundamental opposites of repulsion and attraction, sundering and uniting, analysis and synthesis, which impelled themselves upon me in the course of one of my manic periods. While these phantasies were in possession of my mind, I was filled with the light and certainty of ineffable revelation referred to in Chapter II. I was quite sure I had the secret of the Universe, a sort of open-Sesame to all knowledge of creation, history and life. As we have seen, this sense is a widely found phenomenon of trance. According to Leuba it always recurs in connection with something baffling expression.† One of the few intelligible descriptions is that of William James, quoted in Chapter I.‡ He refers to "the opposites" as being "melted into unity", and in my own case that was certainly the keynote of the whole experience. Yet it hardly baffles expression. Though often illogical and chaotic, it was detailed, explicit, and illustrated with innumerable visions.

At the outset I should perhaps make clear that the subjects of nature religion, orgiastic rites, Great Mother worship, occultism and so on, with which this series of phantasies was

* Leuba, op. cit., p. 33.   † Leuba, op. cit., p. 274.   ‡ P. 14.

largely connected, were, at the time when they first appeared, a closed book to me. I had little or no knowledge of psychology, and I had never read Jung, whose ideas, as will be seen, correspond remarkably closely with those which seemed to be "revealed" to me. The whole experience, indeed, opened with a vision of what was undoubtedly the "anima" Jung describes.

It was towards the end of the last war, in the late autumn of 1944. I was at the time engaged in exacting Intelligence work, involving long hours and much night duty; nervous breakdowns were not uncommon among us. One night, when I had just got home from work, a little patch of damp on the wall opposite my bed took on plainly the shape of a gorilla.

It so happened that I knew a girl nicknamed "Gorilla", and I immediately associated the vision with her. The figure was clearly feminine. But why should she appear to me?

For a day or two my mind had been engaged in off moments with speculations about the evolution of man. How, in particular, did the step to *homo sapiens* actually take place? It may seem a curious subject to be occupying the mind of a very ordinary intelligence officer, but at the moment work was slack, and I had just picked up in the village bookshop a remarkable book called *Darkness and the Deep*, by Vardis Fisher.* This contained a strikingly imaginative preface describing the evolution of the world from the spiral nebula onwards, followed by a sort of novel whose characters were actually anthropoid apes in the process of evolving into men and women. It was a real *tour de force*, showing the genesis of language, tools, weapons and so on. The heroine was an ape-girl who "got her man", thus obeying the primary law of life as laid down by G.B.S. By judiciously refusing sexual satisfaction to her man and spurring him on with analogous feminine tricks, she gets him to murder the Old Man-Ape, father and boss of the primeval horde, and to reign in his stead.

* Published by Methuen, 1944.

The book is written on the Freudian lines of "Totem and Tabu", and is fairly orthodox modern thought. Sexual frustration and sublimation were shown as the primary motive-power of man's conquest of his environment. Evolution was portrayed on the Shavian lines familiar from *Man and Superman* and *Back to Methusaleh* as a painful struggle upwards.

I was not quite satisfied. Where was the "fall of Man"? When mania is approaching my mind is, wholly dominated by an urge to synthesise. I strive to reconcile conflicting ideas, and in this case it was the religious conception of the fall which needed reconciliation with the scientific conception of the evolutionary climb.

So as I looked at the visionary gorilla on the wall of my little bedroom, I spoke to her. "Who are you?" I asked. "Are you the Eve in this little book, the Eve who worked and struggled for the sake of her man and her children, or are you someone else?"

I did not actually hear her voice replying; I have never experienced true auditory hallucinations. Yet she spoke to me quite clearly in my inner consciousness. "I am the other Eve", she said, "the Harlot Eve who fell. Satan, who is the Serpent in Man, tempted me to my fall, but I rose again. For I am Astarte, I am Ashtaroth, I am the Great Whore of Babylon, yes and Aphrodite of the Greeks and Cleopatra and Helen of Troy, too. Look on me, man, as I really am."

And as I looked, the gorilla in the patch of damp seemed to take on the shape of a lovely woman. I do not really know whether she was dark or fair, though I have the impression that she was dark, like Rider Haggard's Ayesha in the caves of Kor. At the same time the voice became softer and sweeter. "P.B.", she said, using a family nickname, "I am many others, too. I am all fallen women since the world began; I wantoned in the groves of Nineveh and Babylon; I danced before the Golden Calf of Bethel and upon the hillside of Greece in the wild worship of the young Dionysus; and as Mary Magdalene I loved the Lord Jesus and for once knew peace. But I know it no longer, for I represent the great Negative Path which the world today has neglected and forgotten, so that it is chased to its destruction by all the furies of Hell." The vision disappeared. I realised that an elated period was coming on, so the next morning I got leave and went home. Within two days I was in hospital with acute mania.

Such was my first meeting with the "anima". Since then I have seen her in many forms; in mania she is always near me. And she is invariably plainly associated with the concept of a "Negative Power" or "Path".

Positive and Negative. How can I explain these concepts, born of the ecstasy of mania? With the vision of the anima it seemed to me that I had got beyond Good and Evil (like Nietzsche), and it was crystal clear that both were like "heads" and "tails" of a coin, equally necessary.* Satan had been cruelly maligned. In my delusion of grandeur I was Satan in person, yet I was "the servant of all" as Our Lord had commanded. Without Satan there could, I saw, be no creation.†

There was a fundamental opposition in the universe, but it was not the opposition of good and evil. I seemed to see, like a flash, two vast lines of connection stretching right back into the evolutionary process, which I could not help calling the "Positive" and "Negative" Powers of God. The image was plainly of an electrical circuit with positive and negative poles, and I made many attempts to draw it. Sometimes it seemed as though two currents were involved, running in opposite directions. Whichever way I conceived it, the electrical analogy seemed the most appropriate.

Yet it was also associated with sex, and directly derived from the vision of the male and female organs which is always behind the ideas which come to me in a manic period. Male was "positive" and female "negative"; in most of my

* Cf. Jung, "Anima is Life beyond all Categories". "Integration of the Personality", p. 78.
† Cf. Toynbee's theory of Satanic challenge and Divine response. "A Study of History", vol. I, p. 270 et seq.

drawings the "positive" and "negative" poles are given the appropriate sexual form. The power or energy involved was in fact sexual rather than electrical, though it sometimes seemed as though the physical force of electricity was in fact part of it. The analogy with the "libido" of Freud and Jung is of course obvious, but at the time it did not occur to me, as I had read practically no psychology. I was quite clear, however, that this was the basic power of creation.

These "Positive" and "Negative" Powers were also plainly identical with the forces dominating me in the depressive and manic states respectively; in my manic ecstasy I knew without any doubt that I was experiencing impulses through "contact" with the "Negative Power". This idea of "contact" impelled itself very forcibly and in many forms on my consciousness.

Here there may perhaps seem to be a contradiction between the electrical analogy of "positive" and "negative" and the idea of forces of "repulsion" and "attraction" associated, as I have explained above, with "dividing" and "uniting". Why should the attracting, uniting, synthesising force of the manic state be regarded as "negative" and its opposite force of repulsion as "positive"?

Certainly there was no doubt in my mind at the time. The association of the male and female principles with this opposition had a good deal to do with it; male would normally be regarded as "positive". But another and deeper reason was, I think, that in the dim, phantastic vision of the creative process as I seemed to see it, the initiative unquestionably lay with the Positive Power.

In the beginning was the undifferentiated All, the primal Chaos, Darkness, which was somehow also God, the Perfect self-sufficient Individual, the One. Creation was only possible by division, differentiation, by producing the Many from the One, by God going out of Himself in the creative act. This produced in the first place Light—in Darkness there is no division. The drive towards clarification through division is thus the initial creative force, the Outflow. That is the "*male*" Positive Power, "repulsion".

But Outflow implies Return. Divided, differentiated individuals yearn to be reunited in the All from which they emerged. Created souls long for God. And God, having gone out of Himself in creation, must return to Himself, or rather to Herself, thus healing the primal split. This is the "female" Negative Power, Goethe's Eternal Feminine, "attraction".

It is easy to see how these two Powers could seem to be symbolised by the male and female organs I had seen in my vision some four years before. They had appeared to me, although separated in space, in the act of orgasm, with the male expelling and the female attracting or sucking. Outflow and Return, dividing and uniting, analysis and synthesis; all were activities of the Positive and Negative Powers —of God, or of Love.

In a series of kaleidoscopic phantasies an extraordinary number of associations with these Positive and Negative Powers appeared to me, until, as I have said, it seemed possible to classify the whole of creation under one head or the other. The essential basis, however, remained at once sexual and religious.

Subsequent study has shown me that the positive and negative concepts of my phantasy were identical with a fundamental religious antithesis, which can be traced right back into the pre-historic past. The ethical worship of a Father-God stood opposed to the nature-cult of the Great Mother, dating from Palaeolithic times.* This opposition came out quite spontaneously in phantasy, although at the time I knew nothing of the Great Mother or her worship.

It is, I believe, well-established that this worship has been generally attended by sexual release through orgiastic celebrations and ritual prostitution. It makes no attempt to oppose harlotry to maternity. Thus although in my vision of the anima she appeared—as she often does according to Jung †—as a Harlot, a fallen Eve, opposed to the Christian

* Cf. G. R. Levy, "The Gate of Horn".
† Jung, "Contributions to Analytical Psychology", pp. 128–9.

concept of maternity, she was none the less a manifestation of the fundamental female or Mother-principle. At any rate my vision set in train a series of phantasies of two main types of approach to the Unseen.

I seemed to see man evolving from the anthropoids, and in the process dividing into two great streams. There was both a Rise and a Fall of man, in the sense that some worshipped the Positive and some the Negative Power. The earliest tribes and civilisations seemed to me to favour the Negative, achieving contact with the Unseen by the orgiastic road, by excess, by letting-go, by relaxation. They followed my fallen Eve, and she gave them visions, sometimes visions of wonder and beauty, but often of horror, of snakes and toads and other repulsive objects which they worshipped.

Among other groups of men, however, a sense of disgust, revulsion and sin appeared, and with that sense came a new approach to the Unseen. Individual sacrifices and mortification of the flesh were stressed; sex was repudiated. The visions thus achieved led those who had them to take up the moral struggle in an extreme form. The main example of this "positive", ethical development appeared to me to be the Jewish worship of Jehovah, or Yahveh.

In the dramatic antithesis which the Bible brings out between the stern religion of the Jewish prophets and the sensual nature-worship of the surrounding peoples of Palestine and Syria, my phantasy had as it were something to work on. I saw the "high places and images and groves", the wild, ecstatic dances, the ritual prostitution, indeed all "the abominations of the nations which the Lord cast out before the Children of Israel".* The great prophets appeared, Elijah and Elisha, Amos, Isaiah and Jeremiah, thundering their denunciations, while Israel went "a-whoring after strange gods".

Of these strange gods and goddesses, there was one which very powerfully affected my imagination. Solomon, it is recorded in a passage which stuck in my memory, "went after

* I Kings 14, 23, 24.

Ashtoreth the goddess of the Zidonians". * Ashtoreth, or Ashtaroth, was always in my mind. She was, as I have said, identified with the anima in my vision, and seemed to me to typify the Negative Power. At the time I knew little about her, except that I had an idea she was the consort of Baal and vaguely connected her with the Phoenicians and Carthage. By a curious chance, just as my mind was running on this subject, I picked up in the library of the Mental Hospital where I was confined a book of short stories, by John Buchan. One of these was of a Scotch Presbyterian who discovered, on an up-country South African station, an ancient altar and grove of Ashtaroth, which had bewitched the owner of the station. Somehow or other the power of the goddess had preserved the grove, originally established by wandering Phoenicians; even the doves, her emblem, were still there. But the power and wrath of Jehovah rose in the Presbyterian blood of the Scotchman; defying the remonstrances of the bewitched owner, he cut down the grove, scattered the stones of the altar and shut the doors, using appropriate texts from the Bible as exorcisms. It was the last refuge of Ashtaroth on earth, and as it was destroyed, the companion of the Scotchman, who tells the story, felt very strongly that something which, though it might appear evil, was in reality good and kind and loving, was being driven away for ever.

Buchan's tale fitted in exactly with the pattern of phantasy I was weaving. Of course I accepted it as "guidance". It confirmed what I knew in any case with complete inner certainty. Not only Ashtaroth, my beloved Goddess, but the whole Negative Power associated with her was good. What did it matter that it included all the witches, devils, goblins, snakes, toads, spiders and other traditional symbols of evil which appeared to me in my visions? What did it matter that it involved wild orgies, loosing the dammed-up floods of primitive instinct? It was not the Power behind the pipes of Pan, the Power which made all Nature and all creation one, which was wrecking the world. On the contrary, surely the

* I Kings 11, 5.

balance of evil inclined to the Positive Power, the Power of division, separation, analysis; surely that was where cruelty, fanaticism, intolerance and hatred really came from?

Yahveh, the solitary god of a people set apart, unique, "chosen". He seemed to me symbolic precisely of the dividing and separating characteristics of the Positive Power. Yet I was also clear that those characteristics were the main-spring of progress, the driving-force of evolution and fresh creation. Intellect, for example, derived from them, whereas the instinctive, emotional side of being was mainly "nega-tive".

In a sense the Positive Power seemed to look to the future, whereas the Negative was turned rather towards the past. The future separates itself from the past, discards it; it is "positive". But the Negative Power discards nothing; it harks back to the past, to lost causes and abandoned paths of evolution, all of which have to be included in its all-em-bracing synthesis. Thus in my visions I sometimes saw the Negative Power as a vast line of connections stretching right back through the infinite past to the Eternal God, while the Positive stretched forward to Him through the equally in-finite future. The whole was a completed circuit, in which Time disappeared. The fall of Man was thus a fall back-wards into the ancient caverns of Instinct and the Uncon-scious; the Rise was the evolutionary struggle for higher differentiation and greater self-consciousness. But both were necessary, since only so could the ultimate contact be achieved and the All be perfectly reconciled.

This "Negative" characteristic of belonging to the past is emphasized by Jung as pertaining to the anima. "But the anima", he writes, "is conservative, and clings in an exas-perating fashion to the ways of earlier mankind. Therefore, it likes to appear in historic dress, with a predilection for Greece and Egypt." * It is also particularly interesting in this connection to note that, as opposed to this association of the anima with the past, Jung finds that the "animus", the

* Jung, "Integration of the Personality", p. 78.

corresponding male image in women, is generally associated with the present and future.* Thus it seems fairly clear that the anima is what I have called "negative", while the animus is "positive". Moreover, if the "positive" tendency is to divide or differentiate, the positive "animus" would tend to be plural, as Jung says.

In the analysis of the Unconscious given in "Integration of the Personality", the anima is closely associated with darkness, with the "shadow", the Satanic reverse, to which Jung actually applies the same term, "negative".† It is also associated with water, "the dark mirror that reposes at the bottom".‡ These associations were very plain in the whole series of phantasies. All Satanism and witchcraft was obviously "negative"; so were streams and rivers with their attendant spirits, generally female, which became almost tangible Presences to me, whenever I had any contact with water.

A point stressed by Jung is that most of the troubles of modern life, notably in the depersonalised Protestant world, are due to the suppression and neglect of this "negative" side of things owing to the lack of concrete symbols in which it can express itself. This view of the "neglected Negative" impressed itself very strongly on my consciousness (long before I had studied Jung's works), and my anima, my Negative Eve, actually used the word "neglected" in my vision. It was clear to me that the Negative is preparing a terrible revenge on modern civilisation, and that revenge is closely connected with the political phantasies with which I shall deal later.

Although much of the Unconscious is "negative", it is not possible to say, for example, that the positive–negative antithesis is the same as that between consciousness and the Unconscious. As we have seen, the animus in the female Unconscious seems to be positive, although I have of course no personal experience of this. Other powerful forces in the Unconscious, however, seem to me most emphatically positive; for

---

* Cf. Jung, "Contributions to Analytical Psychology", p. 133.
† Jung, "Integration of the Personality", p. 92.
‡ Op. cit., p. 65.

example the sense of sin in general, and above all, perhaps, the drive towards a Puritan repudiation of sex and the body, the "flesh", which has played such a large part in the development of the great religions during the past two or three thousand years.

I have perhaps sufficiently indicated the association of "paganism" in the sense of the ancient nature religion, and the gods and goddesses derived from it, with the Negative Power. Ashtaroth, Astarte and Aphrodite, Eros, Pan and his train of satyrs and nymphs, Dionysus; all these are obviously "negative" figures Though they have been banished from most of the great modern religions, they are deeply imbedded in the Unconscious, as is shown by their tremendous appeal to the imagination when artists, as for example at the time of the Renaissance, bring them to the surface of consciousness. In the manic state they appear to me over and over again, and their banishment seems to me to be at the very root of the troubles of modern civilisation. As I have said, they demand their revenge.

Yet it seemed perfectly plain to me that this whole aspect of things was falsely placed in opposition to Christianity. One of the keynotes of the reconciliation of opposites which the manic state brings is the certainty that there is no real conflict between Jesus and Pan or Dionysus. I cannot help seeing Our Lord as leader of all that is good and lovely in the galaxy of gods and goddesses in which the infinitely varied imagination of man has embodied its worship of the invisible Powers. In Him Positive and Negative are reconciled. That reconciliation is for me inherent in the personality of Jesus, friend of "publicans and sinners", of social outcasts and harlots. And somehow it all centres round my favourite saint, Mary Magdalene, who is plainly identified with my anima, my Negative Eve.

The meeting between Jesus and the Magdalene, which I always see in my visions as the lovely incident of the anointing of Our Lord's feet with oil, appears to me as an event second only in importance to the Crucifixion itself. It symbolises the meeting of two worlds, the final contact between Positive and Negative; it completes the inner development of Jesus in a perfect synthesis of humanity and godhead; it is the triumph of the Power of Love before the great sacrifice.

Surely no one could have been opposed to the "positive" doctrines of Pharisaism and Puritanism than Our Lord? Yet they soon crept back into Christianity. I see St Paul, with his Positive Pharisaic background, contributing much to this; then comes the fatal rejection of "eros" for "agapé" in the very language of the Gospels; and finally St Augustine produces the concept of Two Cities in *De Civitate Dei*, in which practically the whole of what I call the Positive Power is attributed to God, while the Devil has the Negative all to himself.

All my religious phantasies in the manic state show me this development as a distortion of Christianity, centring round two ideas: the repudiation of sexual love as "original sin", and the doctrine of eternal Hell. Both of these are clearly Positive and can, I think, be logically traced to Positive aspects of the Unconscious.

I have tried to show how the Positive Power includes all that tends to divide and differentiate, analysis as opposed to synthesis. It is Logos, as opposed to Eros, the ultimate yearning of individuals to unite; the repudiation of Eros as inherently sinful is the quintessence of the "positive" as I see it. The tremendous force of this idea in Christianity and elsewhere is itself a proof that the vast cosmic forces of the Unconscious are at work.

Similarly the doctrine of eternal Hell, of an ultimate and irrevocable division between God and some of His creatures, between the elect and the damned, is entirely characteristic of the "positive". Analysis, cutting up as opposed to uniting, could scarcely go further.*

As we have seen, the depths of my depressive periods are

* Cf. Blake's attitude towards analysis, "dark Satanic mills". Also cf. Aldous Huxley, "Good is that which makes for unity; evil is that which makes for separateness".

dominated by the idea of Hell, of the final separation of my soul from God and His creation. The Positive Power is then in complete control of my soul. But as depression gives place to elation and the Negative Power holds sway, one of its first conquests is of Hell and all that that implies.

To illustrate this, let me describe an experience which came to me at the outset of the same manic period which produced the positive–negative antithesis. An inner voice seemed to tell me that there was only one way to conquer the Powers of Hell, and that was to offer myself as a sacrifice. I fell on my knees and prayed that I might be worthy. Then I went out into the garden and challenged in a loud voice all the Powers of the Universe to dare to condemn a human soul to eternal torment. If any soul had to bear it, let it be me. But in the name of Jesus of Nazareth, my Master, I defied all Powers, Gods or Devils, to do their worst.

No doubt this sounds very trite and silly heroics. But it should be realised that the Powers of the Universe are intensely real to anybody in my condition. It is remarkable that those who have made attempts to describe such states usually seem to be impelled to use the word "Powers".* They certainly were Powers; I could see them all around, flashing in the evening sky; I could feel intense "electric currents" between them and myself. It seemed to me that a sort of battle was really going on. I felt that I was running a real risk, and for a time I felt afraid. Then I realised that I had won. Hell really was conquered; Jesus had conquered it and I was merely following in His footsteps. Yet innumerable souls were still in Hell. Heaven and Hell seemed to open before me, and I could go where I liked, but I must choose Hell as long as a single soul was in torment and could be helped.

At the same time I was appalled at the wickedness of those who have imagined a Hell for others, while they expected a Heaven for themselves. I seemed to see in a series of visions

* Cf. particularly August Strindberg, "Inferno", and Gérard de Nerval, "Aurélia".

the men who had distorted Christian doctrine in this way. Tertullian was particularly plain, so were Augustine and Calvin, and I felt that the Hell of their imagining would do them good.

All these men were obviously "positive". On the opposite "negative" side in Christianity, I saw men like Origen,* St Francis—who heard a voice which told him that God would never refuse pardon to any sinner in the world—and Martin Luther. Broadly speaking, thus, the Puritans stand opposed by all those who place love, charity in word and deed, at the centre of their religious life

Yet this is certainly not the whole truth. I was always clear, for example, that Catholicism, which has by no means always placed great emphasis on charity, was Negative, as opposed to Protestantism; the Reformation was a wholly Positive movement. Presumably this is justified by the considerable number of pagan survivals in the worship of the Virgin Mother and the Saints. It is of interest in this connection that Jung lays stress on the ability of Catholicism to take care of the Unconscious, with its Negative side, by absorbing it into dogmatic archetypes, so to speak without remainder.†

As I saw it in my vision, the great problem of life is always to bring Positive and Negative together, into contact, thus reconciling the opposites and allowing power to flow freely and harmoniously. That reconciliation seemed to me complete in the personality of Jesus and in the true Christianity based upon it; it was also to be found in something near perfection in the great days of Greece.

Again and again visions of Greece appeared to me, little though I knew of the classics and classical civilisation. And always the Greeks appeared to me quite unique. They alone of all peoples had achieved a Golden Mean between Positive and Negative, and it was to this perfect balance that their amazing achievements appeared to me to be due. In charts I

* Note: It is of interest that Jung puts Origin in fundamental opposition to Tertullian. "Psychological Types", p. 22.
† Jung, "Integration of the Personality", p. 60.

drew at the time attempting to classify the peoples of history according to their Positive and Negative elements, the Greeks always came along a central line. Through the Golden Mean the Kingdom of God had very nearly been created on earth.

But more was needed. The Greek balance was soon lost; in any case it affected only a few. Jesus had come, however, to enable mankind to re-establish it, and on the basis of the Golden Mean to build, through love as well as reason, the Kingdom of God for all. That was why He had been born at a a time and place where the ultimate Powers so nearly coincided. There was the extreme Positive Jewish religion; all around were the remnants of the Negative, surviving from the Sumerians, Babylonians and Egyptians. And Greek civilisation, with its balance between the two, covered the whole area.

Why Jesus had not succeeded at the time, why another two thousand years of struggle and tension had been necessary was not clear to me. Perhaps struggle and tension would always prevail on earth. At any rate it seemed plain to me that in the course of our Western history the Negative Power had been driven back again and again, creating, as it were, an increasing "potential". Somehow balance would re-establish itself. The tremendous currents coming to the surface of this tormented age were clear proof that the Negative Power was coming into its own again.

In order to make this Positive–Negative antithesis comprehensible, I have tried to give the opposites which appeared to me in as logical and coherent a form as I can. They were, none the less, typical products of mania; that is to say they were forced upon me in an overwhelmingly powerful flight of ideas quite independently of any conscious ratiocination. In the blinding light of this illumination, or apparent illumination, from the depths of being, practically everything in Heaven and Earth seemed to fall on one side or the other. Let me try to give an idea of the wealth of material involved.

God Transcendent is Positive, God Immanent Negative.

Moral struggle and tension are Positive; forgiveness and moral release are Negative. Within Christianity, as I have said, Protestantism is Positive as opposed to Catholicism, while within Protestantism Lutheranism seems far less so than Calvinism. Most of the great religions today are mainly Positive, except for Hinduism, which is clearly largely Negative. Mahomedanism seems to me, however, to have a Negative streak in its very sensual Heaven, and perhaps in its emblem of the crescent moon. In China, Confucianism is positive, while the philosophy of Lao-Tse and the Way of the Tao are Negative, the two together forming a remarkably balanced whole, as Lin Yu Tiang, among others, has pointed out. African negro beliefs and practices are, on the other hand, almost entirely Negative, and I cannot even now meet a negro without a very strong instinctive feeling of contact with the Negative Power.

The Positive sun (Light) opposes the Negative moon (Queen of Darkness), the starry sky faces the Negative Mother Earth, yet solid Earth is Positive as compared with rivers or sea or any form of water.

Nature, and particularly organic Nature, is Negative; the inorganic has a Positive quality. In the human—or animal—body, everything associated with the reproductive function is Negative and with the nutritive functions Positive.

Science is Positive, art Negative; intellect is Positive as opposed to Negative instinct. Within the arts the same opposition can be traced. In music, for example, Positive classical music opposes the highly Negative negro jazz, whose popularity is a plain sign of the Negative forces just below the crust of civilisation. Yet Wagner and the Romantics are Negative as opposed to Bach's extremely Positive Protestant music, while Beethoven's superlative greatness seems to me to be due to his having achieved a more perfect contact between Positive and Negative than any other musician. The last movement of the Ninth Symphony is an orgiastic rhapsody of the Negative which goes straight back to the Dionysiac thiasos. It is perhaps not without significance that during the three days of acute mania which I spent in the padded cell at Brixton I was generally singing either the choral part of the Ninth or else "Old Man River", interspersed with snatches from *Tristan* or the *Ring*.

Dancing is a Negative activity which derives plainly from the ritual dances of the worship of the Negative Power; no doubt that it is why it is so abhorred of all Puritans. Modern ballroom dancing, with its negro origin, is of course at the extreme of the Negative scale.

The transition from primitive religious painting to the sensuous glories of the Renaissance was a transition from Positive to Negative; the Renaissance was a great outburst of the Negative Power. The Reformation on the other hand was mainly Positive, although episodes of collective intoxication like the short-lived Anabaptist millennium at Münster are of course pure Negative. Lutheranism, as I have said, seems partly Negative, but Calvinism, and most of the movements which trace their origin to it, such as the Puritan republicanism of the seventeenth century, Whiggery, and to some extent nineteenth-century Liberalism, seem to me Positive. Toryism I cannot help instinctively associating with the Negative, and Fascism seems Negative as opposed to Socialism and Communism, though of course all mass collective movements have a strong Negative element.

As I have continually stressed, all the classifications given above, self-evident though they appear to me even now, are of instinctive origin. They are derived, that is to say, from the Unconscious, as is the whole conception of Positive and Negative Powers. I now want to consider to what extent any intellectual validity, any "reality" or "meaning", can be attributed to the whole complex of ideas I have described.

3. *Some Analogies*

It will be remembered that at the beginning of this chapter I gave quotation from Leuba's *Psychology of Religious Mysticism*, in which he distinguishes a fundamental opposition obviously analogous to the positive–negative concept.

Of the two main drives, towards sundering on the one hand and uniting on the other, the latter in his view obviously dominates both the religious mystics and psychopaths like myself who have had analogous experiences. Yet he stoutly denies all real validity or meaning to the sense of unity or to the experiences associated with it.

In particular, he denies meaning to the peculiar certainty or clearness with which ideas appear in ecstatic or trance states. This is merely due, he says, to benumbing of the higher mental faculties and the resulting mental simplification which, "by eliminating contradictions or complexities that might be the occasion of doubt, tends to produce assurance as to what remains in consciousness".* He will not even admit the hypothesis, put forward at the time he wrote by William James and Flournoy, of inroads from the Subconscious. The whole experience is a pure illusion, produced by "a progressive dissociation of the nerve elements, i.e. . . . the undoing of that which takes place when knowledge is gained".

Since Leuba wrote, however, the work of Freud and Jung has been generally accepted by psychologists and the vast influence of the Subconscious or Unconscious has been recognised. It seems therefore not unreasonable to claim, as I have, that my experiences have at least the validity or "reality" of being effects of the released Unconscious, acting on the contents of my consciousness. In the particular case in question, the Positive–Negative antithesis or opposition, additional proof of its derivation from the Unconscious lies in the fact that the principal figure in my visions, my Queen of the Negative as it were, was a typical anima-archetype of the Unconscious as analysed by Jung, appearing as harlot, goddess and saint.

It seems to me, however, as I have foreshadowed in Chapter I, possible to put forward a further claim in the form of two simple propositions:

(1) that "instinct" or instinctive factors (which express

* Leuba, op. cit., p. 277.

themselves as inroads from the Unconscious) can complement "intelligence" or the "rational faculty";

(2) that mystical, ecstatic or psychopathic experiences are due to the greater freedom given to instinctive or unconscious factors. They thus provide some sort of more complete vision in the Bergsonian sense which, in view of the limited nature and capacity of human consciousness, can only be obtained by excessive simplification and elimination of normal hindrances to rational consciousness and perception.

It will, perhaps, be agreed that I shall go some way towards establishing the truth of these propositions if I can show that my "instinctive" perception of the Positive–Negative antithesis tends to correspond to fundamental distinctions made by serious philosophical and scientific writers.

Of all the great philosophers, the one who delved most deeply into the Unconscious was probably Friedrich Nietzsche. And it was in the Unconscious that he found the crucified Dionysus who obsessed him throughout his tragic life and was one of the principal factors leading him to reject Christianity.

Nietzsche's fundamental pair of opposites, as set out in his work *The Birth of Tragedy*, was that of the Dionysian versus the Apollonian principle. The Dionysian principle is obviously almost exactly what I have described as Negative; Nietzsche sees it as unbridled instinct or "dynamis", a frenzy which dissolves the ego and unites man with his brother-man as well as Nature; "estranged, hostile, subjugated Nature celebrates once more her feast of reconciliation with her lost son, man".* The Apollonian principle on the other hand, is measure, number, limitation and order, the separation of the individual from the mass by a process of individuation, the separating out of the elements of experience by orderly analysis. It thus has the character of division which I have attributed to the Positive, though perhaps the elements of

* Nietzsche, "The Birth of Tragedy", translated by Haussmann. Edinburgh, 1909, p. 26.

"repulsion" and strife which I also regard as Positive are less clearly to be seen in it.

Apollo was the Greek God of the Sun, and it may not be without significance that the Sun always appears to me most emphatically as Positive. Incidentally Nietzsche's view that the Greeks owed their greatness to the reconciliation of the two principles, of the Delphic oracle with Dionysus, is a perfect intellectual formulation of my vision of Greece as a Golden Mean between Positive and Negative.

The same basic opposition can be traced in Goethe and Schiller. To Goethe it appeared as systole, a withdrawing inward, and diastole, a great sweeping outward movement embracing all creation. But he also sensed it as a struggle between Christianity and Paganism, the mediaeval and the classic world, which he strove so magnificently to reconcile through the anima-figure of Helen in the second part of *Faust*. The whole of *Faust* has a tremendous appeal to me in the manic state—I cover copies with annotations—and the Eternal Feminine seems to me, as I have said already, a fundamental manifestation of the Negative. So is Schiller's "Ode to Joy", which Jung quotes as a supreme example of Dionysiac feeling,* of a diastolic embrace of all creatures. To Beethoven's setting in the Ninth Symphony I have already referred.

Jung's primary psychological classification, introvert–extravert, has obvious affinities with what I am trying to convey, and I have noted above that I spontaneously classified Tertullian, given by Jung as a typical introvert, on the Positive side (mainly owing to his attitude towards Hell) while Origen, whom Jung cites as the main example of extraversion in early Christianity, I placed on the Negative side. Jung also stresses the Apollonian–Dionysian opposition. Speaking from my subjective experience of the manic and depressive states, it is evident that in mania the Negative Power attracts me out of myself in an extraverted Dionysian expansion towards all outer objects, whereas in depression the Positive

* Jung, "Psychological Types", p. 179.

Power isolates me and forces me in on myself, that is to say to extreme introversion.

The Apollonian–Dionysian opposition has been emphasised in a most interesting manner by Berdyaev. For him the Dionysian principle is essentially orgiastic, involving loss of personality, and in Christian terms what he calls "impersonal salvation". He opposes this to Apollonian form, measure, individuality and aristocracy—personal salvation. The two principles are reconciled by the ultimate Christian Salvation of all men, "in sobornost", to use a Russian word implying the "togetherness" of the whole universe, and he stresses the noble belief of Origen that Christ would not accept the damnation of a single human being.* It is particularly interesting for me that in Berdyaev's mind there seems to have been the same association of the Dionysian Negative with the rejection of damnation for any soul that appeared in my visions. I could not—and still cannot—for a moment conceive of my own salvation unless the ultimate salvation of all creatures were assured. Mr C. S. Lewis's book, *The Great Divorce*, for example, strikes me as appalling blasphemy. The Negative Principle, with its Dionysian link with the whole of creation, fundamentally repudiates the concept of any final divorce between Heaven and Hell, at least as far as individual souls are concerned. Thus William Blake's "Marriage of Heaven and Hell" is a typical work of the Negative, and Blake's visions in general, particularly those recorded in his Prophetic Books, have distinct parallels with my own.

Berdyaev develops an extremely interesting view of the changed relationship between Man and Nature which made modern Science possible. Prometheus, he writes, freed man from subordination to the gods of nature. But this could not be completed without Christianity. "The gods die, the Great Pan disappears into the depths of nature and remains imprisoned there." This was of immense importance, since "a pagan attitude of dependence upon it made it impossible to

* Berdyaev, "Freedom and the Spirit", pp. 227 et seq., also p. 325.

know nature scientifically and so to master it technically" . . . thus . . ."paradoxical as it may appear, it is precisely Christianity which favoured the development of the natural and technical sciences".*

The work of the Positive Principle during the past two or three thousand years could scarcely have been better expressed. The Positive Apollonian tendency towards order, measure and analysis weakened the negative Dionysian link between man and the rest of creation; the immensely powerful Positive forces in Christianity broke it finally, and sent the Negative Gods and Goddesses in which it found expression back into the collective Unconscious. Thus man, and particularly Western man, has consciously conquered Nature, while the Negative Nature forces from the Unconscious look, in revenge, like reconquering, and perhaps indeed completely destroying the race that challenged them.

It is this antinomy, this tragic aspect of the Positive–Negative opposition, which underlies the whole work of another —and a very different—modern writer. If Nietzsche was haunted by Dionysus, the crucified Pan was always before the eyes of D. H. Lawrence. *Lady Chatterley's Lover* is essentially a plea for the rehabilitation of the Negative.

Lawrence expresses this quite plainly in his little apologia *A Propos of Lady Chatterley's Lover*. The "rhythm of the cosmos", the relation between man and the universe, has been lost, and only a profound and essentially phallic regeneration will re-establish it. What the early Christians destroyed of symbolic festivals and cosmic ritual the Roman Catholic Church wisely re-established to a very large extent, but Protestantism and the Nonconformity which followed it have made a clean sweep. What began with the grand idealists, Buddha, Plato, Jesus, with their underlying pessimism as regards life, their doctrine that the spirit demanded divorce from life, has been completed. And now "the universe is dead for us, and how is it to come to life again? 'Knowledge' has killed the sun, making it a ball of gas, with

* Berdyaev, op. cit., p. 226.

spots; 'Knowledge' has killed the moon, it is a dead little earth pitted with extinct craters as with smallpox; the machine has killed the earth for us, making it a surface, more or less bumpy, that you travel over. How, out of all this, are we to get back the grand orbs of the soul's heavens, that fill us with unspeakable joy. How are we to get back Apollo, and Attis, Demeter, Persephone, and the halls of Dis. How even see the star Hesperus, or Betelgeuse? . . .

"There are many ways of knowing, there are many sorts of knowledge. But the two ways of knowing, for man, are knowing in terms of apartness, which is mental, rational, scientific, and knowing in terms of togetherness, which is religious and poetic. The Christian religion lost, in Protestantism finally, the togetherness of the body, the sex, the emotions, the passions, with the earth and the sun and the stars."*

Spirit as mental, rational, "apartness", flesh as "togetherness"; the antithesis sensed by Lawrence is precisely what I have tried to express. He is really revolting not so much against Jesus, Plato and Buddha as teachers as against the whole strange Puritan revolution which swept through the various separate parts of the Eurasian continent during the first millennium B.C. As a Catholic writer, Christopher Dawson, has stressed, during that period new spiritual forces were introduced which have been active in the world ever since. The Hebrew prophets, the Greek philosophers, Buddha, the authors of the Upanishads, Confucius, were manifestations of these forces.† The Positive Principle or Power began its great attack.

At bottom that attack was directed against the religion of the Great Mother, the real basis of the Negative Power, as I stressed at the outset of this chapter. During the last three thousand years something has been destroyed which can trace its roots back for tens if not hundreds of thousands of years. Miss G. R. Levy's anthropological researches, em-

---

* D. H. Lawrence, "A Propos of Lady Chatterley's Lover", pp. 50 et seq.

† Christopher Dawson, "Progress and Religion", p. 119.

bodied in *The Gate of Horn*, to which I have already referred, show with a wealth of illustration and documentation, the enormous part played by this Stone Age Goddess and her spouse, the fertility-God, above all in Europe and the Near East. Figurines of the Mother have been found dating from Aurignacian times, at least. And now the "togetherness" of man and nature which the cult pursued and symbolised, has been lost. In exchange we have idealism, abstraction, "knowing in apartness", another Great Divorce between man and his Mother Nature, a largely—and for Protestantism exclusively—ethical approach to God, vastly intensifying moral tension, and above all, the tremendous, indeed terrifying increase of man's power through applied Science.

.The idea of increasing tension, of dammed-up forces of nature within the soul of man awaiting some sort of catastrophic release, forced itself again and again on my consciousness. To a considerable extent this is now a commonplace of modern thought. It dominates the picture presented to us by the psychologists; it lies behind theological and ethical works like those of Berdyaev and Reinhold Niebuhr; somehow it is in the air of what Mr Winston Churchill has called "this terrible twentieth century".

That somewhat unorthodox thinker, Mr Gerald Heard, goes so far as to maintain that the tension is a sign that a new step in the evolutionary process is at hand. Man has lost, he says, the "togetherness" and contact with "higher Powers" which the ancient fertility or Life religion gave. This was indeed necessary to enable him self-consciously to master his environment. But now the powers over Nature that he has won will only enable him to destroy himself unless he makes the further step of regaining union with "higher Powers" and his fellows through psycho-physical "Enlargement of Individuality".* In other words, Positive self-conscious Science has lost intuitive contact with the Negative, and the tension

* Cf. Gerald Heard, "Source of Civilisation", especially pp. 136 et seq., and "Ascent of Humanity", especially pp. 162 et seq.

can only be relieved by regaining contact through a radical evolutionary mutation. Whether Mr Heard, or his colleagues Aldous Huxley and Christopher Isherwood, who are apparently attempting to adapt Indian mysticism to the Western World through a rather esoteric group in California, will achieve their objects,* whether, in fact, glorified Yoga can save the world, may be open to doubt, but the attempt is certainly significant.

The tension of the twentieth century is a manifestation of what Professor Arnold Toynbee, in his monumental *Study of History*, calls "schism in the soul", and can be traced wherever there is a tendency for civilisations to disintegrate. For Toynbee, the Positive–Negative antithesis between ascetic self-control and *abandon* (in the French sense) is at the very root of this schism.

Toynbee maintains that when, in a disintegrating civilisation, the general faculty of creativeness is lost, *abandon* and ascetisim are the two ways of personal behaviour in which the soul seeks a substitute for the exercise of this faculty. In *abandon* (ἀκράτεια) the soul "lets itself go", in the belief that by giving free rein to its own spontaneous appetites and aversions it will be "living according to nature" and will automatically be receiving back from the lap of this mysterious and therefore possibly puissant goddess, the precious gift of creativity which the sick soul has been conscious of losing. The active alternative to this passive *abandon* is an effort at self-control (ἐγκράτεια) in which the soul "takes itself in hand and seeks to discipline its natural passions . . . in the opposite belief that Nature is the bane of creativity and not its source".†

These two reactions, "passive" and "active" (or "negative" and "positive" in the terminology of this chapter) are, Toynbee writes, apt to be exhibited by human beings in every kind of circumstances.‡ In primitive societies they appear as

---

* Cf. "Vedanta for the Western World", edited by Christopher Isherwood, Allen and Unwin.
† Toynbee, "A Study of History", vol. V, p. 377.
‡ Ibid., p. 399.

an orgiastic and ascetic vein predominating according to the seasons; they can be traced in the growth stage of civilisations; but in disintegration they are more clearly distinguishable as they show up as an unreconciled opposition instead of a creatively harmonious rotation. The examples given include the Epicureans and notably the Hedonist distorters of the doctrine, as opposed to the Stoics; the Chinese Hedonists who followed and distorted Yang Chu and were castigated by the "positive" Confucian and Mencian moralists; lingam-worship as opposed to Yoga in India; temple prostitution as opposed to the astral philosophy of the Babylonians; the Hittite contrast between the orgiastic and ascetic aspects in the worship of Cybele and Attis; and in Renaissance Italy the opposition between the Medici Circle and Savonarola.

In view of the fact that I instinctively associated the Negative with the past and the Positive with the future, it is noteworthy that Toynbee connects the two main political trends in a disintegrating civilisation—Archaism and Futurism—with these two basic attitudes. The affinities between archaism and the Return to Nature are obvious, and he would presumably agree with my classification of Fascism and Nazism (typical manifestations of the Archaist reaction) as "negative" and of Communism (futurism pushed to the limit) as "positive".

Toynbee regards these two attitudes as quite fundamental and associates them with that elemental rhythm of the Universe distinguished by the Chinese as Yin and Yang, which he puts at the centre of his whole philosophy of history.* It is the rhythm of the Erdgeist in Goethe's *Faust*:—"In Lebens-fluten, in Tatensturm, wall ich auf und ab"—it is Challenge and Response, and Withdrawal-and-Return and Relaxation and Strife; in the Chinese concept it is female and male, from which ultimate division of the very stuff of life I have suggested that the Negative and Positive Powers must be derived.

With the above instances, which are by no means exhaus-

* Toynbee, "Study of History", vol. V, p. 324.

tive, I can perhaps claim to have shown that the Positive–
Negative antithesis really has some meaning. In one way or
another it has been sensed by many writers and thinkers,
some of the very front rank.

There are, of course, a good many real or apparent logical
contradictions involved. The Apollonian principle of order
and measure does not at first sight seem to coincide with
Leuba's concept of a sundering force dividing the individual
from his fellows and his surroundings; nor for that matter do
either look exactly like Toynbee's concept of ascetic self-control. The connections between Ashtaroth and Yin, Yahveh
and Yang would be hard to establish logically, however
clearly the intuitive light of my manic phases seems to have
shown them to me.

None the less, I cannot help feeling that a case of sorts has
been established for my two propositions. The instinctive or
intuitive perceptions and visions, which arose in my consciousness when wholly dominated by a maniacal flood well-
ing out of the Unconscious, do seem to some extent to be
capable of rational interpretation; they have obvious affinities with similar intuitions of thinkers, poets and philosophers
with whom I would not presume to compare myself in any
way. Thus it is not wholly absurd to suggest that what I saw
or sensed was a complementary or more complete intuitive
vision in the Bergsonian sense, and that it may give clues to a
fundamental opposition or rhythm in human life, and
perhaps in the Universe itself.

CHAPTER V

DELUSION AND REALITY

1. *The Opposites*

IN CHAPTER IV I endeavoured, on the basis of a hypo-manic phantasy, to give an idea of the concept of "opposites" as some power outside or inside my psycho-physical system seems to compel me to visualise them. I referred to three main concepts of "opposites" developed by writers of established reputation.

The first is that of Jung. His division of human creatures into two basically different psychological categories—introverts and extraverts—has already been dealt with at some length. The second is the Greek opposition of systole and disastole as sensed by Goethe and developed by Nietzsche. The third is the old Chinese opposition of Yang and Yin, light and darkness, which Professor Toynbee regards as not only having vital religious and philosophical implications, but as bearing directly on the whole question of periodicity of history which he is primarily investigating. These three fundamental oppositions and a number of others seemed to me to fall into the two general categories of Positive and Negative, male and female, upon which the whole experience of my manic-depressive psychosis seems to have been based.

For reasons which I must try to explain logically in this chapter, I was "instinctively" or "unconsciously" impelled to put under the general heading of "positive" Jung's introversion. Goethe's systole and Toynbee's Yang, with its essential implication of the light aspect of creation, while under the heading "negative" came extraversion, diastole, and Yin, or the dark aspect of creation. Moreover the first three seemed "dividing", or analytical, in their ultimate nature, whereas the last three were "uniting" or synthetical.

There are, of course, many obvious apparent contradictions in this classification. War, to take the most salient example, is obviously analytical; it divides, it cuts up. Peace is equally obviously synthetical; it unites. But why should war be light and peace dark? Where do good and evil come in, a problem which I have largely evaded as yet but which cannot be avoided? Is war good, for example, and peace evil, a conclusion which should follow from the connection between war and light, peace and darkness?

It may be noted in this connection, however, that the associations between Yang, war and light, on the one hand, and Yin, peace and darkness on the other, were familiar to the Chinese. Yang is an ancient Chinese word which originally meant the side of a valley on which the light (say of the rising sun) shone, whereas Yin was the side which was in darkness. Yang was later, as Toynbee explains, developed to mean the analytical, divisive, aggressive male principle in all things, while Yin was the synthetical, uniting, pacific, female principle. If this classification is accepted, of course, my addition of "positive" as a covering concept for the first group, and "negative" as a covering concept for the second should be agreed to without difficulty. But what of good and evil? And where do Jung's extraverts and introverts come in?

2. *The Philosophy of the As If*

Before trying to answer these difficult questions, I must refer to the views of the late Professor Dr. Hans Vaihinger, of Halle. Professor Vaihinger published just before World War I a work called *Die Philosophie des Als Ob*.* This created at the time real stir in philosophical and scientific circles. After the war, in the disturbed twenties when German thought had largely lost it bearings and was feverishly seeking a lead, the *Philosophy of the As If* seemed to many to provide it, though Vaihinger was never as popular as Spengler. There was a cult of Vaihinger in intellectual

* For a simple introduction to this, see "Einfuehrung in die Philosophie des Als Ob", by Bernhard Fliess. Velhagen and Klasing.

circles; he was even referred to as a philosopher greater than or at least as great as Kant.

This, incidentally, is the view put forward by Bernhard Fliess in an excellent introduction to this philosophy. "And so I have no hesitation", writes Fliess, "in placing the 'Philosophy of the As If' on a level with the principal work of the great philosopher Emmanual Kant, the *Critique of Pure Reason*, published in the year 1781. At that time Kant put an end to all the following of will-o'-the-wisps and phantasies by philosophers before him, on the basis of reason (previously considered to be infallible), about God, the world, and all questions of existence. He showed coolly and clearly that our reason was in no position to answer all questions 'in Heaven and earth': bounds had been set to our perception (Erkenntnis), and we could make no certain statements whatever about all things beyond our external and internal experience (äussere und innere Erfahrung). This demonstration by Kant had at first a destructive effect, since all the airy thought-constructions which the philosophers had set up with the aid of that sole mother of happiness—reason (alleinselig machende Vernunft), fell down at one blow like houses of cards. But the work of Kant also exercised a liberating effect, since even the most dogmatic affirmations of the greatest thinkers had never lost the stamp (Gepräge) of uncertainty; they had never been able to remove the irritating feeling that the whole truth had not been attained to (errungen) in spite of the most beautiful proofs. And so Kant's demonstration that this could not possibly be otherwise, since insurmountable barriers were set up precisely to bound our rational perceptions (vernünftige Erkenntnis), came as a real redemption."*

Vaihinger, as I can testify from personal experience, also has a truly redemptive effect. He demonstrates that everything that we think and say about "God", the world and even our own existence has—and must of necessity have—something false and contradictory about it. We cannot know

* Op. cit., p. 13.

if it is "true". "What is truth?" said doubting Pilate, and the
Roman philosopher-administrator, whom an all-wise Providence may well have sent to Jerusalem precisely for the purpose of washing his hands to absolve his people for all time of
responsibility for the crucifixion of Jesus, was wholly justified. If I look at this paper on which I am writing, feel the
pen I hold in my hand, listen to the conversations I hear in
the "refractory ward", in which I am writing it, how do I
know that all or any of these things are "true" or "real"?
I am said to be "insane"; I have even a certificate to prove it
of which I am inordinately proud. Why should I not be
living in the midst of a completely hallucinatory world,
visual, tactile, auditory and so on? It is absolutely impossible
for me to prove to myself or to anybody else that I am not.
If, for example, I am ill-treated in this ward; if I am knocked
about, kicked, jumped on, as I have been in another Mental
Hospital,* how can I prove that this treatment is not a
"hallucination" or "delusion"? I cannot legally, *de jure*, of
course, since as I am certified "of unsound mind" by due
process of law it would be impossible for any court of law to
accept my word—at any rate if it were contradicted by
"sane" witnesses.

That is what all or most mental nurses with whom I have
had disagreements of a serious nature have told me as soon as
I threatened appeal to the "Board of Control" or legal action.
They will hang together, they say openly, for fear of hanging
separately; the doctors will be on their side; and I shall have
no chance. A specific assurance of this nature was made to
me by the Charge Nurse of this particular ward when I
arrived about a fortnight ago.†

Nor can I prove the *de facto* "truth" of what has happened to me while I was "mad" to any "normal" person,
even to my own family. My wife believes me more or less,
though she probably thinks my mania leads to exaggeration,
even though I am generally given to extreme under-state-
ment in "normal" life. My children are frightened of the

* See Appendix A.   † Also see Appendix A.

whole idea of having a "mad" father; not unnaturally they put it out of their minds and do their best to forget all about it.

Finally I cannot prove the "truth" of my "ill-treatment" in any satisfactory manner even to myself. I know that in acute mania, and even in hypomania, actual sensory changes have taken place. My perception, all my perceptions—of smell, taste, sight, hearing and touch—are at any rate slightly changed. May they not have been radically changed without my "ego" realising it? Perhaps I find myself in a different "stream of consciousness" altogether.

Rationally speaking, I can hardly believe that the mere writing of my name on a piece of paper called a "certificate" marked with certain signs which (I am told) "means" that my "mind" is not "sound", that I am "non compos mentis" as (I am also told) "the ancient Romans" (whom I have in the nature of things never seen) used to put it, can have brought about a complete change of consciousness, have immersed me in another "stream" or translated me into another "dimension". I know, moreover, that those about me within this hospital for the most part agree with me upon common experiences. We see the same things more or less, as far as I know; the curious smell I noticed a few moments ago was also noticed by Michael, the student nurse sitting beside me, for example; it may have been a hallucination common to the two of us, but it was not peculiar to me.

But once I get out of a Mental Hospital all this changes. I find myself in a totally different "atmosphere". I cannot, however hard I try, get even my most intimate relatives and friends to understand or take any interest in what may or may not have happened to me during my "madness". Gradually the vividness of my memory fades; like my relatives, I try to put the whole experience out of my mind, and in fact it does to a certain extent disappear into "lower levels of my Unconscious". Then I find myself genuinely wondering whether these memories, so far as they are conscious at all, are not "delusions", "hallucinations", as "unreal" as the actual technical hallucination I know I have had and have described earlier.

I remember being hurt and shouting out in agony. I remember seeing angry "men" rushing at me immediately prior to this experience. But I also know that many mental patients shout out in agony when shut up alone in padded or side-rooms. What are they "seeing", "hearing", "feeling", "smelling", "touching"? In what essential way does their experience differ from mine? I can find no difference—as soon as I am outside the asylum atmosphere and can no longer see and speak to the individuals present at the time of my sufferings. Even if I returned there and spoke to them, they would, as has been said, deny the whole affair, as a simple matter of self-preservation, of bread and butter. No doubt they can hardly do anything else. They exercised their natural "sadism" in a way they could not help, largely, as I explain elsewhere, because I used all my talents to induce them to lose control.* But they have been taught that "sadism" is wrong; they are ashamed of it; they try to forget it; and finally they succeed in repressing it into their Unconscious and convincing themselves that it did not happen.

It is even theoretically conceivable that they did not fully know what they were doing or saying. They were dominated by extreme anger, not unjustifiably. They let go the full force of their innate impulse to hurt me, if not with the permission of the law, at least with the express or implied permission of their medical chiefs, who for them must have represented an "authority" far more real than that embodied in any distant courts of justice. They thus acted just like any unfortunate murderer—I purposely do not mince my words—who in a fit of sadistic impulse, in "blind rage" as the saying goes, murders someone and then is horrified at the result. How can he "prove" that he acted in a fit of total amnesia? But the murderer finds himself on the wrong side of the law; the nurses in question can be sure of remaining on its right side as long as they hang together. This they do, largely "unconsciously" or "instinctively" if it should be that

* See Appendix A.

they are conscious of what happened; if they have total amnesia about what happened; if they genuinely believe that I was merely "violent" and that they "restrained" me as the law allows, then of course I can "prove" nothing. It will be best for my own peace of mind to forget all about it, to put out of my mind any idea of trying to "prove" to others that I was the victim of injustice and that other people may well be so also, and just to admit that I was "mad" and should thank God I am "sane" again at last.

That is, I venture to suggest, what happens in the large number of similar cases to my own which I assume, on *a priori* grounds, must exist, though of course I do not "know" anything of the kind. They are told, if they seem to harbour resentment against the hospital or any of the authorities responsible for their treatment, that this resentment is a typical sign of "delusions of persecution", the commonest of all delusions in asylums. In order to prove their fitness to be let out, they "repress" or in the most fortunate cases succeed in "suppressing" their resentment. It disappears into their Unconscious; they really do "forget it" as they are generally expressly urged to do. But, as Freud has shown so clearly, the repressed resentment only in due course finds another outlet, and many poor unfortunates come back again where they started. I believe that the failure of discharged inmates of Mental Hospitals fully to sublimate the resentment which they, rightly or wrongly, have come to feel during their stay within the hospital walls, is responsible for a large percentage of the failures to achieve permanent cure.

I use expressly the phrase "within the hospital walls". For these are very real "walls"; there is a very real "barrier", or "curtain" separating life outside from life inside. There is an almost equally real "barrier" separating those on the right side of the keys from those on the wrong side, or even visitors from patients. That I can vouch for as a fact of practical experience. In the course of my career I have perhaps developed a peculiar sensitivity to "barriers" of this kind, which I have noticed in particular to exist wherever different kinds of life, especially life subject to control by arbitrary authority and life governed by the principles of freedom, came into juxtaposition.

I first noticed this on a visit to Soviet Russia in 1924. I was an ordinary visitor to the country and had no official backing; in those days such a simple private visit was still possible. There was something indefinable about the atmosphere of the Customs House on the Leningrad quay which I had never felt before, although I had travelled almost all over Europe. The atmosphere seemed to lurk in the peculiar smell, in the rigid postures of the sentries, in the observant mobile eyes of the Customs men, and so on. I was very frightened, though as a matter of fact I was not even searched. I had nothing dutiable on me, I may say, though that has, I sadly fear, rarely been the case when I have passed other Customs barriers. I had therefore less reason to be frightened. But I was far more frightened—terrified would be no exaggerated description of my internal state of mind.

I spent about a month in Leningrad, adjusted myself, received nothing but courtesy from the Russians I met, and in due course returned home. In many ways I enjoyed myself. But as I passed the Customs in the outgoing direction I felt a great weight as it were lifted from my mind. The "curtain" dropped behind me, and I heaved a huge sigh of relief. I was safe and free, over the Latvian border (I returned by train). At that time, of course, the term "Iron Curtain" had not been invented, but I vaguely remember picturing the "barrier" as some sort of "curtain".

When Hitler developed Gestapo terror in Germany, I sensed a similar change of atmosphere, but to a lesser degree. I did not really feel the same psychical—and physical—sensations until I found myself in gaol in 1939. (It will be remembered that in the first Mental Hospital I went to I was voluntary.) But as soon as I was taken to the police-station, searched, and put in a cell, it seemed to fall down behind me like the famous rocky door with which Gagool shut Rider Haggard's immortal three into King Solomon's mines.

Thenceforward, until my release, I consciously pictured all those on the official side of the barrier as my enemies—or at any rate as opponents. I felt one with those on the wrong side of the keys, with the prisoners and outcasts, with the lunatics and sinners, with the desolate and oppressed. And this feeling, which was quite involuntary, helped me through the experience and gave me the strength to face the three days of solitary confinement in the padded room.

When I was in a Mental Home suffering from acute depression as described, the same sensations returned in full force, though I was voluntary as I have said. I used the metaphor of something "clanging in my soul" when the door shut behind my wife, my chief contact with the world outside. I pictured myself as in "Hell"; the outside world was "Heaven"; my wife and mother were visitors from "Heaven"; the white-coated attendants angels sent by God to keep me in Hell for my sins, and so on. These associations forced themselves upon my consciousness. Although I have long since adjusted myself to the peculiar atmosphere of Mental Hospitals and can make myself pretty well as happy inside them as outside, I still "see", "feel", "hear", "smell" and "touch" the barrier, the curtain. Moreover I have noticed similar "barriers" between the different wards, and the patients in them. The whole concept is best pictured on the analogy of circles of Hell, purgatory, etc., as described by Dante.

Of course I know that these barriers are not "real" in one sense of the word. A free man with the requisite permissions and keys can walk into this hospital, from ward to ward, and walk out again without hitting against anything physically impassable. But I am not free. And, partly perhaps because I am not free, and partly because of my mental state, I feel or sense the barrier as something just as "real" as any physical barrier, impassable in the ordinary common-sense meaning of the word. It "hits me in the eye" as it were. When I escape, I have just the same feeling of a barrier or "curtain" dropping behind me that I have described.

What is "delusion" and what "reality"; what is "a mere figment of the imagination" and what is "hard fact"? Without Vaihinger's help I should be hopelessly at sea.

But by accepting the principles of the Philosophy of the As If, by admitting that we "know" nothing for certain, that "reality" always eludes our grasp, but that for the purposes of practical action we must set up fictions, or postulates, or hypotheses, and act "as if" they were true, merely judging by practical results how near to the "truth" we have got, life becomes comparatively simple.

If, therefore, I say, as I do say, that I postulate (and have postulated since well before I was first thought to be "mad") that there is a God, that all the experiences through which I have passed, am passing, and must pass are experiences sent by Him for my especial benefit, that it is His Will that I should endure them and that if I will accept His Will and learn all I can from them I can achieve many of my most cherished ambitions, that He is the Way, the Truth and the Life and is ever at hand to guide me, I cannot possibly be accused of being "mad" for that reason. I say that I have found as a matter of practical experience that my "God" works; I say that my determination to act "as if" there were a God has shown me that for me there really is a God, or rather that there is something or somebody in the Universe (perhaps only "the Unconscious") which acts on my consciousness as a "God" might be expected to act. And I am being strictly rational, whereas an atomic scientist who—being unfornately untrained in the humanities—is unwise enough to assert that "atoms", "electrons", "protons", "neutrons", or "deuterons" "certainly" or "really" must exist just because he has managed to blow up Hiroshima and Nagasaki with their aid is talking utter rubbish. I act "as if" there were a God; he acts "as if" there were atoms, electrons, and all the rest of it. That is all.

Moreover I do "know" from the Bible and from historical sources generally that countless generations in the past have acted "as if" there were a God, saints, prophets, and so on, and that it appears to be on record that their postulates worked. In more ancient times, as well as in many "heathen" lands today people have acted and act "as if" there were many gods and goddesses, devils, fauns, satyrs, nymphs, sirens, and so on. And with the aid of these postulates they achieved, and still achieve, results, according to credible reports.

Is it not therefore reasonable to suggest that "Gods", "saints", "prophets", "goddesses", "devils", "fauns", "satyrs", "nymphs" and "sirens", are as "real" as protons and electrons? In fact since they have produced recorded results for thousands of years, whereas protons and electrons have only been postulated for thirty or forty years at most, they would appear to be even more "real". As William James maintained,* scientific theories and postulates are mere fashions, and the ancient fashion of postulating natural forces as persons—the demon-theory—is in his view certain to return in the long run.

For the theories which I am putting forward in this book this ancient fashion has proved itself a most successful postulate, as will, I hope, appear. As suggested above, I have been impelled to adopt them. When I think, for example, of the planet Mars, an inner voice "tells" me to remember that Mars is a very important god and must be treated with the greatest respect. When I see the lovely planet Venus in the morning or evening sky; I seem to "see" the form of the goddess in some trick of the light—no doubt an ordinary illusion. So I pray to "Venus" and I pray to "Mars"; I postulate that they are "real" persons; and effective results from my point of view ensue.

In so doing I seem to myself to be doing only what Kant maintained that "practical reason" was bound to do by a sort of law of its own nature. Kant, in *Die Kritik der praktischen Vernunft*, invented a concept which he termed a "Postulate". This was not exactly what is meant—in England or Germany—by the word today; it can be better ren-

* See especially W. James, "Collected Essays and Reviews", p. 487.

dered by the German word Zwangsbegriff, *anglice* "compulsory concept". My "postulates" are really postulates in the Kantian sense—compulsory concepts. They are something, a sort of fixed form or forms, which may perhaps be likened to a definite pattern of "pipes", or a system of electrical wiring, which my psycho-physical system—conscious and unconscious—has to work with for practical purposes, to achieve any satisfactory results in the struggle for existence.

3. *The Problem of Evil*

For Kant such postulates were "God", "freedom" and "immortality". For me they are these three and much more besides. My principal "scientific" postulate, as explained in Chapter IV, is that all things in this Universe—which, as Einstein showed, may be "finite yet unbounded"—can be classified as either "positive" or "negative". My principal religious postulate is that there is a "God" and that there is a "Devil". But neither instinctively nor logically can I equate "God" with the concept "positive" and the Devil with the concept "negative". The concept "positive" is for me, as I have explained, the "Positive Power of God" and the concept "negative" the "Negative Power of God". Both as far as I can see must be equally necessary in the eternal scheme of things, just as no electrical machinery can work without both positive and negative poles.

There is, however, a strong tendency in my Unconscious to equate "God" with the Positive Power and the "Devil" with the Negative Power when I am in a depressive phase, and, conversely, "God" with the Negative Power and the "Devil" with the Positive Power when I am in a manic phase. The tendency has been fully described in previous chapters.

This brings me right up against the problem of good and evil. If I assume, as seems reasonable, that there is nothing basically wicked, no element of "Absolute Evil", in either the manic or the depressive state *per se*, then the fact that "God" and "the Devil" are as it were able to change places points to the conclusion that both are necessary aspects of "reality", or in other words to Jung's view of "the Devil" as the "reverse aspect of God".

Fools rush in where angels fear to tread, and on the basis of my experiences both of the outer world and of the world within me, I am impelled to postulate with Mrs Eddy that there is no such thing as Absolute Evil, or, if there is, that it is just as necessary as Absolute Good. On the principle of Opposites, if there is Absolute Good, there must presumably be Absolute Evil to balance it; it then, however, appears to be a necessary factor in Absolute Good, a sort of part of its machinery, and is therefore no longer Absolute Evil in any rational sense of the words.

The Absolute, however, is a very difficult concept, as all who have studied Hegel are aware. In order to develop it fully, Hegel was compelled to admit the essential identity of A and not-A, which makes logical thought virtually impossible. Though on the whole I agree with Hegel, readers will perhaps forgive me if I leave the question to philosophers.

I do postulate, however, that, whatever may be true of "good", "evil" is a relative term. I may perhaps be compelled to admit the existence of something more than relative evil in myself; there is certainly plenty of "sin that worketh in me". But in the outside universe, in so far as I can distinguish it from myself, I can see nothing either essentially evil or even useless in itself.

Both evil and lack of utility seem to me to be a question of false relationships or of degree. I was once asked by a friend to give an illustration of a useless object. Being unable to do so, I asked him if he could, whereupon he replied:—"What about a glass eye at a keyhole?"

Let us take the all too familiar instances of the horrors of war and the tortures of disease. War is, after all, as German philosophy has consistently maintained, a form of the struggle for existence, of the fundamental competitive method which Providence has chosen for the evolution of life. By what right can I describe it as useless or evil *per se*? Similarly, disease in its bacteriological forms is another aspect of the eternal struggle; my good is the evil of the plague bacillus which attacks me, and vice versa. I may say that Providence should not have allowed bacilli harmful to human beings to evolve at all, but how do I know what function they serve in the scheme of things, or whether the evolution of life would have been possible without them? Most other diseases are functional disorders—inevitable errors of the life process, as it were—or are part of the process which leads to decay and death. Would life be possible without death? On the principle of opposites it certainly would not.

Or take the question of pain, which I as an individual fear and loathe. Yet I know that it is a biological necessity without which I could not possibly survive. Certainly I can legitimately strive to avoid or mitigate it in reason, but I cannot even wish it to be abolished.

The old religious idea of the value of suffering is out of fashion today. We live in a sentimental age to which the infliction of pain seems inherently wicked and even the caning of a naughty child is looked at askance. Yet few ages have seen more cruelty and suffering. Perhaps this paradoxical result is designed expressly by Providence to teach us the lesson that apparent evils are necessary and that to accept them, adapt them and turn them into good is the true way of salvation.

Looking back on my own life, which has not been without periods of suffering, I can sincerely say that were I now given the chance of living my life over again without those periods, with all the happiness and none of the misery, all the ups and none of the down, I would refuse. Theoretically at any rate, though I daresay not in practice, I would choose rather than that to live my life with all the suffering, the misery and the downs and none of the happiness and the ups. For, wonderful though the experience of the mountain-tops has been, I know that I have learnt far more in the valleys, and I believe that what I have learnt is of permanent value.

May it not be that the typical modern attitude to suffering, to the apparent evils of pain, disease and so on, is due to the

decay of the belief in eternal life beyond the grave? If there
is a Resurrection, as the Christian and most other religions
teach us to believe, then the question so often asked of why
God allows such and such evils, such and such pains, misery
and suffering, especially of innocent people, children for
example, is quite easy to answer. Suffering is a necessary
part of the education of souls, more particularly since it is a
pre-condition of sacrifice—the only true way to salvation.

Is it really possible to visualise an eternity of absolute
happiness without suffering, sacrifice and effort to balance it
in some way? Would not any such existence be inexpressibly
boring? It is a common observation of experience that those
things are most prized which are most hardly won. Things
which come to us without effort on our part—the charity of
others or of the State, riches which we obtain by chance or by
inheritance without responsibility attached, even the goods
of nature and freedom, the air and sunlight, the smell of
fresh herbage and flowers, the song of birds; all are eventually taken for granted unless they are endangered or
actually lost. That is what Goethe meant when he did not
admit security into Faust's final Utopia, but said that all
things must daily be conquered anew. What seems to be a
law of life may well also be a law of eternity.

If there really is an eternity to look forward to, there is no
reason to suppose that anything in this life is wasted or lost or
without value in its true relationship, not even sin. Here I
know that I am trespassing on dangerous ground which is the
special province of the theologians.

What value, it may be asked, can there possibly be in a
really foul sin, let us say in a brutal, ruthless and cowardly
murder? At first sight there seems to be none whatever.

Yet if we consider the question of sin closely the matter
takes on a different aspect. Was it not Napoleon who said
that he who does not make mistakes will not make anything
else? Sin is error; it is a mistake or series of mistakes in the
moral sphere, and it is only the fact that morality is the most
important part of human life that makes moral errors worse

than errors, say, of mathematical computation or even in games. If I commit a brutal murder I am no doubt doing something worse than if I merely miss a six-inch putt to win a University match at golf, but the essential nature of the two acts is the same; they are more or less unpardonable errors for which I am responsible.

If I miss the six-inch putt, it shows that I have not trained my "nerves", the actions and reactions of my psycho-physical system, properly, as I probably could have done with more effort and study; if I commit a brutal crime it also shows faulty training of my psycho-physical system, only this time in the moral sphere.

In both cases, the possibility of redemption remains. In the one, I pay a penalty by a guilty feeling of having let my side down, and this may lead me to a course of determined action which cures me of the jitters; in the other case I pay penalties of remorse, in all probability of being hanged, and perhaps in some sort of purgatorial after-life, which cleanse my soul from the evils which dog it and enable me to start afresh to face eternity with the sense of my sins having been washed away.

I hope sincerely that readers will not feel this comparison to be an irreverent trifling with serious things, which is very far from my intention. I merely want to stress the value of all error or "sin" in so far as it leads to a changed course of action on the part of the person who commits it. The commission of some really foul crime indicates as a rule that there is something radically wrong with the soul of the person in question. The fact that the crime has been committed does not make the soul or character of that person any worse; the criminal action is merely the natural result of the evil which was already there. What it does do quite often, however, is to bring the individual up with a round turn and make him face the facts. In the case of a murderer who is caught and executed, that is almost certainly true, and it is therefore a not unreasonable assumption that the value of the crime lies in the fact that it is a necessary part of the process of redemption of the particular criminal.

What of the victim's case, however, it may be asked; surely from his point of view the murder is an unmixed evil? That certainly seems so, though whether death is an evil at all is very debatable. Schopenhauer did not think so. In any case from the victim's point of view it is probably no worse to be murdered than to be killed in a motor-car accident or in any other of the innumerable ways in which life can be lost.

These arguments are, of course, dependent on the postulate that there is an eternity in which all injustices can be remedied, all frustrated desires fulfilled, and the development both of the individual and of the race continued. This is a postulate which I am compelled to make; it is for me a necessity of practical reason, and I am fully prepared to base all my actions upon it. The arguments are further dependent on the postulate that eternal Hell, in the sense of the final damnation or destruction of sentient souls, is no part of the purpose of God, but at the most a theoretical possibility which may never be put into practice. In other words, in the ultimate scheme of things the extraverted view of Origen, St Francis and Martin Luther, will prevail over the introverted view of St Tertullian, St Augustine, and Calvin. The Negative, diastolic, uniting, Yin, female power in this sense just, but only just, conquers the positive, systolic, dividing, Yang, male power. "Das ewig-Weibliche zieht uns heran."

4. *Life and Death*

The victory of the negative, of Yin, can however only be the prelude to further activity by the Positive Yang Power. The eternal struggle must go on, or the Universe really would run down like a clock, as according to some mathematico-physical theories it is inevitably destined to do. The prospect, or at any rate the possibility of something of this kind happening, or, alternatively, of the end of the attempt of consciousness, through Life and Man, to inform the Will and fashion all things new, has been the nightmare of serious philosophical and scientific thought ever since the nineteenth century undermined the old-fashioned faith in a per-

sonal God. It has never been better expressed than by
Arthur Balfour.

"The energies of our system will decay, the glory of the sun
will be dimmed, and the earth, tideless and inert, will no
longer tolerate the race which has for a moment disturbed its
solitude. Man will go down into the pit, and all his thoughts
will perish. The uneasy consciousness, which in this obscure
corner has for a brief space broken the contented silence of
the universe, will be at rest. Matter will know itself no longer.
'Imperishable monuments' and 'immortal deeds', death itself, and love stronger than death, will be as if they had not
been. Nor will anything that is, be better or worse for all that
the labour, genius, devotion, and suffering of man have
striven through countless ages to effect." *

That is a consummation which my "practical reason" refuses to accept. Perhaps that is what Kant sensed when he
insisted on immortality being a necessary postulate. I postulate that it is not so; I act "as if" it were not so, but I do
not pretend to know.

This pessimistic view of the Universe must, of course, be
sharply distinguished from that of Schopenhauer, who would
have welcomed the inevitable end of Life on principle. Just
as Balfour's vision expresses the pessimism of those who love
Yang, creation, struggle, life, so, conversely, Schopenhauer's
expresses the pessimism of those who crave Yin, annihilation,
peace, death. In the terminology outlined, Balfour's is the
pessimism of the Positive Power, Schopenhauer's that of the
Negative Power. Balfour was shattered at the prospect that
life and action might cease, Schopenhauer at the prospect
that it might continue. But is not the truth that there is
eternal life and eternal death, eternal action and eternal in-
action, eternal struggle and eternal peace, all equally necessary, and all perfectly reconciled in God? The time will
come, we can be practically certain, when owing to physical
changes life will perish from the earth. But if there is eternal
life, nothing of the great achievements of man, and of the

* "The Foundations of Belief", p. 30.

animals and other creatures lower down the scale of the great evolutionary climb—let us never forget them—can be lost in any real sense. Even if there is no eternal life in the personal sense of which I am writing, modern scientific technique offers the prospect of Life through Man conquering the stars as he has conquered the earth—if he can conquer himself. And even if the physical, measurable universe of scientific thought must of necessity run down like a clock, may it not be that there are other universes, other "space-time continua", other "dimensions", in which Life can continue, taking with it all its achievements and knowledge of itself and of matter? All created things need rest; all created things die; men and women, nations, civilisations, animals, vegetables, perhaps even all matter, all planets and suns, all nebulae, all atoms, protons, neutrons, electrons and deuterons. They die, and others take their places; but creation continues. Why should not the whole physical universe run down like a clock and die, that another may take its place and that the Spirit of Life may prevail and achieve even greater self-understanding?

Thus, in the sense in which the Positive is Life and action and the Negative Death and rest, the Positive must prevail. Death, as the laws of my practical reason compel me to see it, is not a final extinction, but a rest, or perhaps rather a sexual death, a return to the womb of the Great Mother for fresh creation. All created things perish; all created things are born anew. That is the rhythm of the cosmos, a rhythm which governs animate and inanimate, matter and life or "spirit"; the most insignificant atom or electron, and the greatest saint or leader. Matter, so science assures us, is indestructible; so, my practical reason assures me, is life or "spirit". Both can and do change their form; that is all.

5. *Matter and Spirit*

The latest physical theories, however, which have been developed since Eddington wrote *The Expanding Universe* in 1932, seem to indicate that some sort of fresh creation of matter may be taking place. It has been suggested by Hoyle and Lyttelton that hydrogen may be the raw material of the Universe, and that out of it first helium and then the other elements are built up in the stars. They begin, on this view, as a small knot of unevenness in the "hydrogen cloud"—the cloudy matter which cuts out our view when we look out into our galaxy—and grow by pulling in hydrogen when they find it on their courses.* This theory, as developed by Hoyle, is associated with another, advanced by Bondi and Gold in this country and by Jordan in Germany. The "expanding Universe" loses gravitational energy as it expands, and this energy reappears in some way as matter. Bondi and Gold point out that according to the Theory of Relativity the laws of the Universe must appear at all times the same to all observers. From this it follows that the average density of matter in the observable universe must appear the same at all times, so that of necessity matter must be being created to keep pace with the expansion of the Universe. Assuming that this matter is being created as hydrogen thinly spread out in space, it provides the substance from which Mr Hoyle's stars are to thicken and grow as they sweep along. If these theories are true, the universe may not be running down at all, but merely running on.†

In that case it may be that the physical universe, understood in the true all-embracing, original sense of the word, may be permanent, one of the eternal aspects of "God". "Spirit", which to me seems inseparable from and in fact virtually identical with Life, could then be another aspect, but one essentially inseparable from the material.

"God is Spirit", said Jesus, but He did not say that Spirit had no material aspect. My practical reason, as well as the whole of my visionary experiences during my illness, drive me irresistibly to the conclusion that Spirit and matter

---

* See especially F. Hoyle, "The Nature of the Universe", Blackwell.

† In writing the above, I was greatly helped by a reviewer in "The Sunday Times", whose name I have unfortunately forgotten owing to my mental state at the time. I may even have used some of his phrasing. In any case, I trust that he will accept this as a grateful acknowledgement.

are essentially one, that the fundamental division made by Christian theology, which is traceable far more to St Paul than to Jesus Himself, is based on false, or partly false, premises.

It may well be that this misapprehension of Our Lord's teaching was necessary in the historical circumstances; in fact I believe that it was necessary. As Berdyaev * and others have pointed out, man had to detach himself from Nature with all the power of his soul, thus destroying belief in the ancient Nature-Gods, in order to attain to the objectivity which modern science demands. In other words, matter had to be repudiated. The Puritan hatred of matter and the body, the extreme expression of the minds of great introverts from St Paul and St Augustine to Aldous Huxley, was a necessary phase, but only a phase. And now the time has come to reverse the process and accept matter and the body as wholeheartedly as they have hitherto been rejected by our most influential Christian thinkers. After all, the Resurrection of the Body, not some vague, impalpable "Spiritual" existence, is a fundamental article of the Christian faith.

As I have perhaps sufficiently emphasised, the acceptance of the body, of "the flesh" in its full sense, seems to me to be a basic characteristic of the Negative Power, of Yin. At first sight there may seem to be a contradiction here, inherent not only in the very word "negative", but also in its association with the concepts of Yin, darkness, rest and death. How can positive acceptance of matter and the body be described as "negative", or as associated with darkness and the death which seems to be their negation?

Paradoxes, however, seem to be inseparable from philosophy. And this one is only apparent. The solution, I would suggest, is to be found in the domain of psychology, particularly in the concepts of extraversion and introversion.

The natural extravert does in fact accept matter and the body, the world and the flesh, if not also the Devil. Great lovers such as Casanova and Don Juan are typical extraverts, so are conquerors, statesmen, big business men, organisers of

* See Chap. IV, p. 104.

"reality" in one form or another. They look outwards to the
world and seek to mould it according to their desires or
ideals. They are "diastolic", not "systolic".

And yet they are, in the view which my practical reason
compels me to take, essentially Yin-men and not Yang-men.
They seek, that is to say, to unite rather than to divide, to
synthesise rather than to analyse, for in synthesis there is rest.
Their ultimate aim, their guiding vision, is peace, not war.
Even Napoleon, like all other really great conquerors, aimed
at peace, at the political synthesis of the known world which
he sensed to be possible, however much he used the instrument of war to attain his ends. He was a Yin-man, but he
came before the time was ripe.

The real dividers, the real apostles of strife *per se*, the real
Yang-men, are the introverts, however quiet and sedentary
their lives may appear to be. They look inwards, and there
they see the ultimate division of all things, which is within the
soul of man and not without it. They may seek peace, but
they find strife—eternal, irreconcilable, absolute strife. And
the symbolic expression of that division, of that eternal strife,
is the split between Heaven and Hell, regarded as the
apotheoses of "spirit" and matter respectively.

In an interesting review of Aldous Huxley's *Themes and
Variations* * published in *The Observer*, Miss Kathleen Raine
deals with Huxley's essay on Maine de Biran, another
of the great philosophic introverts. Like Huxley and St Paul,
de Biran hated his body. "He hated the world", she writes,
"but could never refuse an invitation to a party. Because he
could never give anything up, he spun himself a cage of intellectual and social complexities from which he could never
escape, but in which he could never be happy . . . a modern
predicament and one that Mr Huxley well understands."

Modern thought, modern man, modern science, have
reached, by the positive, Yang, introverted method, the cosmic gulf. They have cut themselves, and therewith everything that is, up into little pieces. They have divided the All

* Chatto and Windus.

into tiny watertight compartments as it were; and they are thus hopelessly lost, as in a maze.

The greatest example of this Positive analytical process is undoubtedly Albert Einstein. In the fourth edition of his famous book, the great physicist has incorporated an appendix in which he endeavours to unify the equations relating to gravitation and electro-magnetism.* Whether he has succeeded in this, time alone will show. Probably only about a dozen men in the whole world are capable of understanding what he has tried to do, and it may take a generation or so to verify or disprove his theories. Even so, he has made no attempt to bring in the third series of equations used in modern physics—those applying to the atomic nucleus. The maze remains impenetrable; the synthesis is still elusive. And it will, I think, remain so.

For if analytical thought is inward-looking, is introverted, as I have suggested, and if that is where the ultimate cosmic gulf is to be found, then no amount of work on the same lines will bring about the desired result of synthesis, of unity. That lies in Yin, and Yang alone will never achieve it. The Eternal Feminine will prove eternally elusive. The Goddess must be wooed and won, not by analytical intellect alone, but first and foremost by love.

At this point it will perhaps be convenient to give two flights of hypomanic ideas bearing directly on this subject. They were written while I was in a state of extreme elation, one shortly after I returned after my first certification as "of unsound mind" last October, and the other rather later. They were, I postulate, messages from my own Unconscious, straight out of the horse's mouth as it were.

"THE ETERNAL SCHIZOPHRENIA

The great physicist Clerk Maxwell introduced into science the curious concept of 'Sorting Demons'. I came across the idea in Sir James Jeans' very illuminative works, and it has stuck in my mind. Sorting Demons, or Sorting Valkyries, as I prefer to call them in memory of Brünnhilde and her maidens, are necessary concepts in the ultimate analytical process of cutting up the uni-

* "The Meaning of Relativity", Albert Einstein, Methuen.

verse into little bits of which modern physics consists. This process is, in my tentative terminology, the Positive Power of God, Yang, pushing Himself to the uttermost limits of space and cutting himself into an infinite number of little pieces, all bravely guarded by Sorting Demons or Valkyries with flaming swords, mounted, let us say, on the immortal horses like those we have at home—Darkness, Shadow, Warlock and so on.

Or perhaps we might conceive of another category of immortal 'Sorting Swine'? In our little pig-farm at home we have already raised fifty-two large Whites and Wessex Saddlebacks. Our fertility record is unrivalled as far as we know—above twelve per sow—and we propose to breed on an increasing scale. The series of names we have started, viz: Cleopatra, Aphrodite, Diana, Ashtaroth, Astarte, Isis, Buddha, Confucius, and so on, seems to me very suitable for immortal Sorting Swine.* I feel, moreover, impelled to classify the animals at home with Maxwell's Sorting Demons. They seem to me quite plainly to have something to do with cutting the Universe up into little pieces, or perhaps rather with the opposite, the Great Uniting in the Negative Power of Attraction which makes the Universe whole again in Yin, or Peace, the Immanent God within all Life. With that diastolic uniting I would couple the lovely words of Goethe at the end of *Faust*:—

> 'Alles Vergängliche ist nur ein Gleichnis,
> Das Unzulängliche, hier wird's Ereignis,
> Das Unbeschreibliche, hier wird's getan,
> Das ewig-Weibliche zieht uns heran.'

> 'All temporal things are but an equation
> (or symbol, or metaphor): the unattainable
> becomes reality here, the indescribable is
> done here; the Eternal Feminine draws us
> upward and ever on.'

With these lines I want to couple three more quotations which seem (inductively) to contain the elements of the synthesis which I, now aged 49, am trying to make.

The first is from the Roman poet and lover of good things, Horace:—

> 'Eheu fugace, Posthume, Posthume?'

The second is another couplet from Goethe:—

> 'Zwei Seelen wohnen, ach! in meiner Brust,
> Die eine will sich von der Anderen trennen.'

The third is the opening of Dante's *Inferno*, which has always stuck in my memory:—

> 'Nel mezzo del camin de nostra vita,
> Me ritrovia per una selva oscura.'

I have for some time been exercised in mind about my real

* Alas! I have had to revert to more prosaic names suited to the Herd Book.

position in the Space-Time Continuum. I have even considered the possibility of taking a 'sight', say through my spectacles, in order to verify it. On reflection, that appears to me to be obviously impossible. My spectacles, which as a matter of fact are borrowed from my club, where they are, or were, available for any member to use, are plain magnifying glasses. They are not specially made to correct my astigmatism—a 'double astigmatism' in optical parlance—but they do in fact enable me to read and write accurately.

But although I may not be able to take a 'rational', 'positive' sight to fix my position in space-time, I have in the three quotations immediately preceding, taken by 'negative', 'instinctive', or 'spiritual' means a sort of 'spiritual sight' which gives me a clue to my real position as an individual.

I have just said goodbye, like Horace, to one of my nearest and dearest, my beloved mother, who breathed her last quite peacefully, after a long illness, not quite a fortnight ago. She has passed beyond the Great Divide between Life and Death, yet it seems 'as if' she were in the room with me now, guiding my pencil. I am far nearer to her now than when she was alive, when all sorts of evil influences kept us apart and I often could not even go into her room to talk to her, though I knew she was lonely and miserable. Well she knows, and I know now, at last, what divided us. It was the Power of Evil, or Hate as Empedocles called it.

'Two souls dwell, alas! in my breast; the one wants to divide itself from the other.'

What was true of Goethe is true of me. I have two souls. What are they? They are male and female, positive and negative, deductive and inductive, Yang and Yin. And they want to divide in a sort of eternal schizophrenia. Well, let them go. I, quite an ordinary person, have reunited them and I tell them to go where they will. I have a split mind. I was a manic-depressive; let us say for the sake of the argument that I am now a schizophrenic.

As I have said many times in the book I am writing, I have only had one technical hallucination. It is therefore not likely that I should have had another at this time. But I am in an excited mental state, and I postulate that some sort of schizophrenia has taken place in my own psycho-physical system. I am firmly convinced that a man in this hospital has confessed to me that he was guilty of the Setty murder. I went up to London and reported this to the police—since the doctors refused to listen to me. As the result of this I was sent to ——, and certified as of unsound mind. It appears that the man could not have done the murder, so I must have been misled.*

* The fact was that he never said anything of the kind. I remember clearly convincing myself that he had because it fitted in with some phantasy in my mind at the time.

It will be remembered that I have written in Chapter IV of my book of God going out of Himself and returning to Himself (or rather Herself) in an eternal circular movement. That is something eternal, indivisible, and to all intents and purposes invisible. It is the infinite expression of the Negative Principle or Power, what Goethe called diastole as opposed to systole. It is the release of all joy in the final chorus of the Ninth Symphony; it is the love-scene in the second act of *Tristan and Isolde*; it is the Eternal Male going out into the Infinite and being attracted back by the Eternal Female.

That is, in the terminology I have adopted, the Negative or diastolic Ring. There is another Ring, the Positive or systolic Ring. This works, as might be expected, the other way round.

The Eternal Feminine, or Female, is an abstraction and, like all abstractions, has no 'real' existence. It is therefore necessary to think of a 'real' female, for example of a female newt. What does the female newt do? She attracts the male newt from a distance, he carries out quite complicated evolutions, emitting bright colours, and so on. The sperm and ovum come together; a circle is completed from afar. But the female newt, like the male newt, has a body, and that body has an ordinary digestive system. Now the digestive system is as much a circle as the sexual system, only it works by the 'power of repulsion'. Food attracts, it is true, as it enters the body; but it passes through the alimentary canal and, as the result of the digestive process (after a large proportion has been absorbed into the cells of the body), the residue is excreted. The excreta are expelled from the body by muscular spasms acting by virtue of this 'power of repulsion'. The natural tendency of all life is to part from, to repel its excreta.

The digestive system is thus, at least in part, worked by the power of repulsion as the reproductive system is worked by the power of attraction. My postulate, which should be experimentally verifiable in time, is all attraction is the same attraction and all repulsion the same repulsion. Thus, for example, the power of attraction (gravitation) that holds the planets on their elliptical orbits round the sun is the same power that attracts Mr Smith to Miss Jones; and the counter-force that prevents the same planets rushing back to the sun, that is to say, the power of centrifugal force, is the same repulsion that eliminates the excreta from the body and makes it normally distasteful or disgusting, particularly to man, to have anything to do with his own or other people's excreta.

It may seem an absurd theory. But if the Universe is really one all repulsion must surely partake of the same essential nature. All modern sciences are increasingly finding out that their various little channels of analysis are coming to an end and can only be explained by a single Universe ruled, perhaps by a 'God', or

'All', or 'Absolute' (according to the point of view of the particular observer).

It is interesting to note that the same theory was put forward by one of the early Greek philosophers, Empedocles. He said that the Universe consisted ultimately of a power called Love, opposed by a counter-power he called Hate. Following his line of thought I postulate that these two powers, one uniting and the other dividing, one synthesising and the other analysing, one bringing together and the other cutting up into little pieces, one Yin and the other Yang, one Eternal Female and the other Eternal Male, one reproductive and the other digestive, one 'negative' and the other 'positive', one minus (—) and the other plus (+), are the keys, in fact under 'God' the actual creators, of all that has been, is, and is to come.

The reason that I am putting forward this theory or hypothesis is quite simple. I have experimented with it in my own person. During manic periods I have been under the domination of the attractive or Negative or diastolic Power; in depressive periods the Positive systolic Power of repulsion has held sway. How these two Powers work in me has been described in my book. I stand under an internal and/or external compulsion—in German I would say 'ich stehe unter einem ausseren bezw inneren Zwang'—to postulate that there is a fundamental 'split', a 'schizophrenia' in consciousness, and an equally fundamental re-uniting of the split forces, one or other of which, however, always tends at a given time to dominate the outlook of the individual and perhaps the general consciousness. Split or reuniting, systole or diastole, positive or negative; the state of a particular human mind or of the human Collective or Group Mind in general depends entirely upon which 'force' or 'series of forces' is in control."

The above is, as I have said, almost exactly as it appears in the original pencilled MSS, except that here and there I have made a minor addition, corrected an obvious mistake or chosen another word or form of words to make the meaning clearer. But although written in hypomania it is what Jung calls "directed thinking" as opposed to "phantasy thinking". Since it is quite impossible in "directed thinking" to give the whole contents of consciousness, I am giving also the following specimen of my writing partly at the same time and partly later, in which I deliberately tried to give as far as humanly possible the whole contents of my consciousness—"directed" as well as "phantasy thinking":—

"THE ETERNAL SCHIZOPHRENIA
(Space-time Continuum, actual dimension X)
+

'The Eternal Schizophrenia' may seem a strange title. If I were asked to state, at this precise moment of the space-time (Interjection from Madame de Pompadour, Grand Hotel, Heaven, never repeat never waste love/light you old sinner, end of message, Medical message: ECT never necessary sgd. Harvey) continuum, what I mean by this particular form of words I should find it somewhat difficult. For I chose the title as it were by instinct, by induction; it came of itself into my mind as a line of verse comes to a poet. I have not yet attempted to put (squeaks from padded room next door) into motion the opposite process of deductive reasoning which is needed to justify the title. (Note: nails in mourning).

I have to choose my words very carefully. For what I am doing is, I believe, something which has not very often been attempted (BEELZEBUB ON BED in form of blue fly). It is to think at precisely the same point in the space-time continuum by both methods of thought (coughing, running at the nose, bottom of feet wet)(blue check handkerchief)—inductive and deductive (so hot, have to remove coat and purple pullover query CAESAR'S) artistic and rational (itching), negative and positive—in the terminology expounded in Chapter IV of my book.

First of all it seems to me (had to open window owing to extreme sense of heat query 'real'?) essential to fix my exact position (fly on pipe) in the space-time continuum, at any rate by what sailors call D.R. (dead reckoning query alive or dead?)

(Interjection by Lord Crawford, Huntly and Palmer's biscuits:—Room probably 'really' cold and advises me to go on writing (fly on + temple) to get warm (fly buzzes and settles on + THUMB (TOM) − SHIRT).

I am at this present fleeting moment of time (1750/29/10/1949 B.S.T. equals 1650/29/10/1949 G.M.T.) sitting on my bed in X 1 ward at ————— Hospital, —————, ————— England, World, Solar System. I can check this statement by going to the other end of the ward—where I have actually no business—and looking at the clock. Dates, times, and everything coincide; today is Saturday tomorrow will be Sunday, Oct. 30th. Thus the statement I have written (must pump ship)(Balaam—arse/ass—says normal reaction to excreta) above should, rationally speaking, be correct. I can make it for the sake of the (Query SOCRATIC) argument with a positive or + sign.

Now I called this statement a statement of position by D.R., or dead reckoning. I did this instinctively; that is to say I wrote it down without fully reasoning out in my head what its implications were. It was therefore a statement as it were from the negative or inductive side of things represented by the — sign, and I must now reason out positively, or rationally, exactly what I meant.

(Frederick the Great agreed that my room is now hot and advised me to open top window also. Have done so. Am sitting in shirtsleeves on January 1st/1950, defying the cold coming from Russia. Holy Year is working signed St Theresa +/St Ignatius Loyola T.O.O. (time of origin) x — y).

Dead reckoning is a navigational term (Drake) meaning the position according to course and speed, making allowance for any winds, currents, etc. and $\left\{\begin{array}{c}\text{RESUME PURPLE EMPEROR}\\ \text{shut bottom of window}\end{array}\right\}$ calculated according to the ship's chronometer by plotting a line on a/the chart. My position as described above is stationary (engine, reciprocating, piston and cylinder, male and female), in so far as this planet is "stationary"; it is estimated according to the hospital chronometer, or clock. It is, therefore D.R. in exactly the same sense that a navigational D.R. position is.

(Interjection by St Thomas:— doubt above X
              (Apostle)

                                        STOP OK

Light Programme   Leave off writing sgd. KOKO RT 1937/ 1/1/4/50 Pack up your troubles in your old kit-bag and smile signed   Angels of MONS/BEF/OK)."

6. *Guidance and Reason*

The above example of the irrational mingled with the rational, the inductive with the deductive, is not very easy to make clear to the general reader. Every word is clear to me; as I have now written it with one or two minor corrections there is not one·comma or stop or bracket, not one jot or tittle, without a perfectly explicable reason for its exact position. The words in brackets represent of course the actions and reactions of that part of my whole consciousness which I did not succeed in directing to the matter in hand; they represent "phantasy thinking". Thus in my imagination Madame de Pompadour, Harvey, Beelzebub, Lord Crawford (whose name I noticed in a newspaper announcement), Frederick the Great and St Thomas, not to mention the more hypothetical Angels of Mons, appeared to send me messages exactly as I have written them down. They controlled my pen; I acted as a sort of medium for what they wanted to say. In my consciousness there was no doubt about it; nor could I have written anything else however hard I tried.

For my consciousness those "messages" were as "real" as the pen with which I was writing or the table at which I was sitting. But I was, of course, in a hypomanic state. Now that I am, according to medical authority, no longer hypomanic, how "real" do they appear?

They were certainly real messages of my own Unconscious; of that there is presumably no doubt. Phantasy thinking is always to some extent dominated by the Unconscious, and in "insane" states, as well as in those of trance or of drowsiness between sleeping and waking, that domination is far more powerful. In so far as the Unconscious is "real", the messages were therefore "real".

But how did they arise, and what did they mean? Am I, now that I am in my "normal" frame of mind, prepared to say that they were what they purported to be, namely "real" messages from people who had (with the possible exception of Lord Crawford) passed beyond the barrier of death and were in actual communication with my conscious mind?

There is, so far as I know, no *a priori* reason why this should not be so. My religion, which I "believe" to be true though I do not "know" it, assures me that the personalities in question continue to exist in "reality", and its founder assured His followers that there is a Holy Spirit, a Comforter, which speaks to man and guides him. It may not be Protestant orthodoxy to believe that the technical means used by the Spirit consists of such factors as the voices, "real" or "imaginary", of the "dead", of common objects (like a fly) which produce certain reactions by association of ideas on consciousness, and so on, but the whole experience of my illness goes to convince me that something of the kind does take place, and that a measure of "truth" is to be found in it.

It seems therefore not unreasonable to postulate that these messages from the Unconscious, whether or not the historical characters Frederick the Great, Madame de Pompadour, etc., had anything to do with them, had the validity of communications from the instinctive or Negative side of things, and as such are just as deserving of attention as purely rational considerations derived from the Positive side. That is the principle upon which my experiences have taught me to work; it seems to be a necessity of my practical reason; and I act, and propose to go on acting, "as if" it were "true".

My experiences, however, have also taught me that "messages" from the instinctive or Negative side are not always what they seem, and are to be interpreted with a certain degree of caution. I have noticed in particular that while the details of any particular "message", or, better, of my interpretation of the "message", are liable to be inaccurate, the general trend of the messages taken as a whole seems invariably to prove correct. Moreover, looking back, even my misinterpretations and errors always seem to have had a purpose. They have never led me into really serious trouble, and they have gradually taught me how to use the Negative, how to combine instinct with reason. And unless the whole thesis of this book is unsound, this is the only way to attain even to an approximation of "truth".

The particular "messages" of the Negative under consideration, those which came to me while writing the second passage headed "The Eternal Schizophrenia", all carry with them the idea that I am being guided and helped by factors outside my normal consciousness. This idea, as has been explained, always takes hold of me in mania, only to be reversed in depressive periods. I have, however, not had a serious depressive period of this kind for over ten years, and in the meantime, although I often lose temporarily the sense of guidance and help, and get depressed as a result, somehow the sense seems not to be far below the "threshold" of my consciousness, and it soon returns, particularly when really needed. Whether objectively "true" or not, it is of immense assistance to me in innumerable ways, and, in fact, I could not now face life without it. It is, therefore, a necessity of my practical reason, and I act "as if" it were true, both in small things and in great.

Let me take a simple example. This hospital is situated about six miles from a golf-course where I play nearly every day. The buses are not very convenient; a change is involved, and the times do not fit. Moreover there are no buses at all on Sunday mornings, when I generally want to play. I therefore often have to hitch-hike, which, since the route is somewhat complicated, does not appear easy. Before doing so I invariably pray, receive an answer in some form—the toss of a coin is as good a way of taking the omens as any—and, if the answer is in the affirmative, I set out So far I have never yet failed to get there and back without difficulty.

A somewhat more important illustration is the writing of this book. From the very first I have gone on the principle of "guidance". It seemed to me that I had to write it, that the words and ideas came from outside myself rather than from within, that I should not write of myself but whatsoever I should hear, as the New Testament puts it. I have therefore consistently accepted all suggestions, however apparently irrational, which came into my mind, and merely endeavoured to put them in logical and comprehensible form. Moreover, I have, especially in what has been written while confined in Mental Hospitals, used only the books and other outside sources which happened to be at hand. I have assumed that what was at hand was sent to me for the purpose, and that I need not bother about getting anything else. In so doing, I have acted on precisely the opposite principle to the one employed in my previous literary work, when I have often spent weeks in searching for the sources I needed.

Finally, I propose to act as far as possible on the same principles for the rest of my life. One of the most persistent messages of the Negative in my consciousness is that we are living in an apocalyptic age in which practically anything can happen at any time, and in which another World War is to all intents and purposes certain. I first saw this vision of World War III at the end of 1944, when we were still fighting the Germans, and I have seen it again and again. I have no reasonable doubt that it is true, and as far as I can I am ordering my own life and that of my family on the assumption that it is. Our investments have been and are being selected on this assumption, and our major decisions are guided by it. We do not, as many appear to do, put the spectre of another war out of our minds, saying that if it comes it will be "the end of everything". We simply take it as a probability and act accordingly. If there really is going to be an atomic end of the world—which does not, according to the practical Civil Defence experts, seem likely as yet—it will come, and we shall have to face it like everybody else. But the lesson of recent history seems to be that wars are not quite as devastating as they appear in heated imaginations before they break out, and if the world is to go on we may as well make all the rational preparations for that contingency that we can. In the long run, I may perhaps add, the messages from the Negative seem to indicate that better things are in prospect for mankind; World War III is merely a thorough, but very necessary, purge of the manifold evils afflicting this tormented planet.

7. *The Revenge of the Negative*

It will be recalled that in the vision of the anima described in Chapter IV, from which this whole concept of Positive and Negative with which I am dealing has been derived, the anima-figure seemed to indicate that the neglected Negative would take a terrible revenge on modern "positive", mechanical, scientific, analytical civilisation.* Every experience that I have had since then has tended to confirm this view, and to emphasise that this "revenge of the Negative" is the underlying force which makes World War III inevitable.

Rational considerations, moreover, strongly support these repeated "messages" from the Negative. As a matter of historical fact, the probability of another war has steadily grown more evident ever since I had the original visions in

* See pp. 87 et seq.

question, though at that time few realised it. The line-up of forces, moreover, is between those which can reasonably be classified as Positive on the one hand, and as Negative on the other. Since some apparent contradictions are involved here, it is necessary to deal with the matter in some detail.

To my instinctive consciousness it is plain that the Stalinist attempt to conquer the world is a supreme attempt of the Positive Power, of Yang, to achieve final victory on this planet. Yet, it may be argued, I have defined the Positive Power as something that divides, cuts up, analyses, something basically schizophrenic as it were. Surely the concept of Communism, allied with the managerial dictatorship which Stalin has introduced, is something which tends towards unity, and which I should therefore classify as Negative. Many intellectuals are already tending to accept Stalinism precisely because it seems to offer the only possibility of the world unity and order for which they are yearning.

In the first place, order is not unity. This was brought out in Chapter IV, in connection with Nietzsche's basic opposition of the Apollonian and Dionysian principles.* The Stalinist managerial dictatorship, in which every single individual is ticketed, labelled, and confined to his or her own little pigeon-hole under the direst pains and penalties, is the Apollonian Positive principle carried to the very limit. Although the original motive-power of Communism, as of many other mass revolutionary movements, was in part the Negative Dionysiac thiaisos, as immortalised for example in Schiller's "Ode to Joy", the urge to unite in God and in Love; and although every attempt is made to keep a vision of this kind before the eyes of the deluded masses; yet the practical working of Communism is purely Apollonian. The ancient, instinctively rooted examples of the aristocratic Apollonian principle, such as monarchy in particular, are all attacked and overthrown in order to substitute a brutal pseudo-aristocracy of jumped-up, bureaucratic jacks-in-office.

In the second place, nothing could be more opposed to the

* See p. 102.

instinctive unity in love which is the goal of the Negative
Power than any system of government which forces the free
spirit of man into rigid forms. Authority is Positive, Yang,
male; Freedom is Negative, Yin, female, as her invariably
feminine personification in statues of Liberty goes to show.

The ruthless exercise of authority within the Stalinist em-
pire is another example of the old process by which a change
of government, welcomed by the governed as promising an
amelioration of their condition, in fact produces a far more
ruthless tyranny. Whips have been exchanged for scorpions,
the knout for systematic mental and physical torture on a
scale unparalleled in history. And all has been done in the
name of a Utopian future in which the State is supposed to
"wither away".

It will be recalled that in Chapter IV * I referred to Professor Toynbee's association of the basic Yang–Yin opposition
with Futurism and Archaism, which he regards as the two
main trends in a disintegrating civilisation. Thus he would
probably agree with me in classifying Stalinist Communism
as a Positive Yang-manifestation. The opposite to this, however, archaism, which in our civilisation has shown itself in
the various forms of Fascism, can scarcely be associated with
freedom. There is a contradiction here which is worth going
into at some length, since it involves fundamental problems of
political philosophy.

Freedom, I have suggested, is essentially Negative. In the
final analysis, freedom is freedom to do what we like, the freedom of the released Id in the Freudian sense, freedom from
laws, restraints and inhibitions of all kinds. That is the
Dionysian principle as opposed to the Apollonian, and it is
basically anarchic. That such freedom is practically speaking impossible in a world where men have to live together,
and thus to reconcile their instinctive urges, does not prevent
it being a basic goal of the human psyche, and indeed of all
life. But as the ultimate aim of the Negative is, as we have
seen, to unite all creation in God and in love, the unin-

* See p. 109.

hibited freedom it offers is that sensed by St Augustine in his famous phrase: Love, and do what you like. As a matter of hard practical fact here below, it shows itself in mass movements, where the released Id is collective rather than individual and, within the mass at any rate, overcomes individual conflicts.

Both Communism (as we have seen) and Fascism utilise this Negative motive-power for their purposes. Both say in effect: join our gang, love our gangsters, and do what you like. Both, in practice, instead of giving the bread of freedom, give the stone of tyranny. But Communism, looking as it does to the Positive future, contains within itself an inner contradiction from which Fascism is free.

As I have tried to explain, the Negative, with its intimate association with the anima, looks to the past rather than to the future, though in pursuance of its synthesising aims it endeavours to unite both in synthesis. The Positive, whose very nature is to divide and cut off, draws a rigid dividing-line between the past and the future, rejecting the past *in toto* in order to make a clean sweep for fresh construction. Thus, in its extreme political manifestation it is quite logical that it should cry: "Get rid of all the useless lumber of tradition, destroy the institutions, liquidate the leaders, and when the last king has been strangled with the entrails of the last priest, when the last kulak has been drowned in the blood of the last capitalist, there will be a new heaven and a new earth, for the former things will have passed away."

But the past cannot be cut off; it cannot be banished into the limbo of forgotten things; it is, like the poor, always with us. The more it is rejected and ignored, the worse the revenge it takes. That explains why Communism so effectively demonstrates the truth of the parable of the Seven Devils by providing far more ruthless wielders of power than the kings and priests, kulaks and capitalists who are replaced. For the past is instinct, and instinct is, very largely, the past. You cannot use Satan to cast out Beelzebub; you cannot use the Negative motive-power, as Communism tries to do, to cut yourself off from the Negative past. You may want a "dictator of the Proletariat", but you get a ruthless priest-king.

That is why I believe that the only hope for humanity lies in accepting the Negative. The real way to build a new world is to keep the firmest possible grip on the past and to use all its forces to effect the transformation you desire. Freedom in particular demands that firm grip; only tradition can guide the released instincts into acceptable paths and avoid anarchy. It is as a reaction against the Positive destruction of traditional, instinctively rooted forms that archaist Fascism has developed; and it is only by a rational, "Conservative" acceptance of these forms as a base of fresh construction that the coming victory of the Negative can be prevented from taking a Fascist form.

There is no doubt whatever in my mind that in the coming apocalyptic clash the victory will lie with the Negative. There is an inevitability about the process as my experiences seem to have shown it to me which far exceeds in degree Marx's determinist vision of the inevitable decay of capitalism and the victory of the "proletariat". For nearly three thousand years,* since the great Puritan revolution at the beginning of the first millennium B.C., the Positive elements have preponderated, at any rate in the main stream of civilisation. Now the wheel has come full circle, the pendulum of evolution has reached the limit of its swing.

In Stalinist Communism, moreover, Positive aspects have been pushed to such extremes that the struggle against it is coming more and more to be identical with the eternal war between good and evil. If evil is, as has been suggested, primarily a question of false relationships and extremes, then, however good and necessary the Positive aspects may be *per se*, by being pushed to the limit they automatically become evil. Good is, I believe with Aristotle, to be found in the mean, and that mean can only be attained by redressing the balance through a victory of the Negative after its long eclipse. Today, far from the Devil having the Negative all to

* See p. 106.

himself as may have been the case when St Augustine was writing, he has, I believe, an almost complete monopoly of the Positive.

But the Devil will not win; nor, at bottom, does he want to. The gulf fixed in the soul of man which to the great introverts has seemed an unbridgeable gulf extending infinitely throughout the cosmos, is neither infinite nor unbridgeable. There is a marriage of Heaven and Hell, and when it is consummated both Man in himself and Man and the cosmos are united. But Man will not achieve it by looking within; he can only do so by looking outwards to the cosmos and to God.

The gulf is within; unity is without and is only attainable by the diastolic movement embracing all creation under God which Goethe, more perhaps than any other poet, sensed and saw. Yet the ultimate bridging of the gulf takes place, I believe, within the soul of man, within life, that is to say, and not outside it.

It is, as I have repeatedly emphasised, the essential thesis of this book, which will be developed formally in the next and final chapter, that "spirit" and "flesh", life and matter are one, and that the keys to the understanding of them are to be found within the psycho-physical systems of living creatures. More particularly, of course, they are to be found within the psycho-physical system of Man, the creature through the instrument of whom Life is struggling towards self-understanding, that is to say towards the understanding of both Life and Matter.

In my library at home there is an old book entitled *The Universe, or the Infinitely Great and the Infinitely Little.* May it not be that in the last analysis the Infinitely Great and the Infinitely Little meet as it were, and are, if not actually identical, at least intimately associated?

Professor Einstein, as we have seen, has left out of his latest theoretical speculations the equations relating to the atomic nucleus, or the Infinitely Little in so far as our present scientific methods are able to apprehend it. Whether his attempt to unify the other two series of equations relating to the physical universe—those of gravitation and electro-magnetism—will succeed, remains to be seen. If the views put forward here contain even a measure of truth, no unification or synthesis of ideas or theories relating to the physical world alone is even theoretically conceivable, since the physical world or Universe does not exist in its own right, but only in intimate association with Life or "Spirit".

In the cosmic view or "Weltanschauung" to which my experiences have led me, and which my "practical reason", the system of "wires" or "pipes" in my conscious and Unconscious self, compels me to accept, provisionally at least, the question so often disputed by biologists and other scientists regarding the origin of life has no meaning whatsoever. Where there was no life there was no matter, and if life should ever vanish from the Universe there will be no Universe.

Similarly, or perhaps conversely, if the physical Universe should ever vanish or run down without being replaced in some physical and tangible form, life, and "Spirit", will run down or vanish with it. I am thus venturing to put forward a view which is neither the Hegelian idea that all things depend on Mind, nor that of his opposite, Marx, that Matter is primary, but rather an attempt at a synthesis between the two.

It is, perhaps, absurd for an amateur, a dilettante, and a very ordinary lunatic to boot, to attempt anything so ambitious. Yet the vision has come to me, in however "insane" a manner, and I cannot help trying to convey it to others. In the next chapter I shall try to state it in such a form as to make it verifiable by the normal scientific method of experiment.

CHAPTER VI

THE THEORY OF ACTUALITY

1. Why "Actuality"?

I AM COMING to the end of this book. The time has arrived
to draw together the threads of my somewhat rambling and
inchoate descriptions of mental states and more or less phantastic ideas into a coherent theory. I am optimistic enough to
hope that this theory will be taken seriously, at any rate by
psychologists, and possibly by the scientific world at large.
For there to be any possibility of this, the theory has to be
formulated in such a way as, to some extent at any rate, to be
verifiable by experiment. This is of course peculiarly difficult for an amateur and dabbler like myself lacking detailed
knowledge of the latest developments in the sciences concerned.

The irritating thing is that the theory is all ready at the
back of my mind, beautifully reasoned, and with a whole
string of quite irrefutable proofs attached. Like William
James' ideal philosophical discourse,* were I only able to set
it down on paper I verily believe that it would be taken as the
last word in both philosophy and science. It would prove the
doctors to have been wrong to tell me I could not expect to
solve all the problems of the Universe. It would give everybody a logical, intelligible and satisfactory way of life for this
world and the next. It would be an indispensable vade
mecum for every sensible person. And, last but not least, it
would make both my reputation and my fortune.

But, as with James, this wonderful compendium of all the
answers refuses to take shape in prosaic words. It persists
perversely in flickering and twinkling at the end of distant
vistas of thought, in inviting me to follow, and vanishing even

* James, "Collected Essays and Reviews", p. 407.

while inviting. Only now and then, when I am in an excited state bordering on acute mania, will it emerge from its elusive retirement and allow me to get it down. Unfortunately, when I come to read what I have written in cold blood, after the manic excitement has passed, I can barely make head or tail of it and very often its appalling egocentricity nearly makes me sick.

Elusive though it be, the theory really does exist, and it is primarily a theory of life, of practical life in the world. I have verified it experimentally to my subjective satisfaction, and I seriously try to base all my actions, important and trivial alike, upon it. It is frankly derived from the experiences of my illness, from what I have sensed and seen in both mania and depression, combined of course with my "normal" experience of the "real" world. I call it the "Theory of Actuality".

The choice of designation came about—I was going to say by pure chance, but as the "Theory of Actuality" does not admit the existence of "chance" I had better say "by the intervention of the goddess Tyche". One of the male nurses in this hospital asked me one day why I used the word "actually" so often, and what I meant by it. I tried to explain, but found I could not do so. There I was, a supposedly educated man, continually using quite an ordinary word, and "actually" unable to say what it meant. I thereupon started to reflect, and suddenly realised that this was the ideal name with which to christen the infuriating theoretical will-o'-the-wisp which haunts me. By giving it a good, solid, tangible name like "Actuality", perhaps I could induce it to behave itself and allow itself to be comprehensively tied down and labelled.

The dictionary meaning of "actuality" is "reality" or "realism", and the meaning of "actual" is given as "existing", "real", "present" or "current". Thus "actuality" and "actual" taken together convey a sense in the first place of "reality" and in the second place of something current or contemporaneous in time. A Theory of Actuality should therefore deal with "real nows", with present "realities". Since, however, according to Kant and Vaihinger, whose systems are the philosophical basis of the theory, absolute or objective reality always eludes us and can therefore never be precisely established, the use of another word may help out of the difficulty. As far as I am concerned I can establish precisely what actuality is, since for the Theory of Actuality I define it as it were from scratch. I propose to use the words "actuality" and "actual" to indicate "reality" and "real" precisely as apprehended by my psycho-physical system, and furthermore to indicate contemporaneity, in the sense that everything "actual" for me must have some sort of effect on my psycho-physical system, conscious or unconscious. Outside "Actuality" as so defined, I acknowledge and take account of nothing whatever; for me it does not exist.

At the present moment of time I am sitting in the garden of ————, the topmost purgatorial circle of this hospital. The blue sky above, and the grass, trees and flowers around me are actual objects which all remind me of the actual God Whom I worship, and of the innumerable actual shapes and ways in which He appears. The actual message I have just received from a lady in authority requesting me to take myself and my chair away from the only cool and shady place I can find, on the ground that she regards it as her own private plot (which I have never yet seen her use), reminds me of the dog-in-the-manger attitude of the actual Yahveh in the actual Garden of Eden about the actual Trees of Knowledge and Life. The actual tree under which I am now sitting, though somewhat further removed from this lady's window, is still, I fear, in the actual plot she claims as hers; the plot is within the grounds of an actual Mental Hospital in the actual land of England; and the barriers which enclose its peculiar actual atmosphere are actual barriers.

In order to give a clearer idea of the meaning of "actuality" as I am trying to define it, it may help to take this question of "barriers", to which reference has already been

made,* and to analyse it as exhaustively as I can. There are,
I have said, "actual barriers" round this hospital, enclosing a
peculiar "actual atmosphere". What precisely do I mean by
this statement?

At the time of writing I am again a voluntary patient, living
in a section of the Hospital where every door is open and
regulations are reduced to a minimum. My certificate of insanity has been withdrawn on my wife's application, since
there was some legal business to do for which my signature
was essential. I have been home several times on parole
leave; I am free to go in and out of the hospital as I please,
even to go to London if I wish. A good deal of my time is
spent on an excellent golf course not very far away. How then
can I reasonably speak of "actual barriers"?

It is true that I no longer sense these barriers as I did when
I was confined and in a relatively excited mental state. I can
walk out of the hospital grounds without getting anything
resembling the sensation I got when I escaped. Yet I know
that the barriers were "actually" there for me and I infer that
they are "actually" there for others. Should the same circumstances recur they would be sensed or perceived by me
just as before. They are "actual" in the sense in which I am
using the word. They affect my psycho-physical system consciously in the sense that I remember them and thus know
they are there, and unconsciously no doubt in many other
ways, some of which I shall endeavour to suggest in due
course.

It may be said that I am trying to attach some "reality", by
means of a verbal trick with the synonym "actuality", to
what was a mere figment of my imagination, a sort of delusion induced by my mental state and my confinement.
Actuality as I am using the word can perhaps be said to convey a false sense of "reality" to what is not "real" at all. But
that is precisely why I have chosen it. I regard the products
of my imagination, and particularly of the peculiar form of
involuntarily imagination which, as it were, takes charge of

* See p. 117.

my consciousness in abnormal mental states, as no more and no less "real" than, say, the pen I hold in my hand or the deck-chair on which I am sitting. This "equality of reality" is conveyed by the use of the word "actuality" as defined.

A distinction should perhaps be made here between ordinary imagination, which is more or less voluntary, the "imaging" of known or remembered or hypothetical objects, and the involuntary imagination arising out of the Unconscious. For instance, if as a mental exercise or for any other reason I were to imagine that I saw a cat on the bank next to my deck-chair, I would not describe it as an "actual cat", but I would certainly do so were I to see a cat in a hallucination. In that case I should be quite unable to distinguish the hallucinatory cat from an ordinary "real" cat in the common-sense meaning of the word. For my psycho-physical system the cat would be just as real as any other; the only difference would be that others would not see it and would therefore describe it as a hallucination. I am thus quite justified in describing it as "actual" as far as I am concerned; the question of its "reality" I am content to leave to others.

Similarly I am, as far as I can see, justified in describing the "barriers" round this hospital as "actual", since I sensed them quite plainly, though technically they were not a true hallucination. The fact that I sensed them when in a state largely dominated by the Unconscious goes to confirm their "actuality". Products of the Unconscious strike my psycho-physical system with a "force" at least as "powerful", "real", or in other words as "actual" as any solid, physical objects to which the term real would be applied in the usage of common sense. I am certainly justified in postulating the barriers as actually in existence in the sense of the Philosophy of the As If, and I act "as if" they were.

I postulate them, moreover, as enclosing the peculiar "atmosphere" to which reference has been made above. I feel that this "atmosphere" is of the very greatest assistance in enabling me to write this book. As has been made sufficiently plain, the greater part of it has been written in Mental Hospitals, and I now find as a matter of practical experience that I am quite unable to get down to the job anywhere else. At home my books and MSS remain severely untouched; ideas refuse to flow; but as soon as I am back within the hospital walls all is changed, and I take my pen in my hand with comparative satisfaction and enjoyment. I have now quite made up my mind to stay here until the book is finished, and if the doctors should show signs of wanting to send me home, I am quite capable of staging an imitation manic attack for their benefit.

Thus as far as I am concerned the atmosphere is certainly "actual", something which actually affects my psycho-physical system and leads me to a definite course of action. But I have still not clearly defined what I mean by the word "atmosphere", nor, for that matter, what I mean by "barrier".

Why, it may be asked, should I bother about an accurate definition of "atmosphere"? Surely I am making much ado about nothing. Everybody knows what the word means in the psychological or metaphorical sense in which I am apparently using it. Atmosphere is something which is well recognised to influence human beings and to be of vital importance for men such as artists, authors, politicians, public showmen and so on.

No doubt that is so. But what is atmosphere in this sense? What does it consist of; what influences it; what are its causes? Is it something "physical" or is it purely "mental"? Everybody knows its results on the human psycho-physical system, what it is, for example, to go into a room full of people in which the atmosphere is hostile. Does that mean merely that the individuals in the room are antipathetic or in some way opposed to the person entering, or is there, perhaps as a result of the opposition, some "physical" quality in the room, analogous possibly to the ordinary physical meaning of the word "atmosphere", or partaking of the nature of "waves" or "quanta", or other postulated physical entities?

For the Theory of Actuality the question is easily an-

swered. The "atmosphere" is "actual", just as the people in
the room are "actual", as well as the walls, ceiling and floor
which enclose it, the building in which it is contained, and
the earth on which that building stands. The Theory of
Actuality recognises no essential difference between the
psychological and the physical, between Mind and Matter.
Its basic tenet is the intuitive knowledge, which in my mind
as a result of the experiences described in this book amounts
to a certainty, that all things are one, however much the Positive, analytical, Yang Power may appear to divide them up.
That intuitive certainty I take as a fundamental postulate,
axiomatic for the whole Theory, and it appears to me to
follow the "psychological" and "physical" are mainly words
which we apply to two aspects of Actuality, neither of which
is conceivable without the other. Thus "actual psychological
atmosphere" involves *a priori* "actual physical atmosphere",
and vice versa though what both consist of is a matter for
speculation and eventual investigation.

This view is in no way novel, though there is perhaps some
novelty in the formulation. Philosophically it is akin to
Monism, and it is more or less in line with recent developments in both psychology and physical science. The so-called
"primary qualities" of objects, e.g. those of size, shape, hard-
ness, movement and weight, are no longer held to be "real"
properties of matter independent of the sense organs through
which they are experienced.* For psychology they have long
been regarded as no more "real" than the "secondary qualities" of colour, taste, etc., and with the advent of modern
physical theories, among which that of Relativity is the best-
known, physicists are having to adopt the same point of view.
Nearly a century ago, Herbert Spencer put it as follows:—
'.What we are conscious of as properties of matter, even down
to its weight and resistance, are but subjective affections produced by objective agencies that are unknown and unknow-
able . . . symbols of actions out of ourselves, the natures of

---

* Cf. especially C. S. Myers, "In the Realm of Mind", Cambridge
Univ. Press, pp. 161 et seq.

which we cannot even conceive." * For Spencer not only Matter and Motion, but also Space and Time, were derivable from mental relations. And now the physicists are being forced, much against the grain, to discard similarly absolute concepts of form, mass, inertia, gravitation, etc. When we reflect that physical space can only be described by a co-ordinate system applicable to a "reference-mollusk", † or that some ten completely unimaginable mathematical dimensions are required to predict what happens when two electrons meet and that electrons may change in the very act of becoming known to us, it is difficult to maintain that, at any rate as far as we are concerned, anything whatever can be independent of our psycho-physical systems.

The view postulated by the Theory of Actuality is akin to that of C. S. Myers, who argues in his book *In the Realm of Mind* that the notion of any *relation* between mind and body is absurd, because mental activity and living bodily activity are *identical*.‡ Myers also maintains, as a corollary to this, that "the mechanical principles, with which the natural sciences have so far been solely concerned, are only an abstraction from the *quasi*-dual set of principles—direction and mechanism—that govern the activities not only of living organisms but also of lifeless matter and of the entire universe." Direction, involving order, purpose, and end, is not confined to mind; nor is blind mechanism to living or lifeless matter. Both are universally widespread, and both are abstractions from the whole activity.

The notions both of direction and mechanism are, Myers submits, "derived from conscious mental experience, the former especially from our own individual *personal* activities, the latter especially from our common environment, the *public* world in which we live and act: in other words, we realise direction best in mind and mechanism best in external matter." But mental activity, he adds, involves and is con-

* H. Spencer, "Principles of Psychology", vol. I, p. 206.
† A. Einstein, "Relativity" (Methuen), p. 99.
‡ C. S. Myers, op. cit., p. 189.

trolled by mechanical activity—"conditioned" would perhaps be a more convenient word—just as mechanical activity is guided by directive activity. Both are aspects of the
"truth", or of "actuality" as I term it; both can conveniently
be abstracted—our practical reason in the Kantian sense
leads us to abstract them; but both are essentially one.

There is an interesting analogy here with the way in which,
as we have seen, primitive man looks at his world.* Frazer's
distinction of the anthropomorphic view of the world as ruled
by personal spiritual forces, from the magical view of it as
pervaded with the impersonal force of "mana", shows how
these two principles of direction and mechanism were first
apprehended by our ancestors. From the anthropomorphic
view the great religions have gradually evolved; from the
magical view modern science has developed. Unlike ourselves, however, primitive man does not appear to feel any
difficulty in reconciling the two views. He senses the existence of personal spiritual forces and worships them in an
endeavour to persuade them to help him; he senses the all-
pervading mechanical forces of the Universe as "mana" and
strives to use them for his purposes. The work of the Positive
Power in the direction of abstraction and logic-chopping has
not yet destroyed his "sense of the altogether".

Thus in effect Myers is returning to the primitive view in
postulating direction and mechanism as a "quasi-dual", i.e.
essentially united, set of principles acting together in the Universe. And in basing the Theory of Actuality partly on his
ideas, I am deliberately trying to regain logically the primitive "sense of the altogether", which came to me so forcibly
during the experiences of my illness.

The Theory of Actuality is an attempt to reconcile the beliefs of Religion with the theories of Science by postulating
both as "actually true", in so far as they are verified by their
"actual" results or effects. In judging them, moreover, I
endeavour, as far as may be, to apply the same general principles to both. I do not, like some exponents of Religion,

* Cf. Chap. I.

claim that it is "higher" than Science, and therefore that experimental methods of verification should not or cannot be applied to it. By their fruits, I maintain, both Religion and Science, the personal and "spiritual", and the impersonal and mechanical, can be known and tested.

Thus when a physical scientist like M. Pierre Auger tells me that there is such a thing as a "mesotron", and to prove it shows me cloud-chamber photographs of mesotron tracks in a magnetic field,* I am quite prepared to admit that it is a reasonable hypothesis of actuality. And if a Roman Catholic priest tells me that there is such a thing as the Beatific Vision and produces the writings of St Theresa and of St Catherine of Siena or the pictures of Michael Angelo as evidence, I am equally prepared to admit this hypothesis. I see no reason whatever, on the other hand, to allow to the photographs of mesotron tracks, which are actually only the photographs of droplets of water condensed around purely hypothetical particles called "mesotrons", supposed to be exchanged between a "proton" and a "neutron" in certain circumstances, any greater degree of actuality than to the visions of the Saints or the "angels" of Michael Angelo. I have no doubt that Michael Angelo actually saw the shapes of the "angels" in his mind, as I have actually seen the tracks of the "mesotrons" in a photographic reproduction, but Michael Angelo's mind is, for the purposes of the Theory of Actuality, at least as "actual" as any photographic reproduction. Both have physical actuality and thus by definition psychological actuality; both have psychological actuality and thus by definition physical actuality. Michael Angelo's mind has physical actuality in his surviving works, in the physiological mechanism of the innumerable human beings whose conscious and unconscious minds have been influenced by him, and in other traces of his activity on earth; it is also a perfectly tenable postulate and an article of the Christian Faith that he is actually alive as a part of the "Body of Christ". The

* See P. Auger, "What are Cosmic Rays" (Univ. of Chicago Press), Plate XV.

photographic reproduction of the "mesotrons" has psychological actuality in the sense that it reproduces the traces the mesotrons left during their incredibly short lives in a book which has a psychological influence on me as well as, no doubt, on many others.

The priest and the saint and the artist see the universe in terms of personal "beings" which they feel impelled to describe by means of theological dogma, individual visionary experience, or artistic creation; the physical scientist sees the Universe in terms of impersonal physical forces or material objects—since Einstein there is said to be no fundamental distinction between energy and matter—which they feel impelled to describe by means of various mechanical devices, photographic reproductions, graphs and mathematical calculations. But there is no reason why the two views should not be regarded as equally "true", equally "actual".

It may be urged that there is nothing in the least new about this statement, which is but a rehash of ideas as old as those of the Greeks, if not older. That is no doubt true. The only claim to novelty I make for the Theory of Actuality is that the basic concepts of Negative and Positive outlined in Chapter IV and V provide a method by which the two views of the Universe, as directive and personal on the one hand, and mechanical and impersonal on the other, can be both theoretically and practically related one to the other.

2. *Purpose and Chance*

The Theory of Actuality postulates that the Universe is so designed and ruled that it can be logically and consistently interpreted throughout both as the creation of purposive personality, which can be influenced by prayer, supplication and sacrifice, and as the result of "blind" mechanical forces susceptible of mathematical calculation. According to the theory, our primitive ancestors were right both in seeing beings whom they could influence and in sensing forces which they could utilise and calculate. In their view of the Universe as a whole they were, actually, nearer to the truth than we are today in our schizophrenic world of separated water-tight compartments. Regarded personally and purposively the Universe behaves in such a way that its action can be represented with successful practical results as that of a personal Being or beings. Regarded impersonally and mechanically, the whole Universe can be represented, also with successful practical results, by mathematical calculations.

Putting this in another way, we might say that the Being or beings in purposive control of the Universe act in such a way as to make its mathematics work out correctly. Using Professor Grensted's useful phrase, we may say that correct mathematics are a fundamental "condition of reality" of which even an all-powerful Creator must needs, or at any rate chooses to, take account.

Yet a further way of putting the same view, and one which will, I think, give a clearer idea of how the Theory of Actuality can be used in practice, is to postulate the "actual" existence of Tyche, the Greek Goddess of Chance, or Fortune. Let us suppose that Tyche's function in the heavenly hierarchy is to control the operations of "chance" by mathematical and other means in such a way that the laws of probability hold good. In case this hypothesis should offend orthodox Roman Catholics or other Christians, we will postulate further either that Tyche is identical with one of the Christian Saints, let us say St Theresa, or that St Theresa has taken over her functions.

We will further suppose that Mr Smith, a devout Christian, prays for a certain event. Mr Smith's "guardian angel" decides that it would be good for Mr Smith's spiritual development for his prayers to be answered and for that particular event to happen. Reference is made by the "guardian angel" to "Tyche-Theresa", who allows the event to happen "by chance", and makes an appropriate record of it.

Mr Smith, however, has a religiously inclined scientific friend who is much impressed by this, and forthwith organises an experiment designed to establish the possibility of "miraculous" answer to prayer in general. He collects a number of earnest Christians and arranges prayers under laboratory conditions for an event or series of events, the happening of which will show that prayer can influence mathematical probability. The various guardian angels, anxious for the spiritual security of their charges, and desirous of fortifying their belief in the efficacy of prayer, send a round robin to Tyche-Theresa, asking her to allow the laws of "chance" to be transcended for this very meritorious purpose. They receive a firm reply, saying that even goddesses or saints are bound by law, that if she makes an exception in this case it will not only throw the mathematical system of the Universe out of gear, however infinitesimally, but also be a most unfortunate precedent. Other guardian angels would no doubt make similar requests on behalf of their charges, and before she knew where she was, the Enemy would be in a position to introduce disorder and unbalance into the whole scheme of things.

This little fairy-tale is by no means as improbable as it may sound. About a year or so ago, experiments of this kind were actually carried out in the United States. Attempts were made to establish that "willing" could influence the fall of cards and dice in a sense contrary to the laws of probability. In America it was claimed that a statistically positive result had been obtained, but when the experiments were repeated in Oxford, and in general in England, they were something of a flop. I am not quite sure what the final result was—Professor Grensted told me about the experiments, which at that time had not been completed—but at any rate no decisive success was scored.

According to the Theory of Actuality, this is precisely what might have been expected. The "atmosphere" of the United States, with its lack of classical tradition and contacts and its jumble of racial and religious origins, we will postulate as being inimical to Tyche-Theresa and her orderly methods. The enthusiastic American pseudo-scientists and their equally enthusiastic guardian angels were therefore able to secure results, which though not perhaps decisive were yet appreciable. In the orderly classical "atmosphere" of Oxford, however, Tyche-Theresa was able to assert her authority, and the supposed proof of the ascendancy of mind over matter could not be maintained.

I suggest that, if it is true that there was a slight difference in the results of this experiment in the United States and in Oxford and England, this hypothesis covers the facts, and, if it is urged that "chance" covers them equally well, I retort that Tyche-Theresa, as the goddess or saint of "chance", is merely mechanical and mathematical "chance" looked at from another aspect, so that we are arguing about nothing. I point out, moreover, that, as Mr Myers emphasises,* "chance" in the sense of pure luck is "a mere cloak to cover our ignorance of determining conditions: 'accidents'", he says, "are scientific impossibilities". Thus if my hypothesis gives a possible explanation of the actual occurrences viewed from the personal and purposive aspect, and their explanation from the impersonal and mechanical aspect is impossible without bringing in "chance" as a *deus ex machina*, my hypothesis may perhaps be regarded as scientific romanticism but it cannot be ruled out *a priori*.

For the practical purposes of the Theory of Actuality it is necessary, without prejudice to the theological concept of one God, Creator and Ruler of the Universe, to divide the personal and purposive aspect of things up into concepts of various Beings, endowed with personality and purpose, and fulfilling various functions. This is essential for two reasons. In the first place it corresponds with the religious beliefs actually held by the vast majority of human beings since primitive times, which have left indelible traces on the human mind, both conscious and especially also Unconscious. These traces are "actual" in the sense of the Theory, and lead to the conclusion that the Beings in question can also reasonably be postulated as "actual". In the second place, while the Theory admits that the ultimate truth about the Universe is contained in the concept of the One God, which humanity so

* C. S. Myers, op. cit., p. 173.

largely owes to the Jews, it urges that the human mind is bound by an inner necessity—of "practical reason" or otherwise—to work in part anthropomorphically, and that it can more easily apprehend and work with concepts of a God acting and ruling with and through other Beings, as the ancient pagans believed and modern Catholics as well as the adherents of many other religions still believe, than it can apprehend and work with the concept of a single omnipresent, all-pervading and all-powerful Being, acting largely alone.

Here the Theory of Actuality finds some support in the all too brief confession of faith of William James, at the end of the *Varieties of Religious Experience*, where he suggested the possibility of the purpose in the Universe appearing as a plurality of cosmic Beings. It does not agree, however, with James' tendency, notably in the chapters on the One and the Many and on Novelty, in his last work *Some Problems of Philosophy*, to plump for thorough-going pluralism and deny the monistic apprehension of ultimate unity, since without such a hypothesis of unity the concept of many independent cosmic Beings takes on an aspect of horror akin to Thomas Hardy's vision of cruel immortals sporting with poor Tess.

For the Theory of Actuality, both pluralism and monism are "true", or rather aspects of "truth". The Positive Power divides, and we see disconnected plurality, the Many; the Negative Power unites, and we see the One. James argues that in the Universe there are "practical disconnections without number". His pocket, he writes, "is disconnected with Mr Morgan's bank account, and King Edward VII's mind is disconnected with this book. Monism must mean that all such apparent disconnections are bridged over by some deeper absolute union in which it believes, and this union must in some way be more real than the practical separations that appear upon the surface." * Even independently of the Theory of Actuality, however, I would argue that James' instances are singularly ill-chosen. It is probable, for example,

* W. James, op. cit., p. 115.

that James' "pocket" contained some investments in securities quoted on Wall Street, and at that time few, if any, such securities can have been independent of Mr Morgan's activities and thus of James' own bank account. Similarly, King Edward VII was not wholly devoid of interest, as far as I know, in the developments of contemporary philosophy and psychological science, on both of which James' thought, of which his book was one expression, had a very appreciable influence, so that King Edward VII's mind was connected with the book. If we accept, as the Theory of Actuality does, the hypotheses of a Group Mind and a Collective Unconscious, that connection is seen to be quite inseparable and "actual". James argues in the same chapter * that we can easily conceive of things that shall have no connection whatever with each other. We may assume them to inhabit different times and different spaces, as the dreams of different persons do even now. But if there is a Collective Unconscious of which dreams are one expression, all dreams must be connected. Here again the connection is no dimly envisaged deep "absolute union", but something very practical and "actual".

While I can, as James does, conceive of "whole universes so disparate from ours that we who know ours have no means of perceiving that they exist", and while I agree that for practical purposes I can ignore them, as the Theory of Actuality does, I cannot conceive of anything in our whole "actual Universe" (which I envisage as more or less identical with Einstein's "finite yet unbounded" physical Universe) which is not, in however remote a degree, directly connected with myself, and, therefore, at any rate through my psychophysical system, with everything else that is. A star that is wholly invisible to me, possibly one the light of which will not reach the earth for millions of years, may yet be part of a system of "difference of potential"† responsible for "cosmic rays"

* W. James, op. cit., p. 125.
† For a tentative theory of "difference of potential" as a cause of "cosmic rays", see P. Auger, op. cit., p. 119.

which probably have in some way affected my Unconscious, if not my conscious mind, and almost certainly have affected my physical system, however unable I may have been to sense that effect. If a leaf fell from a tree on this earth at some remote time, that tree was in some way affected. It was a part of vegetable life, which is, according to all theories of evolution, connected with animal life, of which I am a part. Had that leaf not fallen, therefore, the psycho-physical entity "I" would have been infinitesimally, but none the less "actually" different, though no doubt I can ignore the difference for practical purposes.

If the logic of the above statements sounds weak, I can only appeal to the intuitive certainty brought by my experiences; I am compelled to postulate connections of this kind as a necessity of my practical reason. James, on the other hand, according to the Theory of Actuality, was compelled to postulate a disconnected plurality in things by a similar necessity of his practical reason. For, "every boy and every gal that's born into this world alive is either a" child of Negative monism or else of the pluralist Positive. The Negative is responsible for me, the Positive for James; there we stand, we can no other.

This, I think, explains the somewhat curt rejection by James of the monist tendency to appeal to mystical experience, which is surprising in view of his general tendency in the Varieties to attribute validity to it. He gives a clue to the underlying psychology of his attitude in a footnote expressing his intense gratitude to the French pluralist philosopher Charles Renouvier for freeing him "from the monistic superstition under which I had grown up". * Feeling "endlessly thankful" to Renouvier for his redemption, James dedicates the book to him. This almost Pauline conversion and liberation from monistic sin seems to indicate that James's innermost being and Unconscious were involved, and the simplest assumption is that "monistic superstition" was basically opposed to his inner nature. His "charge", according to the

* Op. cit., p. 165.

Theory of Actuality, was "positive", whereas mine is "negative".

I will not repeat the attempts made in Chapters IV and V to define these psychological categories and show their applicability to human beings, and indeed in some degree to all life. My object here is rather to indicate how they can be used in practice, and, if possible, to show their intrinsic connection with the basic physical categories with the same name which modern physical science shows to be at the very root of all matter. I sense, as a result of my experiences, this connection to be something very much closer than a mere process of analogy. As I have said, I "saw" the positive-negative opposition as a fundamental but necessary separation of all things, as though the Universe had begun with the choosing of sides—a sort of universal pick-up—for the great game of Time and Eternity. There are thus, I am impelled to postulate, positive and negative Gods, or Powers of God, positive and negative saints and martyrs, angels and archangels, goddesses, devils, warlocks and witches, sirens, fauns, nymphs, sprites, gnomes, gremlins, poltergeists, fairies, ghosts, men and women, anthropoids and animals, birds and insects, fishes reptiles and bacteria. And the positive and negative qualities in these "actual" beings, all of whom are direct manifestations of the personal and purposive, or "spiritual" aspect of things, are connected, in some way which I do not pretend to be able to define accurately, with the actual positive and negative "charges" and "potentials" and "poles" of the impersonal and mechanical "physical" aspect, the two aspects being intrinsically inseparable. The whole Universe is, in actuality, psycho-physical, and all psycho-physical things are by definition positive or negative or combinations of the two polarities, in varying degrees, though they may be "neutral" in the sense that the two "charges", being equal, neutralise each other. This is the condition of "God" in the ultimate vision of Monism. He possesses that peace beyond understanding (impassibility is the technical theological term) in and through which all things are reconciled. But only at rare moments of mystical insight or through the faith that moves mountains can we see Him so; His other manifestations, as transcendent or immanent, as Eternal Judge or loving Shepherd, as jealous guardian of his privileges or sacrificial "Lamb for the redemption of mankind, and so on, are all "positive" or "negative" in one degree or another, and, as such, susceptible of analysis and classification.

3. *Ashtaroth and Moloch*

If any scientific readers have got so far, I cannot help feeling that they will throw down this book in disgust at such lunatic romanticism—to allow it the predicate "scientific" would, they may well feel, be a prostitution of a noble word. Here is a man, they will say, who actually asks us to believe not merely in God, but in "goddesses", "angels", "devils", and in fact in all the outworn superstitions of man, and pretends, moreover, that they are psycho-physical facts, capable of scientific investigation and measurement. Let us call him a crank, or, better still, a lunatic, and have done with him.

My answer is to say that of all the predicates, good and bad, that can be legitimately applied to me, "lunatic" is the one I would least like to dispense with. For it is through my "lunacy", which, though perhaps no longer certifiable, is yet intimately a part of me, that I can alone hope to provide the objective proofs without which the Theory of Actuality cannot possibly establish itself.

The Theory of Actuality is largely derived, as I have sufficiently explained, from subjective inner "visions" and experiences. So, as a matter of fact, are all theories in some degree, however "scientific" and "objective" they and their subject-matter may appear to be. No man can wholly get out of his skin or detach himself from his psycho-physical system, with all that that implies of conscious and unconscious tendencies, prejudices, purposes and mechanisms. The vast "progress" of modern science, in the sense of practical results, is due to the discovery of experimental methods, which enable subjective hypotheses to be tested against objective criteria.

The objective criteria against which the hypotheses of the Theory of Actuality can for the most part be tested are readily available in Mental Hospitals. In any Mental Hospital can be found heavens and hells, gods, goddesses and devils, saints and angels, ghosts, gremlins and all the rest of the denizens of the Unconscious, as well as plenty of human nature with its infinite actions and reactions. The inner visions and experiences which have led me to formulate the Theory are, I maintain, in no way unique—except in so far as the experiences of every human soul are unique. They were the result of the impact of the Unconscious, in a typical form known as manic-depressive psychosis, on an ordinary human mind, and I have no doubt that innumerable manic-depressives, and probably also sufferers from other forms of mental disturbance, have had the same, or at least very similar experiences. If that is so—and it can easily be tested—my experiences have at least the validity of being typical revelations of the working of the Unconscious, that is to say of the normally hidden part of the human psycho-physical system.

It will be recalled that in Chapter I, I expressly repudiated the word "revelation" as applicable to my experiences. I meant by this that I did not regard them as in any way "supernatural" or even unique. On the contrary, they are typical. But they do reveal entities, and methods of operation of those entities, which are, I postulate, inherent features of the human psycho-physical system, whether individuals are conscious of them or not.

Thus I would maintain, for example, that the Goddess Ashtaroth, who represents for me the quintessence of the Negative Power, has an actual existence not merely in the Universe at large, but in the psycho-physical system, let us say, of the Archbishop of Canterbury. I do not, of course, know whether Dr Fisher has ever seen Ashtaroth, but I have no doubt that if—which I pray he may not—he should have a severe nervous breakdown, she would appear to him in one form or another. If Dr Fisher remains *compos mentis* and Ashtaroth remains invisible, some account must none the less be taken of her in any attempt to predict Dr Fisher's actions on a basis of complete causality.

I do not know Dr Fisher though I respect him as an earnest Christian and a very worthy successor to Archbishop Temple. I believe him to have a well-balanced mind, which means that Ashtaroth, let us say in her Christian shape of Mary Magdalene, is on the best of terms with him and is quite content to remain in the background. There are, however, other ecclesiastics with whom this is certainly not the case. Without mentioning names, I would suggest that some are even worshippers of her cruel spouse Moloch. As long as Ashtaroth and Moloch were united by marriage in the minds of the Carthaginians and other worshippers, the love of the goddess sufficed to balance and thus set a limit to the hate of the god. But after the destruction of Carthage a divorce took place. Moloch was freed to add to the accumulating potential of hate in the Universe and in the human Unconscious, which is the effective cause of the troubles of this terrible twentieth century.

Just as Ashtaroth is, as I have said, for me the quintessence of the Negative Power, so Moloch appears as the quintessence of the Positive. He is "God" as I see him in depressive phases, a "positive", angry, hard, cruel force or person who has separated me out for sacrifice and is ready to cut me up and torture me eternally. He is a male aggressive power with his phallic symbol a flaming sword for analysis, division, destruction. He has nothing in common with the "God" I saw in mania, who was both a gentle, loving leader who had redeemed me, and also the ancient Mother-Goddess, with her symbol a perfect circle and her objective a synthesis or reuniting of all her children back in the Eternal Womb in which all their wants are supplied.

It is a corollary of the Theory of Actuality that few things are more dangerous than to destroy forms of worship, however undesirable, which give expression to and thus as it were absorb fundamental tendencies of human nature. A process of repression takes place which is not merely individual but collective and cumulative, and the repressed tendencies are apt to break out later, sometimes centuries later and among quite different peoples, in far more dangerous forms. The Theory postulates that the Collective Unconscious, like the individual Unconscious, contains as it were "reservoirs of potential" in which the repressed forces store their energies until the "pressure" of the "potential" is sufficient to enable them to break through into the world of consciousness.

The two basic tendencies of human nature, as of all life, are, according to more or less orthodox psychological theory, aggression and sex, the will to power and the will to congress, hate and love, or, in our terminology, Positive and Negative. The ancient pagan religions provided for both. When they were superseded by Christianity a process of sublimation had to take place; that process of sublimation has produced modern science.* The sublimation was, however, inadequate to absorb the whole of the suppressed and repressed energies. As Jesus foresaw, He came not to bring peace but a sword. Repressed aggression, the Positive Power, which to some extent had been absorbed by the sadistic religious element of human sacrifice and by analogous ceremonies such as gladiatorial games, returned with redoubled force first as religious fanaticism, and later, in our own day, as pseudo-religious fanaticism like that of Stalin and his "Communist" followers. Repressed sex, the Negative Power, finding even fewer outlets, has either added itself to the potential of the Positive manifestations or—which is perhaps the same thing—has remained repressed, adding cumulatively to the colossal tension which we sense in the world today.

In this connection the researches of Dr J. D. Unwin are of considerable interest. These were based on the Freudian theories of sexual sublimation, leading to the conclusion—as Dr Unwin himself puts it—that "if the social regulations for-

---

* Cf. references to Berdyaev and others, Chap. IV.

bid the direct satisfaction of the sexual impulses, the emotional conflict is expressed in another way and that what we call 'civilisation' has always been built up by compulsory sacrifices in the gratification of innate desires." * After investigating the cultural behaviour of eighty uncivilised and the best-known civilised societies, Dr Unwin found a direct relation between the limitation of sexual opportunity and advance in civilisation, both being measured by carefully defined objective tests. In particular he showed that sexual continence greatly increased the expansive energy of a society.

Freudian theory, of course, only postulates the accumulation of sexual energy in the form of "libido" within the individual Unconscious. It will be recalled, however, that I have assumed for the purposes of the Theory of Actuality the existence of a Collective Unconscious and possibly also of a Group Mind in McDougall's sense. I suggest, moreover, what I seem to have clearly seen in visionary moments, namely that within the Collective Unconscious accumulated and unsublimated sexual energy can store itself in what I can only describe as "reservoirs of potential". If this is so, then the cumulative effect of the Positive Puritan revolution detected by thinkers like D. H. Lawrence and Christopher Dawson in the first millennium B.C. is likely to be enormous.

According to the Theory of Actuality, the actual object of this revolution as designed by the purposive Power or Powers in the Universe was to complete the conquest of Nature. The Negative Power was forced, or agreed, to step into the background. But now that the conquest of Nature has largely been achieved, the Negative Nature-Gods and more especially Goddesses can legitimately demand recognition once more, and until they get it they are likely to produce irreconcilable conflicts and nervous strains. If we are living in a world of catastrophic wars and full lunatic asylums, that is only what is rationally to be expected. We have sat on safety-valves for something like three thousand years, and it is not much use grumbling at the resulting dangers of explosion.

* J. D. Unwin, "Sex and Culture", Oxford University Press, p. vii.

Thus viewed, the problem of modern civilisation is to release the dangerous potential of the collective Id without destroying itself, which is only another way of saying that socially acceptable ways of regaining contact with the Negative Powers must be found. The problem is primarily religious, and it is at least as much a question of restoring religious balance as of reviving religion itself. In this connection the new dogma of the corporal assumption of the Virgin, which has been proclaimed by the Vatican, is of great interest. The Queen of Heaven is the chief and oldest of all Negative Powers.

The Theory of Actuality, I have suggested, can appropriately be tested in Mental Hospitals. It can be tested even better, perhaps, in that great lunatic asylum, the modern world.

4. *Apocalyptic Actuality*

As Le Bon points out so clearly in his *Psychologie des Foules*, the world, in the sense of the sense of the collective or crowd personalities which appear as States, parties, movements and so on, is primarily moved by "la moelle epinière" —which may be aptly if inexactly rendered as shivers down the back.* This has always been so in some degree, as conquerors, statesmen and other leaders have well known.† Today, however, in this terrible age which Ortega y Gasset has described as that of *The Revolt of the Masses*, the influence of shivers—or "bloody shivers", as a schizophrenic lad of my acquaintance in this hospital invariably puts it—is greater than ever before. The masses rule, and the masses are dominated by instinct, by unconscious factors. They are, collectively, Le Bon says, like primitive savages or children and, he might have added, like patients in Mental Hospitals.

Le Bon does not regard the collective personalities of crowds as in any way morally evil. They are, he points out, capable of actions morally much finer than the normal actions of the individuals of which they are composed. If the

---

* G. Le Bon, "Psychologie des Foules", 38th ed., p. 23.
† "It is the stomach which moves the world." Napoleon to Las Cases.

right images are evoked, the right buttons pressed, they will cheerfully sacrifice themselves for their gods, their leaders, or for pure abstractions. If other buttons are pressed, they will commit rapine and murder equally cheerfully. Normal moral inhibitions, mainly, as Le Bon stresses, the result of fear of consequences, go by the board; each man feels that he cannot be held responsible and therefore can let himself go. So do the normal inhibitions of reason; nothing, for example, appears impossible to a crowd; the numbers in themselves give a vast sense of power. When Napoleon said: "It is impossible, therefore it shall be done," he was showing himself a master of crowd psychology. This sense of power is obviously analogous to and probably derived from the same sources as the similar sense in mental patients.

In this age of masses, of crowds, the Powers of the Universe, working through the Unconscious, have as it were a clear field for their apocalyptic purposes. Gods and goddesses, angels and devils, many of them long forgotten and neglected, are on earth once more, doing battle. "And there shall be signs in the sun, and in the moon, and in the stars; and upon the earth distress of nations, with perplexity; the sea and the waves roaring.

"Men's hearts failing them for fear, and for looking after those things which are coming on the earth: for the powers of heaven shall be shaken.

"And then shall they see the Son of man coming in a cloud with power and great glory.

"And when these things begin to come to pass, then look up, and lift up your heads; for your redemption draweth nigh."*

It is a postulate of the Theory of Actuality that this apocalyptic vision seen by Our Lord and thus described, is no mere fable or parable but an actual vision of actual coming events. Since this will no doubt seem absurd to scientifically-minded readers, I will endeavour to give in some detail a description of what I mean, in the course of which wider implications of the Theory will become apparent.

* Luke 21, 25, 28.

The Theory takes as axiomatic, subject of course to the limitations laid down by the Philosophy of the As If, that there exists some possibility of foretelling the future independently of ordinary rational calculations. This is not, I know, scientifically proven, and it may be that it never will be. We will postulate, if that is so, that one of the purposive Powers which influence our actions, let us again suppose that it is Tyche-Theresa, knowing that certainty as regards the future is not good for man, and also that scientists and philosophers must be left with questions like Time, free-will, and determinism to argue about to prevent them getting bored, insists on preserving the element of chance as a possible explanation of actual prophecies. This, however, does not prevent the Theory of Actuality from adopting as a hypothesis that the Unconscious is connected with the future, and with the past, and that in certain circumstances the future, like other aspects of the Unconscious, can therefore be revealed to consciousness.*

In this connection the Theory bases itself not so much upon recorded cases of prophecies which have proved correct, though they should not be disregarded, but upon the mystic insight, which, as stated in Chapter I, seems to involve a denial of the reality of Time. I will not go into the philosophical implications of this, whether, for example, it must necessarily involve absolute determinism, since this would carry me too far afield. Free-will, in any case, is a necessary postulate of our practical reason, and the Theory of Actuality leaves it at that.

The future, the Theory holds, is "actual" in a sense, just as is the past. It has an actual influence on our psycho-physical systems, just as the past has, though in a lesser degree, since it is far more difficult to attain to correct knowledge of it. What I am trying to convey here can be best explained by reference to the work of imaginative writers.

* Tyche appears to be relenting. Dr Rhine of Duke University, North Carolina, and Dr Soul, of London University, have conducted investigations into a so-called "psi faculty" with apparently positive results.

Le Bon maintains that all history books must be regarded as the work of pure imagination. Events, and particularly great and exciting events, are invariably misreported. Hundreds of witnesses often testify to things which never happened at all, and Le Bon even goes so far as to say that the more witnesses can be found to testify to an event happening in one way the more certain we can be that the event happened quite differently, since collective crowd hallucinations are the most common of all. History cannot be accurately established, therefore, by the most meticulous study of original sources.*

According to the Theory of Actuality, the most accurate accounts of historical events are not those given by historians, who mostly endeavour to restrain their imaginations, and therefore repeat the errors of contemporary accounts, or of other historians, but those given by frankly imaginative writers who, by steeping themselves in its "atmosphere", have made the past live again. If, for example, a Time Machine of Wellsian pattern were to be invented, and we could return to the Middle Ages, Walter Scott would be found to be practically accurate, not only as regards general atmosphere but probably also as regards actual events. Even his individual characters may well have had actual prototypes, associated in some such way as he describes. Our Time Machine would in that case show us Cedric the Saxon, Gurth and Wamba, Ivanhoe and Rowena, Front-de-Boeuf, the Templar and Richard the Lion-hearted, very much as a film based on the novel would show them, though no doubt less dramatically. In fact, the Theory maintains that where our great imaginative writers make the past "live again" they do so in an actual rather than in a merely metaphorical sense; they are, in fact, living Time Machines.

For, according to the Theory, the past is actually present in the Unconscious and can therefore be actualised for consciousness. Writers of genius, who study the past and find their imaginations stimulated by it, obtain actual contact

* Le Bon, op. cit., pp. 26 et seq.

with the historical characters concerned, at any rate in some degree, dependent probably on the power of their genius and on the intensity of their study and effort. The past is female, Negative, ruled by the anima; she must be wooed with effort and love, but once contact is made, she gives herself freely.*

The future, as we have postulated, is also present in the Unconscious. But it is not female, in the domain of the Negative, like the past; it is male, aggressive, and ruled by the Positive animus. As Jung has pointed out, the animus is plural. So is the future, being ruled by the Positive principle of division. In the Negative Past there is peace; the fight is o'er, the battle won. In the Positive future there is war—war between a plurality of possibilities.

The future does not require to be wooed, like the past. On the contrary, it woos us; it attacks us, thrusts itself upon us and through us, determined to actualise itself and attain peace in the past. But it does so as it were from a great distance, or, more accurately, from beyond a great gulf. From across the gulf an arm stretches to the blank page of the specious present, on which the Moving Finger writes, and, having writ, moves on. That is the only certain contact with the future which we have. But there is another which can best be described by pursuing the metaphor.

Let us suppose that the gulf is wholly impassable and that the ordinary rational, forward-looking faculties can merely see across it with the calculated foresight based on experience that we all know. That is how we endeavour to grasp and woo the future, with strictly limited results, by means of reason, through the Positive Power in us. But the Positive future is all the time attacking us, wooing us, endeavouring to make contact with us. As it cannot traverse the gulf, which represents, let us say, a vast "difference of potential", it "goes into reverse", and strives to reach us right round the "circuit

---

* The independent operation of imaginative characters has been attested by many writers, notably Shaw, who says he "never knows what his characters will do next".

of eternity", penetrating us by penetrating and intermingling with the Negative Past from the "beginning of Time", and appearing to us in the chaotic visions which are all we generally see of the Unconscious.

I do not pretend that the above is more than a metaphor, and a somewhat mixed metaphor at that. It is an attempt to describe what I seem to have clearly seen in periods of manic excitement, but which now baffles description. All I wish to postulate for the purpose of the Theory of Actuality is that the future also comes to some extent into actual consciousness through the visions and dreams of prophets, poets, and imaginative writers like Mr H. G. Wells, though in far less definite and accurate detail than does the past.

Our Lord's vision of the "Perousia" was, according to the Theory, subject to the general laws and limitations of all visions of the future by human beings. In taking "our nature upon Him", He accepted all our disabilities, and, though His relation with the Eternal was unique, it could only find expression in technical ways appropriate to the human psychophysical mechanism. As human being, Jesus shared in the Collective Unconscious, from which His apocalyptic visions in particular are clearly largely derived.

Cassandras have always been common. There is, perhaps, no more frequent prophetic product of the Unconscious than the vision of apocalyptic destruction. The Bible is packed with instances from cover to cover. Here is a typical example, taken at random from the first Isaiah.

"Fear, and the pit, and the snare, are upon thee, O inhabitant of the earth.

"And it shall come to pass, that he who fleeth from the noise of the fear shall fall into the pit; and he that cometh out of the midst of the pit shall be taken in the snare; for the windows from on high are open, and the foundations of the earth do shake.

"The earth is utterly broken down, the earth is clean dissolved, the earth is moved exceedingly.

"The earth shall reel to and fro like a drunkard, and

shall be removed like a cottage; and the transgression thereof shall be heavy upon it; and it shall fall, and not rise again.

"And it shall come to pass in that day, that the Lord shall punish the host of the high ones that are on high, and the kings of the earth upon the earth.

"And they shall be gathered together, as prisoners are gathered in the pit, and shall be shut up in the prison, and after many days shall they be visited.

"Then the moon shall be confounded, and the sun ashamed, when the Lord of hosts shall reign in mount Zion, and in Jerusalem, and before his ancients gloriously." *

In this passage from one of the greatest of all the magnificent line of Jewish prophets, the vision of horrors to come, the product not only of instinctive apprehension but also of innumerable atavistic memories of destruction, is not unrelieved. The Positive Power makes contact, through its co-operation with the Negative the vision of ultimate redemption breaks through, and shortly afterwards there follows the famous verse which foreshadows the Christian hope of resurrection:—"He will swallow up death in victory; and the Lord God will wipe away tears from off all faces; and the rebuke of his people shall be taken away from off all the earth: for the Lord hath spoken it."

Whether such visions as those of Isaiah—and of Our Lord —were, technically speaking, "hallucinations", "illusions", or merely the inner images of a creative mind, matters little. They were, the Theory of Actuality postulates, messages of the Spirit through the Collective Unconscious, and the Unconscious makes its messages—as Freud has shown—conscious in innumerable ways.† Visions, dreams, absent-mindedness, chance actions or words of oneself or of a fellow-creature, the flight of birds, "pictures in the fire", the movement of the heavenly bodies; all these and many other "coincidences" can be and have been construed as messages

* Isaiah 24, 17-23.
† See especially Freud, "Psychopathology of Everyday Life".

to man. And rightly so, for though not all such communications of the Unconscious are messages of the Spirit of God, direct messages of the Spirit, as opposed to His indirect working through the laborious processes of reason, can come no other way.

If we endeavour, with all reverence, to imagine the inner working of the mind of Our Lord, we must, I think, assume that a great deal of his thought came to Him in such ways as these. No doubt He checked it in every possible way with His reason. He must have had the most powerful mind of His age. No doubt, too, He was well aware of the danger of false guidance, and incidentally, of the similarity between the technical workings of His Unconscious and those of the innumerable false prophets, mostly paranoiacs and megalomaniacs of one kind or another, with which Palestine abounded. Many claimed to be the Messiah.

May it not be that Jesus set out on His mission so late in life precisely because He wished to be absolutely sure of Himself first? In particular, He is recorded throughout the synoptic Gospels as showing an intense reluctance to claim the Messiahship. "Why callest thou me good? There is none good but God." Yet in the passage quoted above, and in many others of like tenor, He asserts the certainty of a "Perousia" as a reward for the service of those whom He asked to abandon all for His sake. How sure must he have been before He did so? In His mind the Second Coming must have been something as certain of actual physical realisation as that the sun would rise on the morrow.

One of the salient features of the Unconscious is timelessness. With His human, time-bound psycho-physical system, Jesus seems to have thought that His Second Coming would take place in the immediate future. He appears to have assumed that it would in some way be associated with the forthcoming destruction of Jerusalem, which He no doubt foresaw rationally as well as instinctively, through the Unconscious. The context of the foregoing passage is strong evidence of this: "And when ye shall see Jerusalem compassed with armies, then know that the destruction thereof is nigh." *

The misapprehension of the time factor, due to the working of the Unconscious, is probably inherent in the very nature of the relations between Time and Eternity. But the fulfilment of true prophecy, however long delayed, does take place. On the basis of the Theory of Actuality it can, I believe, be logically and consistently maintained that the events coming to pass before the eyes of this tormented generation have at any rate a direct connection with those foretold by Jesus on the basis of the Jewish prophetic tradition.

No unbiased person can surely doubt that the actual political, religious, and economic situation likely to develop if the present "cold war" becomes a shooting war will be of an apocalyptic nature very much along the lines of Scriptural prophecy. If a great leader from another planet or elsewhere wished to come "with power and glory" to judge the earth and inaugurate a new era, it seems likely on purely rational grounds that the preliminary events preparatory to his intervention would be something like what we are actually witnessing. Nothing great ever comes to birth without sorrow and sacrifice. But unless the cosmos is a chance collocation of atoms, or solely ruled by demons, cruel immortals sporting with mankind for their own pleasure, we must believe that the sorrow and sacrifice is for a purpose.

The Theory of Actuality postulates, as has been said, both purpose and mechanism. But purpose is paramount. Contrary to what is often maintained, the purpose of historical evolution, at any rate, can be more clearly visualised today than ever before. That we are assisting at the birth-pangs of a World Union of States, or of some other type of world-wide political organisation, is a commonplace of modern political thought. Science has placed in our hands the means for establishing and maintaining such an organisation. It also gives us in the machine the means for superseding the

* Luke 21, 20.

grinding toil which has always been the lot of the vast majority of mankind.

The possibilities of the future are endless. All the dreams of mankind can be realised by rational, technical means. Space can be conquered; interplanetary travel is almost certainly not more than a century away, perhaps not more than a few decades. It may even be that Time can be conquered, possibly by psychical methods, possibly also by some sort of biological change to a "superman", such as has been envisaged by Nietzsche, Shaw, Heard and Toynbee. Western Civilisation, the product of sacrifice, of an unprecedented sublimation as the result of a tension increased to a degree which has now become intolerable, can at last give birth to its promised fruit, a free and full life for all.

Is it possible to imagine that He, Whose sacrifice on the Cross made all this possible, will have no part in it? I do not believe it. The Theory of Actuality postulates that Jesus, as God and Man, is the conqueror, judge and leader, not only of mankind, but also of the innumerable cosmic forces and Beings in this actual Universe. In Him is the conquest of evil and the contact between Positive and Negative which alone can reduce the tension and bring order to the world.

The time is coming when Jesus will show Himself to the world as the fighter that He is. It seems to me that the Christian cause has suffered untold harm from the tendency to a milk-and-watery representation of Our Lord. It was that tendency against which Nietzsche reacted so strongly, which led him to repudiate Christianity *in toto*. That was why Nietzsche's Superman was anti-Christian. But according to the Theory of Actuality, the Superman can only come to birth through the Second Coming of Jesus in the hearts of men, manifesting itself in an action of the Spirit as direct and effective as at Pentecost and among the early Christians.

When Jesus was on earth, He fought his war with the Powers of Evil by propaganda and sacrifice. The Spirit guided Him to choose a war of the Spirit rather than the hot shooting war of conquest which the Jews expected from their

Messiah, and that is why He was crucified. That he had had the other alternative of a war of conquest before His eyes, had considered it, and had rejected it as a temptation of the Devil, is clearly shown in the story of the Second Temptation. The time was not ripe. He deliberately chose a course which, though ultimately calculated to save mankind, involved relative obscurity, apparent frustration, and death for himself. "Verily, verily, I say unto you, Except a corn of wheat fall into the ground and die, it abideth alone: but if it die, it bringeth forth much fruit."

The harvest of fruit is ready for the gathering. When, countless aeons ago, Life emerged from the depths of the ocean and saw the light of the sun and the moon and the stars, the urge to strive *per ardua ad astra* was born. Life reached the land; it mounted with the birds into the air. But without intelligence it could go no farther. Now, at last, with consciously reasoning man conquering the stratosphere and contemplating the conquest of space, the Son of Man truly comes in the clouds with power and great glory. And our redemption draweth nigh.

The Theory of Actuality postulates the conscious leadership of the actual Christ in putting this actual world in order. It maintains that whatever horrors we may have to go through, provided we play our parts manfully and fight with Him, victory is inevitable. For we are really only the organisers of victory; the true victory was won on Calvary. Had Jesus chosen power and glory on earth, all history would have been different and, according to the Theory, neither the conquest of Nature, nor the rational control of man's spirit by himself, would have been possible. For millions of years man might have survived, but, eventually, the sun would have cooled (or heated) and the race would, as Balfour feared, have vanished without leaving a wrack behind. All the work would have had to have been done again from the beginning, perhaps in another planet, perhaps in another "continuum" altogether.

But now Nature has to all intents and purposes been conquered, and what we are witnessing is the judging of the earth, the control of man's spirit by man in the person of the Son of Man, the living Christ. That it is attended by wars and rumours of wars, atomic and bacteriological horrors, cruelties on a scale unheard of since the days of Genghis Khan, the systematic establishment of idolatry of evil men by evil men, is only what was rationally to be expected. All great historical changes have been attended by horrors; they are impossible without attendant modifications of the balance of forces in the Unconscious, which never takes place by peaceful means. Moreover, if the Theory of Actuality is right in holding that a certain degree of prophecy is scientifically possible, some weight must be attached to Biblical and other prophecies. It may well be that those "Fundamentalists" and others who try to show the application of Biblical prophecies to current events are nearer to the truth than those who laugh at them.

In dealing with all intuitions and visions of the Unconscious, the Theory follows Robert Bridges, who wrote, in his *Testament of Beauty*, that the "troublous task" of Reason was

> "to comprehend aright and wisely harmonise
> the speechless intuitions of the inconscient mind;
> which, tho' a naked babe (as men best pictured Christ)
> is yet in some sort nearer to the Omniscient
> than man's unperfect Reason, baulk'd as that must be
> by the self-puzzledom of introspection and doubt."

The Utopian vision of a perfect land flowing with milk and honey, of peace and security and all the freedoms, is no product of reason. It is an intuition of the Unconscious, and of all such intuitions probably the most powerful. According to the Theory of Actuality the following aspects can be distinguished in it.

Firstly there are the Negative aspects in the sense of the Theory. Most important of these is the sexual.

The vision represents, I suggest, the longing for sexual satisfaction and the attendant peace. This, according to Freudian theory, is intimately associated (in the male at any rate; as regards the female the Freudians are less clear) with the regressive longing for the peace of the womb. Being Negative, this aspect is dominated by the anima. The Mohammedan Heaven with its houris is probably its most typical expression.

Connected with this, which may perhaps be regarded as the ontogenetical aspect of regressive longings, is another Negative aspect. This is phylogenetical—the urge to go "Back to Nature", to regain the primal peace of instinct and innocence.

Why the story of the Garden of Eden should constantly have been derided by believers in Darwin's evolutionary theories is difficult to see. If we regard the state of primal innocence as that of the instinctive animal consciousness, before the evolving anthropoids had been unwise enough (from their own point of view) to eat of the Tree of Knowledge of Good and Evil, the story appears as the most perfect parable of the great evolutionary mutation that can be conceived. How many of the miseries of man are due to conscience (intimately associated with reason), only priests, lunatics, psychiatrists and others with practical experience of the inner workings of the human soul can tell us. The Paradise lost by man is one enjoyed by every other member of the animal kingdom—as far as we know at any rate. And as all the experiences of our animal ancestors form, according to the hypothesis which the Theory of Actuality bases on more or less orthodox biological and psychological science, an actual part of our own Collective Unconscious, what more natural than that we should hark back to these experiences and see them, transfigured, as the Heaven or Utopia for which we long?

Secondly, there are the Positive aspects of the Utopian vision. These seem to be connected with the future rather than the past, though in view of the way in which past and future are inextricably mixed in the Unconscious, the distinction is not easy to make.

There is the economic aspect, representing the urge for the

satisfaction of nutritive and other economic needs in the struggle for existence. This aspect probably predominates with the female, who is always preoccupied with the need to feed herself and her offspring—not to mention her bread-winner—during her defenceless childbearing period. Being Positive, it is dominated by the animus, which has, according to Jung, a tendency to appear in somewhat intellectual shape, as a kind of assembly of wise men who are always right.

Associated with this is the intellectual aspect, which in Western man, with his predominantly Positive character-istics, seems to see its satisfaction only in perpetual "pro-gress", largely of a materialistic nature. The typical ex-pression of this is the Socialist or Communist Utopia of modern Left-Wing thought.

It will be remembered that in Chapter IV, I referred in connection with the concepts of Negative and Positive, to Professor Toynbee's distinction of "archaism" and "futur-ism" as the two major tendencies in disintegrating civilisa-tions (i.e. civilisations in which the Unconscious factors are taking charge).* On the above classification, the first two, or Negative aspects, must be regarded as "archaic", and the last two, or Positive aspects, as "futurist". It is only in relation to these four aspects, as thus classified on the basis of the Theory of Actuality, that a clear understanding of the underlying forces governing the course of contemporary history can be gained.

This may seem a large claim. I will, however, as the con-cluding section of this chapter and this book, endeavour to give a forecast of the future which can be tested against the facts in due course. According to the principles of the Theory of Actuality, this must be based on instinct and intuition as well as reason, Negative as well as Positive. The basis of the forecast is the instinctive or intuitive vision of the world and its immediate future which has forced itself upon me as the result of my experiences. I shall try, as Bridges advises, to check, explain and amplify that intuitive vision by reason, in this case by the systematic application of the principles of the

* See p. 109.

Theory of Actuality. I am content that the validity of the Theory should be judged by the degree to which my forecast corresponds with the facts. The *experimentum cruciale* to which I appeal thus takes place in the great laboratory of the world.

5. *The Management of Unrighteousness*

As stated in an earlier chapter, while engaged on Intelligence work in 1944, I had a severe breakdown. I was transported from the atmosphere of my office, where we were engaged in an all-out effort to defeat the Germans, to the solitude of a side-room in a Mental Hospital, where I soon found myself in acute mania, coping with the fantastic creatures of the Unconscious.

As far as I remember it was about three weeks before those creatures began to take political shape. During the interim I read the papers in my more lucid intervals, followed the fortunes of our advancing armies, and hoped for a speedy victory for the Allies. Then one night I had two clear visions, in the technical form of illusions, which inaugurated a profound reversal of my whole political orientation.

I lay on my bed watching the play of light-reflections on the shiny walls of my sick-room. There were two patches of light, one in front of me, and the other on my left. Gradually the one in front of me began to take shape as a definite pattern. I knew that this meant the advent of a vision, and relaxed my eyes and body accordingly.

I saw the mouth of a cave, which appeared to be on a mountain-side, since I could see the snow-caps of other mountains in the distance. The cave-mouth was brilliantly lit by a sort of all-pervading glow, which seemed to come from within. As I looked, a boy or youth—I judged him to be about seventeen or eighteen years of age—approached the mouth of the cave. He was dressed in ordinary Russian style, with a belted shirt outside his trousers, and wore an Astrakhan cap rather like a Cossack. I took him for a lad of the better-off peasantry or lower middle-class.

As he approached the mouth of the cave, an attractive

shape in female form, which however had an indefinable air of unreality about it, seemed to materialise in the mouth. The shape beckoned; the lad followed; and both disappeared into the cave, from which sounds of revelry seemed to emerge.

At that moment I had no idea what was happening, or whom the vision might represent, though I knew the lad must be Russian from his dress. Naturally I was most curious about it. I did feel, however, a strange and rather appalling sense of evil about the cave and the proceedings, which was peculiar in view of my general attitude towards wine, women and song, especially when in manic states dominated by the Negative Power. An inner voice told me to look at the other patch of light, on my left, where my curiosity would be fully satisfied.

There I saw a man, apparently bound to a post by cords about the legs and hips, since the upper part of his body was free to writhe and make various gestures. He appeared to be facing some sort of court, being held in the open air. In front of him was a row of judges seated at a table on a raised dais, who were wearing military uniforms which I could not identify. I could, however, plainly see the prisoner's guards, who were all in the blue helmeted uniform worn by the Berlin city police in the years between World Wars I and II. Equally plain were the face and figure of the prisoner. He was Joseph Vissarionovitch Djugashvili, self-styled Stalin.

I remember being definitely surprised, and expressing my surprise to the dual personality, the inner voice that speaks to me on such occasions. "There is nothing surprising about it," replied the voice. "You see an evil man receiving the reward of his iniquities. Look at the other vision; it shows the beginning of the story."

I looked, and saw the lad, whom I then recognised as the young Joseph Vissarionovitch, emerging from the cave. As he went out, he turned, and prostrated himself on the ground. Dimly, I saw a shape inside the mouth, a shape no longer of beauty, but of inexpressible horror. It seemed to speak to the prostrate figure. "Joseph Vissarionovitch," it said. "Now that thou hast sold thy whole, undivided soul to me, and hast bowed down and worshipped me in token thereof, I give thee all Power, and all the kingdoms of the earth, in full reality. Thou shalt re-establish my priesthood, the covens of my worship, and then shall manage all the world. The black magic of the forgotten past shall live again, and control the science of the future. To thee, and to those whom thou shalt choose to be my managers, shall belong all the riches, all the pleasures that thou canst conceive in thy wildest dreams. All men shall be slaves of my Management of Unrighteousness. Only obey my voice, and when I command thee to slay, then slay and spare not. Through blood alone comes Victory."

The voice ceased; the vision vanished. I turned to the other vision on my left. The scene had changed. The figure of Stalin was still bound to a post, but facing him was a khaki-clad firing squad, in uniforms which I seemed to recognise as those of the Grenadier Guards. Their rifles were levelled at the prisoner, I seemed to hear the word of command to fire, and then a volley. The writhing figure collapsed, and the whole patch of light became once more a blank.

A day or two afterwards, while the flights of political ideas, which these visions had set going in my mind, were in full swing, I had another vision, though one not so clear as the above. The ward wireless was playing some of the Strauss waltzes, which reminded me at once of the film *Congress Dances*. On the wall was a similar patch of light, on which appeared a picture of another Congress of Vienna, in modern uniforms and modern dress, dancing in celebration of another Peace.

I have always admired the Congress of Vienna—to the disadvantage of the Congress of Versailles—for the remarkably successful way in which it pacified and settled a Europe at least as disturbed as that of 1918. Whatever its faults, it gave Europe a century, if not of tranquillity, at least of freedom from a major world war. In particular, I have admired Wellington and Castlereagh for their statesmanlike moderation, and their insistence on the generous treatment of the defeated enemy.

As I looked at this new vision, I seemed to be talking to the Iron Duke and his colleague. "Fear not," they said. "What you see is a true vision, and it will come to pass in your own lifetime. World War II is but an interlude in the great struggle. No peace will follow it, but at most an armed truce. Within some twenty years (the period is clear in my memory) there will have been a third world war, in which we who speak to you will take our full part. Evil, which is not where men see it today, will be destroyed for a season, and what you see is the peacemaking. Vienna will rise again as a city of Peace, and there a reasonable settlement of the problems of a devastated world will once more be arranged."

While I do not for a moment claim that these "visions" and their attendant "voices" were more than the ordinary communications of the Unconscious experienced by countless millions of people in Mental Hospitals and elsewhere, yet they have left with me an inner certainty which no rational considerations are able to destroy. By 1965, I have had little doubt in my innermost heart since then, Stalin, or perhaps his successor, will have been shot, after a trial in which British and Germans will have taken part, and at long last a sane peace will be in the making, probably at Vienna. Whether I shall myself be alive, I do not know, in spite of what the "voices" said; nor do I want to know. What will happen will happen—wholly independently of me.

The two clearest features of the series of visions, the two which have an indelible impression of absolute certainty upon me, are the evil nature of Stalin and the fact that Germans were concerned in his trial. I can see the helmets of those Berlin police now, as I write.

What I have described, I have said, happened in 1944, when Stalin was "Uncle Joe" to most of us in Britain. Admittedly, I had my doubts about Uncle Joe, having been to

Russia, made some study of Russian developments, and read one or two biographies. Admittedly, too, I have had many connections with Germany, where I lived for years, and I worked hard as a journalist to improve Anglo-German relations between the wars. But I had just written an official memorandum, based on information available to me as an intelligence officer, in which I took very strongly the normal view held at that time about the danger of trusting the Germans too much after the war. The visions really did produce a reversal of my attitude, which, in view of subsequent events, very naturally still prevails. In 1947, in a small Newsletter I publish, I gave, largely on "hunch", the correct date of the Russian discovery of the atomic bomb long before the Foreign Office published it, and wrote the following passage:—

"Towards World War III

[The Moscow Conference of April 1947] marked . . . the final defeat of the policy of 'United Nations', the policy for which the Second World War was fought to a finish and Nazi Germany destroyed—the policy of basing peace on agreement between the great victorious powers. And if it is true, as every leading statesman and newspaper from Mr Churchill and *The Times* downwards has told us, that the policy was the only way to reap the fruits of victory in peace, it follows that the points of the world train are set towards war."

When I wrote the above, I had not been feeling the pulse of world affairs in Fleet Street or New York, but had, on the contrary, been into retirement in this very Mental Hospital, when my intuitions of 1944 had returned, thoroughly clarifying and arranging themselves. It is, to say the least, a somewhat humorous paradox that I should get a far clearer and more accurate view of world affairs from within the walls of a lunatic asylum than I do elsewhere.

Yet it is true, and on the Theory of Actuality it is readily explicable.

In the first place the "actual atmosphere" of a Mental Hospital is probably in closer touch with the Collective Unconscious than that of anywhere else. All or nearly all of the varied influences that pervade the Unconscious are there represented. There are men and women of all classes, of many European and other nationalities, in an immense variety of abnormal states of mind. According to the Theory, proximity and personal contact, though no conscious communications or sense-impressions may be received, have an actual effect on the Unconscious. Thus the intuitions or hallucinations or other communications from the Unconscious received by patient A, may be influenced directly by the fact that in a neighbouring ward there is a particular patient B, whom A has never ever seen. This hypothesis has been very strongly impressed upon me in the course of my manic periods, and I assume it to be true, though I have only experimentally verified (as far as subjectively possible) the actuality of "atmosphere" in the sense described. For example, I should not be surprised to hear that, in the hospital when I had the above-described visions of Stalin, there were at the time one or more patients of Russian origin, though I have not been able to ascertain whether this was actually the case. This example is purely illustrative; the full implications of the hypothesis are far wider. Theoretically, the "atmosphere", say, of a building, is influenced in one degree or another, however infinitesimal, not only by individuals and objects present in it at any given time, but by all individuals and objects that ever have been in it, or connected with it. The "atmosphere" of St Paul's Cathedral, for example, where I recently spent a quiet half-hour of meditation, can be assumed to be influenced by St Paul (or by the fact that it is dedicated to St Paul rather than to another saint), by all those who are buried there, by Sir Christopher Wren and his fellow-workers, by the fact that it is situated in London and not elsewhere, and so on. Though I was not conscious of a thousandth, nor a millionth part of these influences, my Unconscious was, and was affected by them, so that, through the influence of the Unconscious on the conscious personality or ego, "I" am slightly affected by the personality, say, of the humblest workman who wielded a trowel in the building, or the poorest citizen who ever worshipped within its precincts.

In the second place, when in Mental Hospitals I am generally in some degree "abnormal" in the sense of being more directly subject to the influence of the Unconscious than when I am "normal". I am, therefore, as it were a better "receiver" for unconscious influences and messages, which I am in some degree able to interpret rationally as well as to sense consciously. Since, however, my rational and critical faculties have been partly inhibited by my mental condition —this inhibition appearing to be in some sense a condition of the free functioning of the conscious-unconscious connection —I cannot place full reliance on my direct and immediate interpretation of what I have sensed. I must wait until my critical reason returns and then endeavour to make the interpretation. If this happens while I am still in a Mental Hospital and influenced by its "atmosphere", so much the better, since it is to be assumed that its extensive contacts with the Collective Unconscious remain with me, though I am no longer plainly conscious of them.

This is my situation as I write these lines today. Though regarded by medical authority as virtually back to "normal" in a mental sense, as the result of a physical infection I have had to occupy a bed in the infirmary ward where I am once more "immersed" in an exceedingly "abnormal atmosphere". I am also compelled to lie in bed, which forces me to concentrate my thoughts and is very conducive to my writing. As a purely personal matter, I postulate that the purposive Power or Powers particularly concerned with me, let us say my "guardian angel", has been able to organise this in order to enable, or perhaps to compel me to finish this book properly. Since this is a peculiarly difficult chapter to write, and since my natural laziness makes extreme concentration difficult when I have full liberty to devote myself to more pleasurable activities, I am duly grateful.

At the present time, therefore, I should be in an advantageous position to do what I am attempting here, namely to "think" by both Negative and Positive methods, or, as Bridges puts it, to "comprehend aright and wisely harmonise the speechless intuitions of the inconscient mind". I ought to be able to take a balanced view.

In order to explain precisely what I mean by a "balanced view", and at the same time to give an idea of the practical application of the analytical methods of the Theory of Actuality to human thought, it is necessary to pursue further the somewhat self-centred and egotistical process of introspection and self-analysis with which this book is all too full. I am, I believe, a natural extravert in the Jungian sense. According to the Theory of Actuality, this really means that my Unconscious, though it contains (like the Unconscious of all creatures) both Positive and Negative influences, is predominantly controlled by the Negative Power. This might be expressed, purely hypothetically, by saying that my "guardian angel" is Negative, with female characteristics, let us say associated in some way with my favourite saint, St Mary Magdalene. There is, however, no need to stress this purposive and personal aspect, which is difficult to analyse scientifically, since the Theory of Actuality postulates that the mechanical aspect of "spiritual" forces is equally "actual". Let us say, then, borrowing from the (equally hypothetical) terminology of the physicists, that I am a human "particle" with a "negative charge".

Pursuing this electrical metaphor, I might say that I am a "human electron", part of a vast "negative electric current" of such electrons, all moving in the opposite direction to the positive current of "protons". My Unconscious demonstrates this to me in many ways, such as, for example, my inner certainty that I am on the side of Origen and St Francis of Assisi against Tertullian and St Augustine, of Luther against Calvin, of the Medici circle against Savonarola, and so on.* This certainty I can describe as being derived from the Unconscious; it is purely instinctive or intuitive; I can find no rational grounds for it—rationally those who believe in the

* See Chap. IV.

eternal separation of God from some of His creatures, which I have described as the quintessence of Positive, analytical doctrine, may equally well be right. But, as I have said earlier, I was born a "synthesist", a particle of the Negative, and there is nothing I can do about it.

Human beings, however, are even more complicated than particles appear to be in the present state of physical knowledge. I am also affected by the Positive and I am affected in two ways. In the first place my rational faculty, with which I cannot dispense any more than can any other human creature, is predominantly Positive. Instinctively I tend to synthesise; rationally I tend to analyse. That is what happens when my mind is working properly. I then have the "balanced view" I am endeavouring to define. In the second place, a possibility appears to be inherent in my Unconscious of changing over to a "positive charge". Tertullian, St Augustine, Calvin and Savonarola take over as it were in my Unconscious; my Positive rational faculty associates itself with them and exaggerates their separationist views; and I find myself wholly separated from God in the utmost depths of depression.

For ten years, however, this has not happened to me. My explanation for this is that my Unconscious is at last stabilised in its natural Negative condition. The Positive forces in it are under complete control; the Negative is in command. This explains why, when my mind becomes unbalanced, I now always have a manic and never a depressive swing. This, I believe, happens, not because of any increase in the Negative "charge" or "forces" in the Unconscious, but simply owing to the diminution of the influence of my "positively controlled" rational consciousness. My "negatively controlled" Unconscious then has a clear field, with the results sufficiently described in this book.

I do not pretend that the above is free from contradictions, or accurately worked out; it is no more than a groping, metaphorical attempt to simplify the true facts. As will be seen, however, it is possible along some such lines to give a rational explanation of the changes in my conscious view of contemporary affairs, which are under consideration.

As an ordinary, rational human being—I hope readers will not wholly deny me the right to the predicate "rational"—I am influenced by the views and beliefs of my contemporaries, and by modern developments generally. My imagination has been stimulated by the Positive, futurist visions of men like H. G. Wells; I am, I trust, not unprogressive; the Socialist, even the Marxian Paradise is not wholly without appeal to me. I sometimes describe myself as a Tory Socialist; and the great movement of Liberal thought in the nineteenth century and after seems to me to have played an essential part in human development. Thus, during World War II, when Britain was fighting essentially on the Positive side, I had no difficulty in aligning my sentiments accordingly, and in entering wholeheartedly into the struggle according to the measure of my capabilities.

Before I pursue the argument, I should perhaps describe exactly what I mean by the "Positive side" in this context. I have already endeavoured to associate Professor Toynbee's concepts of "archaism" and "futurism" with my own analysis of the Utopian vision of man into Negative and Positive aspects, on the basis of the Theory of Actuality. Toynbee regards, as we saw in Chapter IV,* the movements of the extreme Right, such as Nazism, Fascism and so on, as examples of archaism, and those of the extreme Left, such as Jacobinism and Communism, as futurist. The Theory of Actuality follows Toynbee in holding that both have the Utopian vision as their goal, Negative, archaist movements of the Right having before them the vision of a lost Paradise to be regained in the form of a romanticised past, and Positive, futurist movements of the Left the vision of a new Paradise to be created in a never-never land of the future.

In World War II, the Negative, archaist movements were the aggressors, forcing practically the whole world on to the

* See p. 109.

other, Positive side of the Allies, whether the Allied nations thus brought in were predominantly Positive in tendency or not. The fact that the war was for the Allies inevitably a war against Negative archaism, expressed in Goebbels' powerful propaganda, naturally tended to further the political aims of the Positive, futurist movements in the Allied countries. The victory of the Allies thus brought with it a series of Positive political victories in Europe and elsewhere. The surprising post-war defeat of the Tories in spite of their leader's war record was mainly due to this, as were the immense advances which Positive Communism has registered almost everywhere. The Positive Left was in the ascendant.

If I may now return to my personal analysis, I would say that when I left my work as the result of my breakdown in 1944 I was, emotionally as well as intellectually, dominated by the Positive forces liberated by the struggle, and controlling my colleagues and contemporaries engaged in the war. But these forces only had control of the "upper layers" of my Unconscious. As soon as I got out of the "atmosphere" of the war effort into that of a Mental Hospital and, with the progress of my manic swing, my "deep Unconscious" took charge, the Negative forces reasserted themselves. My "visions", flights of ideas, and general political metamorphosis were the result.

It does not, of course, follow from the above that there was any "truth" in the "visions". It can be argued that they were merely the psycho-physical mechanism through which a political point of view which is more or less natural to me regained the upper hand. It may be said that the very precise details of the visions, for example the clear picture of the face and shape of Stalin, and of the German police acting as his guards in the trial, were the result of "chance". But, quite apart from the Theory of Actuality, which regards "chance" as purposive and equates it with "Tyche-Theresa", the great authority of Freud denies that there is any "chance" in the workings of the Unconscious. This is clearly shown in Freud's *Psychopathology of Everyday Life*, where he actually writes of his Unconscious helping him, for example, saving him from foolish mistakes, and by implication almost attributes personality to it.

It appears to me that an important feature is the precision of the "visions", and of my memory of them, which is in strong contrast to the vast majority of my illusions and flights of ideas. As a matter of subjective experience in quite minor matters, I have noticed that although I am often misled by intuitions and hunches, which are very frequent in my manic periods, this is generally either when they are of a vague nature (and thus can easily be misinterpreted), or when they come to me when I am not really under the influence of the deep Unconscious. The nearer I am to a trance state, the more likely the communications of the Unconscious are to be true, and in the case we are considering I was as near as no matter in a state of actual trance. The trouble is that communications from the deep Unconscious generally either have little detail, or else the details are not readily comprehensible. This is, of course, particularly the case with dreams.

What carries most conviction, however, is the fact that, ever since 1944, every single intuition or "hunch", or other communication from the instinctive, Negative side of things, has confirmed what was borne in upon me then. Normally, when my Unconscious makes mistakes—let us postulate that it is through the influence of Beelzebub, a Positive devil for whom I have the greatest distaste—it soon manages to correct them. Alternatively, when I misread its communications, something soon turns up to show me my error.

Finally, my Positive, rational, conscious self, observing the actual course of history since 1944, finds my Negative intuitions confirmed in every respect. It is one of the most important postulates of the Theory of Actuality that when Positive and Negative are brought by the subject into close contact and found to be in agreement and to act in harmony, then the subject has got as near as he can to the actual truth.

All successful human effort depends, in the individual as in the race, on the degree of contact, coordination and balance between Positive and Negative. The age in which we live is one in which—we will again postulate that it is through the conscious purpose of Beelzebub, Lord of Flies (according to Mr Aldous Huxley)—there is neither contact nor coordination, and the balance or pendulum has swung right over to the Positive side. If truth and goodness lie in the mean, as the Greeks maintained,* then lies and evil look very much like prevailing. No doubt Beelzebub, whose dominion can perhaps be assumed to extend to lies as well as to flies, thinks he is doing very well. How can he be defeated, and the balance re-established?

All history, according to the Theory of Actuality, works by opposites. A movement—it may be Positive or Negative in essence—arises, conquers, and through its very conquest provokes a resistance which draws its strength from the counter-Power, until a new balance of forces is achieved. This applies to cultural as well as to religious movements, to economic as well as to political. Thus the excesses of Negative paganism, based largely on Great-Mother-worship, provoked the Father-worship of Positive Judaism; Christianity, Negative in its stress on the loving character of the Father and its reaction against Jewish legalism, soon stressed its Positive aspect in struggling to supersede Negative Greco-Roman culture; Negative Mohammedanism temporarily stopped the expansion of Christianity; the Negative Renaissance of the pagan gods of Greece and Rome led to the reaction of the Positive Reformation, which soon went to extremes in Calvinist Puritanism; the Reformation in its turn was stopped by the Negative Counter-Reformation. In the more specifically economic and political spheres, the Negative feudalism of the Catholic Middle Ages was superseded by Positive capitalism associated with Positive Calvinism; monarchy, whose real strength is Negative (or instinctive), having established its power in alliance with the Positive capitalism of the cities, reacted against capitalism and endeavoured to control it,

* See especially Aristotle, "Nicomachean Ethics".

whereupon capitalism associated itself with Positive republican movements and murdered Kings in the name of Liberalism.

The analysis of the past century is more difficult, possibly because it is less easy to see it in perspective. I have described capitalism as Positive; it is futurist; its vision and motive-power are economic; it is also essentially divisive, combative, analysing, in a word, Yang. Its deep-rooted Positive character was demonstrated particularly plainly by its association with Calvinism.* But if capitalism is Positive, then surely Socialism must be Negative. Yet I have described Communism, an extreme form of Socialism, as the quintessence of the Positive. Is there not an inherent contradiction here which invalidates the whole theory?

The answer is I think that Socialism is largely Negative in its ideals but Positive in its theory. As the situation of Socialist parties in Britain and elsewhere shows very plainly, it is essentially schizophrenic. Its schizophrenia, I will postulate, is probably the neatest job achieved by Beelzebub for at least a millennium.

The ultimate ideal basis of Socialism in the human soul has never been better expressed than in Schiller's "Ode to Joy" as set by Beethoven in the Ninth Symphony. It is Negative in the very deepest sense in which I am using the word; it goes right back to the Dionysiac thiaisos. There is the vision, basically sexual in origin, of a lost Paradise regained, of classes and peoples hitherto strictly separated by "die Mode" reunited in love. Behind it Beethoven expresses the peace that passes all understanding. Yang is finally defeated; Yin and love reign supreme.

It is a curious fact, but readily explicable on this hypothesis, that in many countries Socialism started its reactions against liberal capitalism in alliance with Negative (i.e. moderately archaist) Conservatism. In England it was the Tory landed gentry who carried the Factory Acts under Dis-

* See especially R. H. Tawney, "Religion and the Rise of Capitalism".

raeli and thus produced the first practical improvement in the lot of the exploited urban workers. In Germany, the Junker Conservative Bismarck established the first Welfare State by his extensive and well-organised system of social insurance.

The Negative, archaist aspect of idealist Socialism is very clearly shown in the life and work of William Morris, whose vision of the Utopian future was directly derived from a somewhat idealised past, and who deliberately set out to picture the Socialist Commonwealth as a resurrected Merrie England. British Socialism, in fact, has always been very largely Negative.

The way to the capture of Socialism by the Positive Power was opened, above all, by the theories of Marx. Marx was a rootless, intellectual, Ashkenazim Jew, and as such quintessentially Positive. He was Yang personified. To the very depths of his being he wanted to destroy, to break down, to cut up. His hatred of Society was fanned into white-hot flame by ancestral memories of racial persecution and frustration. With the flaming phallic sword of his ancestral God Yahveh, allied to a supremely powerful intellect inherited from thousands of years of Talmudic study and dispute, he succeeded, like Calvin before him, in dividing society into two, and only two parts, the predestined elect and the predestined damned—good workers and evil capitalists. The simplicity and genius of this tour de force has put his doctrine in a fair way to conquer the world.

Were it not for one factor I have no doubt that it would do so. But that factor renders the ultimate defeat of Marxism quite as certain as Marx himself believed that the liquidation of the wicked capitalists would be.

Marx was a dogmatic atheist. He hated God as he hated society. He set his Positive doctrine in opposition to all religion, the "opium of the people". He made his movement of this world alone, doomed to fight against all the yearnings of man to bring Time and Eternity together. He based his faith solely on materialism and mechanism, working in Time towards a futurist never-never land. And in so doing he cut his movement off wholly from the past, from which religion so largely derives, making it like a severed tree precariously balanced on its stump.

The stump will endure, while the hewn tree is cast into the flames. Today, the power of Marxism is concentrated in Stalinist Communism, whose worldwide aggression is steadily forcing all religions, whether Positive or Negative in their essential nature, into the Negative camp. The situation is thus very much the opposite of that which prevailed before World War II, when the Negative Power was the aggressor. The "revenge of the Negative",* postulated for the near future by the Theory of Actuality, is the just revenge of God in all His diverse aspects, in all the manifold forms in which the spirit of man has been able to apprehend Him, on the aggression of the Satanic hierarchy that is defying Him.

A Management of Unrighteousness of evil men, who have openly cast away, with their God, all regard for moral principle, is steadily and systematically preparing to conquer the world. They know that such a conquest is, at long last, technically possible. The world today is far smaller, far easier to master from the point of view of organisation and communications than was the "world" conquered by Alexander or by the Romans. The dream of all conquerors since the primal horde-leaders can at last come true. The absolute security of a wholly enslaved planet is the clear, and apparently realisable, aim of the Managers of Unrighteousness in the Kremlin and elsewhere.

Stalin and his Management—the term indicated in my "vision" seems not inappropriate in view of James Burnham's remarkable theories of Managerial Revolution—have in the theory of Marx, who with all his faults was a great and sincere idealist, a perfect instrument for their ends. They can pervert it as they will. Marx said the State would "wither away" and leave man free; they are increasing the power of the State to the utmost limits of the possible for their own personal bene-

* See Chap. IV.

fit. They take the great vision of man's future which is in the Unconscious for all to see, and claim it as their Marxist monopoly. Because the masses, being nearest to the Unconscious—except perhaps for lunatics—see the vision most plainly, and because their present condition in many parts of the world contrasts terribly with what they see, they are often easy prey.

For man, as the profound psychologists who run the Management of Unrighteousness well know—the devil is a close student of Scripture and science—must look to a Kingdom of Heaven as a necessity of his practical reason. If his hope of such a Kingdom in the eternal world is finally destroyed, he is forced to project it into an exclusively earthly future, and this (by destroying the deepest basis of morality —the belief in a righteous God of Judgement) eventually allows him to be seduced into any crime to achieve it. Positive futurism thus carried to the limit leads in this way to the bottomless pit.

The real victors of World War II were the Positive futurists of the Management. Our postulated Beelzebub probably thinks he has gained the day. But, according to the Theory of Actuality he is, in the final analysis, only a necessary evil, a necessary political opposition, as it were, in the Universe. He is the means by which the Spirit of God is rallying the forces of freedom and love for another Pentecostal outpouring which will give us the victory.

It seems to be possible to detect in the periodicity of history something in the nature of a two-thousand year rhythm. Oswald Spengler gives two thousand years as the approximate duration of a normal culture-civilisation complex. There is an Eastern belief that great religious leaders, producing profound modifications in the religious structure of society, tend to appear every second millennium. If this is so, must not the time be ripe, and overripe, for a great reversal of the Positive revolution of the first millennium B.C.? *

The whole course of my visionary experiences has forced

* See p. 106.

this view on my rational consciousness. Cold or hot, World War III must and will be fought to a finish, and it will be a war of the Negative against the Positive in which the victory of the Negative is as necessary and inevitable as that the hornèd moon will rise tonight.

For the Positive, in the extreme form in which it is making its bid for world domination, has secured a virtual monopoly of evil, or at any rate of political and social evil. Just as St Augustine saw a world in which the devil had the Negative all to himself, so we, if we look clearly, can see the Powers of Hell monopolising the sheep's clothing of the Positive. They are, behind their façade of order, the principles of unbalance and chaos. Only by defeating them can the balance be restored.

I have endeavoured to convey in this chapter, as indeed in this whole book, an idea of the Theory of Actuality as it appears to me, a rational instrument by means of which it is possible to pierce the menacing war clouds of the present and see the light shining on the future of man. The coming victory of the Negative, according to the Theory, will be, not a return to the past, which is gone beyond recall, not a victory of "archaism" or of "conservatism" alone, but the means by which the past, right back to the earliest amoeba and to the star-burst out of which the solar system is now supposed to have originated,* will be once more linked, theoretically and practically, to the present and future. It will re-establish the Tree of Life firmly on its roots.

In the Garden of Eden story, the Tree of Life was planted beside the Tree of Knowledge of Good and Evil. In the terminology of the Theory of Actuality, the Tree of Life represents the Negative and the Tree of Knowledge of Good and Evil the Positive Power. But the Positive Power of the Management of Unrighteousness has denied its Tree. The Serpent who persuaded Eve and Adam to eat of its fruit and thus started our anthropoid ancestors on their evolutionary climb is now giving us an emetic to make us vomit it up. We

* Cf. Fred Hoyle, "The Nature of the Universe". Basil Blackwell.

are asked to eat instead an artificial apple of moral—and intellectual—"knowledge" produced by the Serpent's Management of Unrighteousness in its own factories. Only eat the apple of artificiality, says the serpent, and you will achieve moral peace, the haven beyond Good and Evil of which Nietzsche had a vision. Let yourselves be wholly "conditioned" by the State, by its Management, and the torments of moral struggle will be at an end.

But the wily Serpent is now telling lies, though to Eve he told the truth. The Theory of Actuality holds that the true destiny of man and woman is first to digest the apple and thus "become as gods, knowing good and evil", and then, after paying the full penalty of the disobedience which gives them such painful knowledge, to return to God, who will give them of the fruit of the Tree of Life, so that they may live for ever. In the Tree of Life alone is the redemption from moral struggle, the peace of Yin that passeth all understanding beyond good and evil. By making the contact between Positive and Negative in his own person, by mingling the apple, in due time and season, with the fruit of the Tree of Life freely offered on Calvary, man can conquer the actual Universe of Time, however many millions of inhabitable planets our astronomical physicists may be able to find in it, and share with his Leader the peace of eternity.

That is the final postulate of the Theory of Actuality, and it is admittedly a matter of faith. There can be no complete certainty here below; the Devil must always have a mathematical chance at least, perhaps even a fifty-fifty chance, or the battle would be unreal. But it is the Christian faith that, whatever his original chances, the Devil lost the battle of the planet Earth on Calvary. Here he is fighting a rearguard action, however he may appear to be advancing at the present moment, during the Holy Year of Grace 1950. No doubt he is preparing a come-back in other galaxies, if not in this one.

Such recondite metaphysical speculations may be left to philosophers and physicists in this world and the next. The Theory of Actuality is more concerned with immediate

Actuality, since the object of its author here is, as I have said, to give a forecast of things to come which will establish its validity by comparison with the facts.

Though it is arguable that the Theory, which I hope will enable a new and more fruitful approach to the Mind-Matter complex to be made, does not wholly stand or fall by the course of World War III that it envisages, I am quite content that it should do so. The only thing I ask is that a little latitude should be allowed in the timing. As I have stressed, timelessness is one of the essences of the Unconscious, and the period of some twenty years from 1944 which appeared to be indicated to me was admittedly somewhat indefinite. My own guess is that by 1965 the final Treaty will have been signed, and I think it very probable that the signature will take place at Vienna. If it is urged that Vienna is a most unlikely city for that purpose, I can only appeal to my vision and suggest, moreover, that by the end of World War III it is by no means improbable that only one or two cities in Europe and America will contain the necessary accommodation for a full-scale Conference or Congress. There is a no *a priori* reason why Vienna should not be one of them. Perhaps the actual spirits of the great peace-makers of 1815 will protect it for the purpose.

I will not venture to predict the precise character of the peace settlement, though at times this appeared quite clear to me. My guess is that the Negative, "archaist" influence will be shown not in any form of Fascism but rather in a return to some extent, most appropriate to Vienna, to the principle of legitimate monarchy, which can alone provide a Negative counter-balance to modern, Positive, democratic forms. It is no coincidence that Social-Democracy today is practically confined to the countries where constitutional monarchy has survived, and it is readily explicable on the principles of the Theory of Actuality. Only where the Negative as represented by ancient and secure tradition has a firm hold, can Positive, rational, "progressive" ideas be put into practice without provoking a violent reaction. To readers of the Positive Left who may be shocked at this prospect, I would suggest that no class of the community has a greater vested interest in peace than kings, who invariably lose their thrones nowadays in the event of a defeat in war. They also tend to have a vested interest in religion, which is intimately associated with their "mystique". This may be put in the form of a brief slogan which occurred to me once during a flight of manic ideas: Princes sometimes pray; Commissars can't. But then I am a Conservative, a "particle of the Negative", born and bred, and so no doubt biased. I even share the view which the late Dr Gustav Stresemann once expressed to me very forcibly, namely that Presidents and Prime Ministers in their dull black coats will never succeed in retaining their hold on popular affections for long, simply because they lack colour and romance, a view which Hitler subsequently showed to be well-founded.

Thus the Utopia of the Negative which I glimpsed in the course of my experiences had a place for the romance of the past; there was, in fact, a slightly Ruritanian atmosphere about it. I seemed to see a Parliament of Man, a Federation of the World, which the influence of hereditary monarchs and their family connections made a good deal more united than the Geneva or Lake Success organisations, as well as much more colourful. I saw, too, a world in which patriotism, local as well as national, had plenty of scope within the world order, resulting in a diversity basically opposed to the appalling uniformity that is the chief characteristic of the dominions of the Management of Unrighteousness. And this diversity was rendered possible by the downfall of that extreme manifestation of selfish nationalism—national "planning" secured by rigid exchange-control; a measure of freedom of trade and exchange made existence possible as well for small nations as for great.

Wishful thinking? No doubt it is. It is the ordinary delusion of a very ordinary lunatic in an asylum. There I am, and there I expect I should remain. But is the outside world any saner?

EPILOGUE

I AM WRITING this Epilogue chiefly at the suggestion of Professor Grensted, who has kindly consented to write a Foreword. He feels that it might be well to make clear to my readers (if any) that I am now out of a Mental Hospital, and officially recognised as *compos mentis*. He also thinks that an indication of my attitude in my present normal phase towards those parts of my book which were written in more or less abnormal phases would be of value.

This is not very easy. The whole book is really the production of what I have called the "manic (or manic-depressive) consciousness", and beyond the indications given in the text of my actual state of mind when writing, there does not seem to be very much to say. Some of the book was written in a state of at least relative "normality". By the end of the last chapter I was, in my own opinion and in that of my wife, as "normal" as I am today. But what is "normal" and what "abnormal"? "Visions" that I had when "abnormal" seemed to me when I wrote the last chapter on the Theory of Actuality visions of a truth at least as "real" as the fact that I am typing this on a Corona typewriter, and still seem so. I base my life upon them, and propose to go on doing so. Is that "normal"? I very much doubt it.

Yet I am certainly not "certifiable" now, whatever I may have been when I was actually certified in that instance. Why not? I am really just as "mad" as ever. The difference is apparent rather than real. I just do not appear to be "mad", that is all. Certainly the apprehensions of the manic consciousness are as it were further away from my "field of vision"; they have receded into deeper layers of my "Unconscious". But they are there, and I know that they are true, in so far as there is such a thing as "truth" at all. As I have said, I go on acting upon them all the time, though I take care to do so in a way which is in accord with commonsense "reality". When I am in any way manic, however, I find this difficult. To some extent I am in another world, on another "plane of Actuality", and I cannot make proper contact with my fellow-creatures. They cannot understand me and I cannot understand them.

That is the explanation, I think, of the distortion which took place when I was certified on one occasion as described in the Appendix. Statements were attributed to me which I maintain I did not make, presumably in perfect good faith and because I was not properly understood. Those statements were the legal basis for depriving me of my freedom. I therefore felt that I had been unjustly treated, and was quite right from my point of view. But the lady doctor and the nurses who were responsible for my certification were equally justified. I was in a borderline state of hypomania, which they could easily recognise from their experience. Owing to the difference of "plane of Actuality", of "atmosphere", I was misunderstood, and as a result distorted statements were put on my certificate. But I was not really "insane" unless this whole book is "insane".

This really raises the question of whether there is such a thing as insanity at all. According to the Theory of Actuality there is not. There are varying states of Actuality, or better, perhaps, of "apprehensions of Actuality". That apprehension of Actuality which is the statistical average over humanity at large, or perhaps only for the particular group, comes to be taken as "normality" or "reality". Those whose apprehension differs are prophets, or geniuses, or lunatics, or merely cranks, all according to the degree of difference on the one hand, and to their ability to relate their apprehension to that of the average on the other.

William James makes considerable use of the phrase "the field of consciousness". He suggests, in particular, that states of mystical intuition may be only very sudden and great extensions of this field.* I have tried to give in this book a series

* See article "A Suggestion about Mysticism", "Collected Essays and Reviews", p. 500.

of parallels between the mystical intuition and the manic consciousness as I have experienced it. It certainly appears to me to be an extension of consciousness, just as the depressive state is a sort of contraction. Both manic and depressive states are in any event changes or modifications of consciousness. Other "insane" states, as far as I have been able to observe them, partake of the same general character. Schizophrenia, for example, seems to produce in some instances much the same states of consciousness, or apprehensions of Actuality, as manic-depression, only they vary far more rapidly, and are probably therefore more difficult to fix and so to describe. At one moment a schizophrenic friend of mine feels that he is a devil doomed to eternal torture and the next that he is a god presiding over eternal bliss.* With a manic-depressive the two apprehensions of Actuality may each last for weeks or even months. The former state, as described in Chapter III, lasted in my own case for over a year. With confirmed melancholiacs it can last for most of a lifetime. Confirmed paranoiacs or maniacs believing that they are God Almighty may remain in that pleasant but dangerous state until they die. But the apprehensions of Actuality are none the less the same. There is, according to the Theory, nothing else to apprehend.

James compares the mystical extension of consciousness to "the state of things which we see on an unusually flat shore at the ebb of a spring tide". An extension of consciousness, involving a fall of the "threshold", is the fall of the tide. "Vast tracts usually covered are then revealed to view, but nothing rises more than a few inches above the water's bed, and great parts of the scene are submerged again, whenever a wave washes over them." The consciousness of insanity seems to me to be of a slightly different nature. Vast tracts of Actuality are also revealed, but they do not disappear. By their interaction with the personality of the viewer they produce a change in his psycho-physical system, which is more permanent and perhaps deeper than in the case of the mystic, and renders ordinary life impossible. The lunatic cannot re-

* See Appendix A.

late his visions to "reality"; the mystic can. Perhaps one might say that the mystic only sees the other and wider tract of Actuality, being in many cases inspired by it to go and do great deeds in the "real" world, while the lunatic insists on running away from "reality" and going to live on the sand- and mud-banks of his dreams. His Unconscious is too strong and takes charge altogether.

The revealed tracts of Actuality are, however, just as actual as so-called "reality". What man would no doubt do in an ideal Universe, what a superman in the evolutionary sense may some day be able to do, what great mystical prophets and even perhaps some geniuses have possibly actually done, is to have it both ways, to live in both worlds. That is one thing that I have tried to express with the concepts of Posi- tive and Negative. Complete contact between them is per- fection; it is both worlds; it is all worlds, the divine con- sciousness itself.

For some time there has been an underlying consciousness in our materialistic civilisation that something of the kind is possible. Men like Gerald Heard and Aldous Huxley have, as we have seen, been thinking on these lines. They have, in particular, been endeavouring to relate the thought of the West with that of the East. Some Eastern philosophers are making similar endeavours from their angle. Mr Sri Auro- bindi, of Pondicherry, has recently published a remarkable book under the title *The Human Cycle*. Basing his argument on Lamprecht's theory of historical development, with its symbolic, typal, conventional, individualist and subjective stages, he maintains that man is moving towards a Spiritual Age at "the end of the curve of reason", in which the achieve- ments of the various stages will be reconciled in the power of the Spirit. I do not very much like the word "spiritual", which has been so sadly prostituted, but I would maintain that the apprehension behind Mr Aurobindi's book is much the same as that of the manic consciousness, which I have tried to systematise in the Theory of Actuality.

The intuition of primitive man, which leads him to see

both the force of "mana" and personal "spirits" in the world around him, produces the symbolic and typal stages as exemplified in the Veda, as soon as civilisation begins to develop. In an individualistic rational age, such as the West is moving out of today, the need is felt to regain the truths of intuition, which lie in the Unconscious. These are, however, incredibly evasive. The reason alone cannot capture them, though it grub away in the Unconscious till Kingdom Come. Intuition is intuition, not reason, and it will remain so. The Negative is not the Positive. These are, I have suggested, ultimate Powers or manifestations of God, and in Him alone lies the "contact" between them, the means of reconciling them.

In religion, therefore, in man's apprehension of the Eternal, the key to a full understanding and appreciation of Actuality lies hidden. But religion without science leads to obscurantism, just as science without religion leads to hubris. Both are needed. What I have tried to do in this book, and particularly in the Theory of Actuality, is to indicate a possible new approach to the scientific study of the religious consciousness, while fully admitting its truth, or rather its Actuality. I believe that God, as manifested in the gods, goddesses and other beings (such as the Devil) whose Actuality man has apprehended in the course of his age-long climb, can be scientifically studied, and that the easiest place to study these is in the consciousness of the so-called "insane". Mystics are apt to be somewhat allergic to the scientific method, the religious records of the past are difficult to relate to present Actuality, and the religions of the present are apt to resent the intrusion of science, particularly when it is, as it must be, essentially sceptical. But the insane, like the poor, are always with us. Once the essential step has been taken of admitting that their "delusions", however apparently absurd, are by definition true apprehensions of Actuality, that if, for example, a lunatic tells his doctor that he has seen a devil, it is reasonable to assume that the devil was as "actual" as the lunatic, and to investigate the particular kind of devil he has seen, results will soon be secured.

In the final analysis all scientific progress, however sceptical the methods used to bring it about, is based on faith. Man had to believe in matter in order to master it. As we have seen, he had to banish the old nature gods and goddesses of the Negative in order to gain the necessary detachment. This was achieved by the worship of a Positive sky-god, who in his turn became increasingly abstract and ethical. Finally, at any rate in our Western civilisation, only the physical and rational Universe was left. Modern physical science was the result. Now, without ceasing to believe in the physical, we must find a way of both believing in and studying the psychical and a-rational. Only if we believe in her will the Negative deliver up her secrets.

Psychological science, valuable though its achievements have been, seems to me to have made the mistake of endeavouring too often to explain away rather than to explain. To trace a given manifestation of Actuality to its logical, Positive cause, is not to destroy its Actuality, which may lie in the Negative. Thus if, for example, our hypothetical devil is traced, on good Freudian principles, to some unfortunate nursery experience of the subject, that does not mean that he has not an objective, actual existence. A child, let us say, who is shut away in a dark cupboard, sees actual devils. In later life, as the result of some maladjustment, those devils return. The psychologist finds out about the cupboard and explains them away. This works a temporary cure. I would suggest, however, that a far more permanent cure would be to put the patient on good terms with devils in general, or alternatively, to give him the power to cast them out. Teach him to roar at them fearlessly and they will soon do his bidding. Martin Luther's inkpot might also do the trick. I can testify from experience that this is possible, and that devils are very useful—in their proper place. If the two who watch me from the bracket above my bath every morning should unaccountably disappear, I should be seriously disturbed. I might even believe that something had gone wrong with my apprehension of Actuality. Fortunately Lucifer and Mephisto remain faithful.

The advantage of this method is that it does not conflict with Actuality. However intelligently the psychologist may argue that the devils were merely the result of the dark cupboard, the Unconscious remains unconvinced, at any rate at the deepest levels. It knows perfectly well that the devils were actually there, and still are, since it is in constant contact with them. Grubbing away at their hidey-hole will only drive them to find cover lower down.

We who profess and call ourselves Christians have the highest authority for saying that devils will yield to the power of truth and love. They did so once, and they will again. But the one thing least likely to vanquish them is incredulity. What would we say of a Commander-in-Chief who refused to believe actual evidence tendered to him by his Secret Service to the effect that there were spies in his G H Q, on the ground that there were no such things as spies? Our Unconscious is our Secret Service, and is worthy of belief.

For the Theory of Actuality, of course, such miracles as the casting out of devils, as recorded in the Gospels, present no difficulty. Nor, in fact, does any other miracle. Indeed for the Theory there is no such thing as a "miracle". There are the Laws of Actuality, which are the laws of God, and are presumably valid for the whole Universe of Actuality. All so-called "miracles", even, if I may say so without irreverence, those of Our Lord, may be presumed to have taken place according to those Laws. Jesus is recorded as having said that all the miracles He did, and greater ones also, would be done by His followers; He never claimed that His powers were unique. It is therefore to be assumed that even such achievements as the raising of the dead will some day be possible to man (or superman).

But they will not be possible if all man does is to follow the Positive line of development which has ended in modern Science. Not of course that this line is of no value; on the contrary its value to humanity is immense. It was no pipe-dream when the nineteenth-century scientists foresaw the conquest of the physical Universe, with all that that implied. But the physical Universe is not everything, and it appear more and more that its conquest can only be achieved by means of a type of knowledge which is essentially schizo-phrenic. I cannot somehow believe that the world will be saved by men who know more and more about less and less.

What is needed today may perhaps best be described as "synthetic intuition"—a synthetic intuition of the Negative. Certainly we must have a technique; we must know what can be done and how to do it. Jesus Himself must have had a technique; He knew, for example, the importance of physical contact—"Who touched me? . . . Virtue is gone out of me". But Negative Actuality does not respond to technique alone, as Positive Actuality appears to do. It requires cooperation with, or perhaps even surrender to, another outside Power, which seems to work through the Unconscious. "The Father that dwelleth in me, he doeth the works."

The "miracles" of Science are, as it were, Positive miracles; they are the result of detachment from at any rate the Negative aspect of the Divine. The "miracles" of the future will require this detachment to be replaced by a new contact, which will, I think, be achieved through the Unconscious, and will be partly of a religious character. It will be "synthetic", in the sense that it will be based on a new "apprehension of the altogether", and will in its turn increase that apprehension.

It should not be thought that I visualise a world in which we all go about healing the sick and raising the dead by the sheer power of our personalities. Powers of this kind will no doubt remain rare, even in the best of all possible worlds. I seem to see rather a state of affairs in which what is at present lumped under the omnibus word "chance" is seen to the controllable through the Unconscious, largely, perhaps, through the power of prayer. Tyche-Theresa, our postulated Goddess and Saint, will be back in action, and with her the Negative as a whole.

I make this prophecy primarily because I, a very ordinary lunatic and a miserable sinner, have personally experienced something of the kind, which has not wholly abandoned me. What I seem to have secured through the strange and unforgettable experiences of manic-depression is precisely the sense of purpose, the "apprehension of the altogether", of which I have written. In ordinary Christian language it is simply faith in God, and an indefinable sense of nearness to Him. "Welt-Angst", as well as other fears which have played a large part in my past life, and particularly in my illness—of poverty, of illness, even of death, have just vanished into the blue. At the same time, the whole of my life, with its dismal tale of failure and frustration, seems to fit into place like a jigsaw-puzzle. So does contemporary world-history and the evolution of man. I seem to feel God working His purpose out, even though the hydrogen-bomb is at hand. According to the Theory of Actuality, the coming apocalyptic horrors seem even to be logically necessary, as the "revenge of the Negative". But this apprehension is beyond logic; it is derived from the Negative side of things, from intuition. The very actual Greek Goddess of history, Clio, seems to say that she knows what she is about.

I have come to the end. To the best of my ability I have tried to put the strange "apprehensions of Actuality", which have come to me in the course of an ordinary period of mental disturbance, into comprehensible form. They have led me far afield. I have not solved the riddle of the Universe —how dull it would be if I had! But I have perhaps shown that there is a wisdom in "madness" which has not yet been fully explored. If I have only done this, my book will not have been written in vain.

MENTAL HOMES AND MENTAL TREATMENT

THE FOLLOWING EXTRACTS on the subject of Mental Homes and Mental Treatment were largely written when I was confined in the Refractory Ward of a Mental Hospital, and were intended to form one of the chapters of this book. They have now been incorporated as an appendix for two reasons. In the first place they do not wholly fit into the general scheme of the argument but are rather in the nature of a digression, and in the second place they have had to be thoroughly redrafted to avoid the danger of libel. This has involved breaking up the connected narrative form in which they were originally couched, as well as, of course, removing most references to personalities.

The question arises whether I am wise to include them at all. I do so largely on the advice of Dr Grensted, who feels that they are an essential part of the general picture. As he says, my account of the inter-relations between patients and the authorities shows how those relations actually appear to an individual patient at the time; they are, as it were, from "the other side of the fence". At the present time, in my relatively "stable phase", I see the point of view of the authorities more clearly than I did, but I still see my own. I am perfectly ready to admit that I was hypomanic to some extent, and that I must have been an appalling nuisance. But that is how a man in hypomania feels and thinks, and re-reading what I have written I still adhere to it. "Sane" or "mad", my description of my own mental state as well as that of others still seems to me true and not unfair. Nor do I think that the suggestions or criticisms I made about mental treatment are necessarily invalidated by the fact that I was hypomanic and legally "insane" when I made them. On the

contrary, it may well be that they are more valuable precisely for that reason.

I have already referred in Chapter V to the difficulty which
a mental patient has in establishing precisely what happened
to him when confined in an abnormal state. If my recollec-
tion is as accurate as it is vivid, I have undergone certain experiences which were both illegal and—in any normal use of
the words—both cruel and sadistic. But, as I have said, I cannot prove that they "really" happened. They may be "delusions". For me they are "Actuality"; as I have sufficiently
explained. I do not know anything about "reality", or even if
there is such a thing. Should there be a libel action, for example, I should have no case whatever; the courts could not
possibly accept the word of a man who was certifiably insane
at the time of the happenings in question. This was sharply
brought home to me by the incident described in the following extract.

Mental Nurses—and doctors to a lesser degree—have to have
the patience of saints. If they sometimes lose their tempers, it is
only human. What is wrong is to pretend that they are perfect
when they are not. Even Dr ——, though he would no doubt
stoutly deny it, is probably as human at bottom as anybody else.
Because he is a doctor with many letters after his name and a high
reputation, he is none the less subject to impulses. I certainly deliberately annoyed him, and I cannot help feeling that there may
well have been an element of personal irritation in his treatment
of me. He actually on one occasion admitted as much to one of
the nurses.
This particular nurse has always been very good to me. When
he told me what Dr —— had said, I asked him at once if he was
prepared to give evidence to that effect should there by any kind
of court case or enquiry about my treatment. He replied that he
could not possibly do so, as his bread and butter was involved. Even
if he were to be subpoenaed, and questioned on oath, he would
not dream of giving evidence against the medical authorities.
I was deeply shocked at this, particularly since this particular
nurse had been present at my certification, and would, in the
event of my case being investigated, presumably be called to
testify to my state of mind. When I protested that surely his conscience would be involved, he said that bread and butter must
come first, and that practically all the nurses in the hospital would
take the same line. It was, he went on, absolute madness for me to

entertain the idea of legal action. I should not be believed, and all the nurses would back up the medical authorities. I should have no chance. This opinion was supported by the Charge Nurse of the ward.

If this is in fact so, it seems probable that legal machinery for the protection of mental patients, such as the Board of Control, as well as, of course, the ordinary Courts, must be wholly ineffective. There is, I believe, hardly any case on record of a mental patient successfully fighting or getting damages out of the institution in which he is, or was, confined. Yet to err is human; mistakes must be made sometimes.

This particular incident could, in fact, be established in Court. I have the names of two nurses who were witnesses of the conversation, and I believe them to be reliable. They both gave me specific assurances at the time that they were prepared to give evidence. I also took the trouble of writing a more or less verbatim account and sending it to my lawyer, since at the time I was actually contemplating proceedings. I have now abandoned the idea, since my only object was to draw the attention of the public to abuses still existing in Mental Hospitals in spite of all the well-meaning efforts of psychiatrists and social reformers, and I feel that this object can best be achieved by my book.

I am encouraged in this belief by the experiences of an American manic-depressive named Beers, which were in some degree similar to my own. After his discharge, Beers wrote a book describing them and started a movement for the reform of Mental Hospitals which is still going strong. Beers wrote many years ago, and conditions were no doubt far worse then. There was certainly more physical ill-treatment of patients, though, as will be seen, this does not appear to me to have entirely disappeared from English Mental Hospitals. Now and then you find a bad atmosphere which brings out the natural sadism of the most well-meaning men. Beers quotes the statement of an attendant to the following effect:—"When I came here, if anyone had told me that I would be guilty of striking a patient, I would have called him crazy myself, but now I take delight in punching hell out of them".* Beers

* Beers, "A Mind that Found Itself".

found by experience that the tactless and often cruel treatment to which he was subjected had a serious effect in aggra-
vating his own condition. When he began his campaign he
visited psychiatrists of wide experience and the highest stand-
ing, who all confirmed this view, saying that an elated or
maniacal patient would obviously be made much worse by
unsound and tactless treatment. It appears to me that I can
claim to have suffered on occasion from tactless treatment, as
instanced by the following extract:

I had been told by the Charge Nurse of the ward that the regulations did not allow smoking in side-rooms. It is true that most
inmates of side-rooms do smoke, with the full knowledge and permission of the nurses, including the Charge, but he has perhaps his
own reasons for showing me how conscientious he is. Anyway he
said that if I wanted to smoke I might, but that I should come out
of my room into the corridor or into the dayroom to do so.
Otherwise he might get into trouble.

Having learnt by bitter experience the importance of obedience
in these places, when I felt I needed a smoke I duly went out into
the corridor and obtained a light for my pipe in the kitchen, in the
presence of the Charge. I could not stay in the kitchen; bed-
patients are not really allowed there, so I went into the corridor.
This is fairly narrow, having the dining-tables all along its length.
There were the usual patients walking up and down, some mut-
tering, some silent and smiling, some silent and miserable, one
singing. I was rather in the way, and I therefore moved towards
the dayroom, where I saw the deputy Charge Nurse sorting out
some clothes.

The deputy Charge is generally rather a friend of mine. I have
known him for some time; he calls me by my initials; and although I was a little irritated when he caught me by the collar
when half asleep on my first morning in the ward and bundled me
roughly downstairs; that is long since forgiven if not forgotten.
Yesterday he told me that a Mental Hospital was not a place for
sane people and asked me what on earth I thought I was doing
there. This was, I thought, most encouraging, but then he was in
expansive mood as his chief was away.

Anyway, to cut a long story short, I approached the deputy-
Charge looking as pleasant as I could, hoping to have a chat with
him. To my amazement he rushed at me as though he was about
to catch hold of me by the collar again and rudely ordered me
back to my room at once. I only just had time to protest that the
Charge had specifically allowed me out to smoke, to which he
replied:—"Well, he has ordered me to keep you in your room

according to regulations. Get out of the dayroom at once or there'll be trouble." So I retired rapidly and somewhat hurt.

There was a time in my early experience of Mental Hospitals when this sort of treatment, which is the regular thing in some wards and with some male nurses, would have made me furiously indignant and might even have brought on an attack of acute mania. I should have considered the sudden change of attitude without reason, on the part of a man who had been friendly, to indicate deliberate malice; I should have brooded upon the injustice done me, have then started to worry about similar injustice being done to others, and my mental health would obviously have been affected. Now, however, I realise that the deputy Charge was merely suffering from suppressed irritation at having been told off by his chief for being too lenient to me. Venting his irritation on me may have been unjust, but it was only human nature.

The point of this little incident—of no particular importance in itself—is none the less absolutely vital for the whole question of mental treatment. It is this—mental nurses are human; mental patients are human; and mental illness is not something which goes on in the mind of patients independently of the men and things around them, but continuing, intimate action and reaction between the two.

One Saturday night I had a dream which, interpreted on the Jungian principles taught me by Dr Grensted, plainly indicated that I was only staying in the hospital out of cowardice, and that my plain duty was to rejoin my wife and face the world. I also had a letter from my wife saying that she was not well, that things on the farm were in a bad way without me, and that the sooner I could get home the better. I therefore decided to hand in the legal notice as a voluntary patient, and discussed the matter with the Charge Nurse of the ward, who raised no objection and seemed implicitly to approve my intention. This was handed in on the Sunday, and I was due to leave on the Wednesday afternoon. I made up my mind, however, that if a serious attempt was made by the doctors or anybody in authority to persuade me on rational grounds to withdraw my notice, I would do so. I had no wish to be certified again, at least no conscious wish, though I did envisage the possibility. No such attempt was made.

On the Wednesday morning I was distinctly nervous and probably appeared excited. This was only natural. When a party of people arrived in the ward which, from previous experience, I knew meant somebody's certification, my excitement increased. I could not keep still (a fact subsequently noted on my certificate as evidence of "insanity"). I determined to make this impending certification a test case. I would ask for what appeared to me to be reasonable rights for a man about to be deprived of his freedom and see what happened.

I was called into a room in which were a young lady psychiatrist aged about 27 or 28 at the most, two local magistrates,
and a representative of the hospital authorities (not a doctor). The
young lady asked me to sit down and tell her all about it. I said
that I fully realised what the object of the interview was, that from
previous experience I knew that things said in such circumstances
might be misinterpreted, and that I would not talk freely unless
some legal representative or representatives were present on my
behalf to note exactly what was said, and in general to see fair
play. This request was noted, I understand, as evidence of
"grandiose ideas". Although I then said as little as I could, it was
evident that I was not going to get away with it. I therefore decided to let myself go and to make one more request which seemed
to me reasonable, but which might perhaps be taken as evidence of
"insanity". As well be hung for a sheep as a lamb!

There was a patient in the ward, an excitable "bully" or pimp
type who found asylum life very comfortable and was largely playing up, more or less shamming insanity. In particular he was
going about saying that he was Abraham Lincoln. The doctor
saw through him and had decided to discharge him the following
day.

Now this man had threatened me on several occasions. Moreover he knew the address of my farm and had taken a particular
fancy to the photograph of my daughter which I had in my room.
When annoyed with me, he invariably warned me that as soon as
he was out he would go to my farm, steal my pigs and rape my
daughter. I knew that in all probability these threats were mere
hot air, but, after all, how could I be certain? So I told the young
lady and the magistrates about this gentleman, said that he
appeared to have the delusion that he was Abraham Lincoln, and
anyway that he had threatened my family. If I was to be confined and he to be let out, surely police protection for my family
would be arranged.

This was the last straw. The young lady and the magistrates
looked knowingly at each other and the party began to retire. I
then played my last card, asked not to be certified and promised to
withdraw my notice to leave and stay in the hospital. I followed
them down the corridor saying so.

But all to no purpose. I was duly certified as of unsound mind,
and the chief ground, I am now informed by the ward doctor (unless I have misunderstood him), was that I "had the delusion that
a patient to be discharged was Abraham Lincoln, and asked for
police protection against him". Perhaps my original request for
some sort of legal or impartial representative to avoid misinter-
tation was not unjustified?

Every lawyer knows how difficult it is to be absolutely sure what
happens at any crucial interview. Two perfectly truthful people

will go into the witness-box and swear to diametrically opposed versions. The "truth" is extraordinarily elusive. That is also why all the majestic and expensive apparatus of the law is required, why there must be representatives of the defence—and of the public—present at a trial, why there is provision for appeal, and so on.

The certification of any mental patient is a sort of trial in miniature. At the worst it may involve the sentencing of a human creature to imprisonment for life; at best it is a short sentence. That is why a magistrate must be present. But to judge from my own experience the procedure is very perfunctory. My own "trial" took five minutes at most.

No doubt I appeared irritable and perhaps elated and "over-active". How do prisoners behave in the dock during their trial, or when they are awaiting their sentence? Are they always calm and "rational"?

Looking back, the extraordinary thing to me is the behaviour of the magistrates, who were presumably there to see fair play, and in a sense to represent my interests. No attempt was made in my presence to establish whether I was or was not telling the truth about "Abraham Lincoln", although there was plenty of evidence available in the ward to confirm my statement. Neither of the magistrates, as far as I can remember, asked me a direct question of any kind. They certainly made no attempt to put me at my ease. I sensed a hostile * atmosphere from the start. Being a sensitive person—and what mental patient is not?—I reacted, which no doubt increased my appearance of "abnormality".

The only rational explanation of the whole matter that I can conceive is this. The hospital authorities no doubt decided that I was unfit to go home—though why they did not try to persuade me of this I have no idea. They called in, as the law requires, an outside psychiatrist—the young lady in question, who can only have just qualified—and the two local magistrates. All these people, and particularly the young lady, stood under the influence of high medical authority. The hospital authorities are leading psychiatrists. The young lady, with her name to make, would hardly dare to disagree with them. She must—subconsciously at any rate—have wanted to certify me. The magistrates, like most laymen, know little of "insanity" and were probably frightened of it. They therefore felt that they must accept medical opinion, as represented in this case by the young lady. How could they presume to decide what is or is not "overactivity"? The latest concepts and definitions of psychology and psychiatry are altogether incomprehensible to most laymen, which is why the judges in courts of law very wisely refuse to accept them without question.

* I am now convinced that the atmosphere was awkward rather than hostile, but the effect was the same.

But in a Mental Hospital the doctor's word is law. Moreover, in this particular case it so happened that another Charge Nurse was on duty when I was certified, and he is perhaps more deferential to authority than his colleague. I have no doubt, from what he has said to me subsequently, that he did his best to back up the medical view, since he maintains that he really feels I was certifiable at that time. So altogether I had little chance.

There is not very much more to say about my recent experience. Owing to what I consider to be mental—and in one case physical ill-treatment (I was seriously scarred by an attempt to force me to drink paraldehyde), I have twice escaped from the hospital. On my recapture (in both cases because I was unwise enough to go near my home, where the police have all been warned about me), it has been made plain that my escaping is regarded as further evidence of "insanity". The doctor has flatly refused to discuss the question of whether a man who escapes from other kinds of captivity is necessarily insane. I am not "in captivity". I am "under treatment", designed by medical authority for my own good. If I escape I must obviously be "insane" and there is no more to be said. The doctor even told me a day or two ago that because my wife did not dissuade me on the second occasion from escaping but agreed to help me, she ought to be confined there too. She tells me to tell him she is quite ready to come, at the Government's expense; it would be cheaper, and perhaps we could have married quarters together. But I have not yet had the opportunity.

The above account of my certification during one of my stays at a Mental Hospital still seems to me objective. Professor Grensted finds it particularly disturbing. It should not be thought that I have any particular objection to being certified when it is really necessary. On the contrary, I have on several occasions gone to a Mental Hospital as a voluntary patient, knowing full well that the course of my illness would soon render certification probable, if not inevitable. On other occasions I have deliberately allowed myself to be certified by my doctor at home for my own protection. For the last ten years, ever since I parted so freely with my money in London as described earlier, I have invariably arranged to get myself to hospital as soon as I felt my illness coming on. The certification of and confinement of mental patients is a necessary protection both of the patient and of society.

It seems to me, however, that a great deal depends upon how it is done. The old principle of justice applies here with particular force. Justice should not merely be done, but should manifestly appear to be done. It is perhaps too much to expect that the procedure should be adequate to convince every certified patient that he has been justifiably certified, but it should certainly not be patently inadequate. In this case I am still left with a feeling of resentment. Every attempt I made to discuss the matter with the doctors was pooh-poohed. I wrote to the Board of Control, which exists specifically for the purpose of appeal by mental patients against unjust certification or arbitrary treatment, but never even had an answer. Subsequently I got my lawyers to take the matter up, but as by that time I had been recognised as "better" by the doctors and had been granted parole, I let the affair drop. One practical suggestion I would offer. Mental patients, however "insane" they may appear to be, should be treated as responsible individuals in everything concerning their legal rights, and more particularly in regard to their certification. If the whole procedure has been absolutely just and above-board; if it is clearly explained to them why they are certified, and they are given a reasonable opportunity to state their case, and to prove it if they can; if their letters of appeal are answered with courtesy and consideration; then it is quite probable that at any rate a part of their mind will recognise the justice of their treatment, and their feelings of resentment will be correspondingly less, with satisfactory results on their mental state and possibly on their ultimate cure.

In my own case I do not of course know whether my return to "normality"—in so far as I am now "normal"—was delayed by my feelings of resentment, but of one effect there is no doubt. The relation of confidence which existed previously between me and the Medical Superintendent of the hospital in question was completely destroyed. However I try to see his point of view, I simply cannot feel towards him as I did before. To some extent this applies to all the doctors at that hospital. The relation between doctor and patient is one of the major factors in the cure of any illness, and in the case of mental illness it is perhaps the paramount factor. All I can say is that after the events related I made no further attempt to confide in the doctors; I regarded them as more or less hostile, in any case as definitely on the "other side of the fence"; I thought out my own course of action, negotiated with the doctors only through my wife, and in due course left the hospital in my own time. The following extract is indicative of my attitude of mind:

Most of this chapter was written, as I have explained, while I was supposed to be "over-active", in a state of "hypomania". At present I am officially supposed to be "cured"; I am going home next week. The doctors have told me how glad they are to see me "myself" again. I have parole, and am leading a more or less normal life, playing golf at the local club and so on. My certificate of "insanity" is being withdrawn on my wife's application. I am once more "responsible for my actions" in the eyes of the law.

Yet re-reading what I have written, apart from minor alterations there is nothing that seems to me unfair or that I would wish to change. I have given a strictly factual account of what happens in a modern Mental Hospital run by medical authorities of the very highest reputation. Now that I am "sane" I feel just the same as I did when I was "mad".

My personality, ideas, beliefs and so on are precisely what they have always been. It is possible that part of this chapter was written in a state of "over-activity"; * all writers and journalists have such periods—it is a professional disease very necessary to make a livelihood possible. But at no time during the past two or three months, at least, have I been in the abnormal state of consciousness which is described in earlier chapters.

Why then have the doctors changed their minds about me? Why do they think I am "sane"? The answer is quite simple. Yielding to the persuasion of my wife, I agreed to crawl to the doctors—no milder word meets the case—to say nothing about any grievances I may have, and to give the impression that I am quite satisfied with my treatment. With the exercise of a modicum of self-control and of all my powers of dissimulation, I have shown myself a model patient, and am now getting my reward.

"Sanity", "normality", in mental treatment today, seems to be largely synonymous with submission to Authority with a big A. The obedient "lunatic" has a reasonable chance of securing his release; the defiant "lunatic" has none. No matter how much injustice or ill-treatment a patient in a Mental Hospital may have

---

* Undoubtedly it was.

suffered—and a modicum is inevitable even in the best-run and most humane—the wise man endures it in silence. Complaints and appeals are practically useless, as I have learnt from bitter experience; they only make matters worse.

Furthermore, while a golden rule is never to complain at all, a silver rule is this: if you must complain, stick strictly to your own case. To complain about the treatment of others is sheer madness and is regarded as such. Anybody in a Mental Hospital who suffers—as I unfortunately am apt to do—from the horrible delusion that his neighbour is a concern of his and that when he sees others stupidly or unjustly treated he should do something about it, is asking for trouble.

A Mental Hospital seems to me, rightly or wrongly, to be the bureaucratic State writ small. To some extent this is no doubt inevitable, and even advisable. A large Mental Hospital is a bureaucratic organisation and suffers from the disadvantages of all bureaucratic organisations. The patients are treated as a mass rather than as individuals. To show individuality or eccentricity is to differ from the "norm", and to differ from the "norm" is not to be "normal", that is to say to be "insane". In a world in which these conditions apply to a rapidly increasing extent, a Mental Hospital serves the useful purpose of being part of the conditioning apparatus which forces individuals to adapt themselves.

When I decided to publish the above, I sent the whole chapter as written to the Medical Superintendent of the Hospital concerned, for his comments. Not unnaturally he took considerable exception to it. In particular, he objected to the word "crawl". "To assert", he wrote, "that a certified patient must 'crawl' to the doctor before he can be discharged is, if you will excuse my saying so, sheer nonsense." I can only say, however, that is how it appeared to me, subjectively. My wife told me that I was stupid to allow my resentment, whether it was justified or not, to get the better of me; the doctors had the power and the only thing to do was to get on the right side of them instead of the wrong. I said I felt that would mean crawling to them, particularly to a certain doctor who happened to be in charge of my case at the time—the word is quite distinct in my memory. It required a strong effort of will to change my hitherto defiant attitude, but my wife persuaded me to make the effort as a matter of practical politics; I took the next opportunity of being particularly polite to the doctor in question, swallowing my pride as I did so; and the results were satisfactory from my point of view. No doubt the doctor did not think I was crawling; I may not have appeared to be crawling; but the word precisely fits my subjective state of mind. All I suggest is that other defiant patients may feel the same, and be unable to overcome their resentment and pride.

In that particular Hospital I was not ill-treated physically; the regulations are very strict on this point. The following extract shows, however, the kind of thing that can still happen in an English Mental Hospital to a patient who gets on the wrong side of doctors and nurses.

I will now give a description of my experience of a large hospital—during a manic period. Perhaps I should say at this point that although, to the best of my knowledge, I have only on one occasion made a violent attack (in mania or in depression) upon anybody—and that was in a brief period of total amnesia—I know that I must be extraordinarily irritating when I am elated. I adopt a deliberately defiant attitude; I swear like a trooper; I am as rude and particularly as sarcastic as I know how; and I set out to "get under the skin" of any doctor or nurse who has (in my opinion) been unjust or unfair. I know, of course, that the consequences will be unpleasant to me, but there seems, though I am not fully conscious of it, to be an underlying masochistic urge in my Unconscious which deliberately invites punishment. This I dramatise to myself as "courage" to right everything for the right, or something of the kind. I also have a sort of feeling that I must "go the whole hog"; "go completely through the mill", "descend to the lowest circles of Hell in the company of the Spirit", and so on.

It is not that I enjoy punishment of any kind, not that I get any kind of satisfaction of a sexual nature in particular out of it. My sexual tendencies are quite "normal", and although I have tried most vagaries as an experiment, I have not repeated any of the "unnatural" ones. Thus though I may invite punishment by my behaviour, when it comes to it I am genuinely frightened and detest the experience, though I subsequently may give myself a pat on the back for having endured it.

There may therefore be some excuse for the degree of sadistic physical torture—no milder form of words will do—to which I was subjected in the hospital in question. To use the actual words of the attendant referred to by Beers, the nurses used "to punch hell out of me", and seemed to me to "take delight" in doing it.

On some eight separate occasions I was subjected to a procedure euphemistically referred to as "restraint". When I got excited, showed defiance, and in particular "adopted a threatening
attitude"—to use a form of words used in Mental Institutions to
justify punishment (refractory ward, padded room, or beating-up)
—four "nurses" would rush at me together. I would be knocked
down (probably making some attempt at resistance); one nurse
would hold or sit on my head, another on my feet, while a third
jumped up and down on my chest and solar plexus and the last
punched me in the lower abdomen or kicked my testicles. Though
at first wild with fury at this "treatment", I would soon be reduced
to an abject wreck howling for mercy.

It was not long before I attempted to escape; in fact I probably
made the resolution as soon as I found that the doctor paid no
attention to my allegations of ill-treatment. He just laughed them
off as though they were a delusion and went on his round.

My first attempt to escape was very feeble; I merely dismantled
my bed and tried to use one of the bars as a lever to open the
shutter and get out of the window. I also tore up sheets to act as a
rope. For this my bed and most of my personal possessions were
removed, and I was given a long spell—several days—of solitary
confinement with only a straw mattress and a blanket or two. I
complained of the cold but without result. Eventually, by good
behaviour, I got myself out and later tried again, this time
successfully, though I was later recaptured.

It was after my return from this second escapade that the whole
weight of instinctive sadism that is inseparable—in my considered
opinion—from any human organisation, large or small, fell upon
me. I was placed in solitary confinement for almost a month,
with no access whatever to fellow-patients. At the same time I
received a number of beatings-up, for which I must admit I gave
some cause.

The worst occasion remains particularly vividly impressed on
my memory, and I think I could even name those concerned; certainly I could identify them in a court of law. The night man on
duty one evening observed me climbing round the closed shutter
investigating the possibilities of escape. He told me roughly to
stop it. I got angry and cursed him for a "lousy Irishman" (he
was in fact Irish). He went off, returned with three colleagues, and
the whole party came into my room.

I knew of course that I was in for trouble. But I would not give
in and remained defiant. I told the nurses—all of whom were
Irish—that I had been unjustly treated, that I would escape if I
could, and ended up by using all my powers of vituperation upon
them and their native country. I deliberately made the matter
political, partly to screw up my own courage by self-dramatisa-
tion, partly because I felt indignant as an officer and ex-Service

man at being so treated by men who were well out of the War. I knew that other ex-Service men in the hospital had been treated in a similar manner and felt equally indignant on their behalf.

So I cursed those nurses for a pack of lousy cowards who kept out of danger and were only ready to beat hell out of British ex-Service men with odds of four to one in their favour. I cursed their government, their country, their race and their leader, De Valera. At the same time I kept my hands firmly behind my back so that there might be no excuse for accusing me of a threatening attitude.

As was not unnatural the self-control of those young Irish nurses broke, and they rushed at me like a pack of hounds. I was knocked down, and the full force of their resentment and sadism was visited upon me in the usual manner. I howled and howled for mercy; I promised to do anything if they would only stop; but the "treatment" went on until I was practically unconscious. In fact I think, though I would not swear, that I actually was unconscious for a short space.

The four nurses then went away. Some time later one of them poked his head in and told me that if I said another word against Ireland or the Irish I would "leave the hospital feet first". Although still in great pain, I managed to say that that would be murder, and there was a punishment for it. The lad replied, as far as I can remember—"We have nothing to fear. There is no witness. All we have to say is that you were violent and that we had to restrain you."

The next morning, still in very considerable pain, I told the doctor, who either did not believe me or did not mind. He refused to look at my bruises or my black eyes—I think it was on this occasion that both my eyes were blacked. A night or two afterwards, in a not unnatural state of depression, I tried to commit suicide by making a rope from my blankets, pinning it to the ceiling light and jumping from the window-ledge (or possibly a chair). The rope broke. In the morning I told the nurse, who laughed. I told the doctor later; he smiled and went on.

I then wrote a letter of complaint to the Board of Control, setting out the details of my "treatment". About three weeks afterwards—they were prompter in those days—I was visited by three doctors, who were introduced by the Medical Superintendent. Two of them were local men; the third was a consulting psychiatrist. The course of this interview is clear in my memory. It is of considerable interest as illustrating the sort of difficulties with which a certified patient has to contend in getting his case reviewed by authority.

The doctors began by putting me at my ease, offering me a cigarette, and encouraging me to tell my story; I did so, though no doubt in a far more discursive and long-winded way than that in which I have set it down here. I was asked a few questions suggesting that I had attacked the nurses and had needed "restraint": the two local doctors were particularly insistent in pressing this aspect of the matter. Exactly how I replied I do not remember, but as I was throughout telling the strict truth I must have stuck to my guns.

The consulting psychiatrist was more sympathetic. His questions seemed to indicate that he thought my story worthy of investigation at any rate. Unfortunately this sympathy led me on to make general charges suggesting that widespread cruelty of the kind I had suffered was going on in the hospital. In particular I remember launching out into a typical hypomanic diatribe against the brutality of Irishmen who beat up unfortunate ex-Service veterans of the 1914–18 War in revenge for their sufferings under the Black and Tans. Because I thus allowed myself to be carried away and thus showed a certain degree of what might be construed as hypomania, I undermined my whole case. At any rate I was not "normal". Could I therefore be believed at all?

That is how I assume the doctors must have reasoned. I saw them look at one another. They took their leave and went. The only result of this visit, as far as I know, was that I was very soon afterwards transferred to another hospital. There I met a completely different, thoroughly human atmosphere. Within six weeks I was discharged, decertified and cured. The experience described seems to me to emphasise the principle emphasised earlier, viz. that mental illness is not something which can be isolated in the mind of a patient, but continuous intimate action and reaction between the patient and his surroundings.

In a general hospital, dealing with physical troubles, although I believe there to be a much greater connection between mental and physical disturbances than is generally recognised, it probably does not much matter if a patient gets on the wrong side of the ward sister, or the doctor (being human) has his likes and dislikes. Both doctor and sister are presumably conscientious people who carry out the regular treatment, though they may leave the irritating patient till last, or not give him a little privilege, or something of the kind. If, however, a convalescent from scarlet fever, let us say, is not allowed out to look at the hospital football-match, though he is an ardent fan, because he has annoyed the sister and she (probably unconsciously) translates her irritation into a statement that he is "not fit enough", no appreciable harm is done. The convalescence may be slightly delayed by the irritation and disappointment felt by the patient reacting upon his health, and to an infinitesimal extent by the loss of sunlight and fresh air. But the patient will within a week or so nevertheless be discharged as cured.

If on the other hand the same thing happens in a Mental Hospital where patients are, by virtue of their very condition, liable to be far more irritating than "normally", the results may be very serious. Only a few weeks ago a young patient, usually very helpful and obliging, became rather over-excited and irritating. This was, according to what he told me, for two reasons. Firstly he was due to play in a hospital football match—he is an ardent footballer. And secondly he had a date for a dance with a young lady patient.

His excitement took the form of extra officiousness, which irritated the Charge Nurse. When the time came for the footballers to get ready, the Charge refused him permission to go. No doubt he has far more experience of mental trouble (from the outside) than I have, and it may well be that, objectively speaking, he was quite right. It is also possible that there was a not unnatural element of irritation unconsciously affecting his decision.

However that may be, the result was that the patient lost control of himself to a degree which made it necessary for him to be placed in the padded room. Not only did he refuse to recognise the justice of the Charge Nurse's decision and became very indignant, but he kept on childishly shouting about his missed football and his missed date. Further, as he has told me, he absolutely loathed the padded room for some inexplicable reason connected with its rubber lining. Finally, he was deprived of smokes, as he (being under "correction") did not get the usual weekly half a crown for his work. All these factors acted cumulatively; he could not control himself, and became a general nuisance. He insisted on signing a notice to leave, as I did, was certified in much the same manner as I was, and transferred to this refractory ward. Here, fortunately, his anger simmered down; he made himself useful, and is now back in his former ward, though he is still, of course, certified.

Now although in this case disastrous results did not ensue from this patient's treatment, they might very well have done so. In any event his departure from the hospital has been very considerably, perhaps indefinitely delayed. His outburst and his classification as "refractory" is now an indelible part of his case record, just as any crime is part of that of a criminal. His certification has changed his whole status. He has no longer the elementary rights of a citizen. Even if he is decertified, any contact with the police during his whole career will inevitably bring the matter up again. Something absolutely final has happened to this young man of 25 as the result (possibly) of a natural and human, but perhaps erroneous decision.

Error is inevitable in this imperfect world. The essential thing is not so much that it should be avoided, but that adequate means should be provided for correcting it. What would have happened, for example, if I had not been transferred from the hospital where it appears to me that I was so badly treated? The Medical Superintendent told my wife right out that he regarded me as incurable, and that she might expect me to be confined for life. It is very probable that in that hospital I would have remained incurable. I was hypomanic and classified as a refractory escapee. Had I not been transferred, natural action and reaction would almost certainly have either kept me in an excited condition or brought on depression; resentment at my treatment would have got deeper; I would have developed true delusions of persecution, of reference, and so on, and these, with the "overactivity" of a man of cyclothymic temperament, might well have evolved into a completely rationalised delusional system impossible to eradicate. It was, as things were, touch and go. Yet transfer to new surroundings, to a new "atmosphere", to use the word which I regard as of some importance for the Theory of Actuality, worked an immediate cure.

"Atmosphere", as I have defined it, is very largely made up of the conscious and unconscious reactions of human beings upon one another. It lies, I believe, at the very core of successful mental treatment. That is the view of a Viennese doctor, Dr Bierer, who is now working in this country. Dr Bierer's psycho-therapic method is described as a "method of treatment by experience, termed situational treatment".* Patients are encouraged to enter into social activities with each other, the special needs of each case being subtly planned and the individual is drawn naturally into doing things of which he believed himself not to be capable. Although Dr Bierer's method is only used for "those who suffer from less severe forms of mental illness, resulting perhaps from unsatisfactory home life or other social frustration", and are not really bad enough for Mental Hospital proper, its essence seems to be the principle I have just formulated, namely that mental illness is—and therefore mental treatment should be—

* "The Times," March 22, 1950.

a question of action and reaction between human beings among themselves and between them and their surroundings.

This principle is of course not new. It was recognised by Freud, Jung and Adler. All schools of psycho-analysis, psycho-therapy and individual psychology now admit, I understand, that action and reaction between the physician and his patient is an essential part of the curative process. In Freudian psycho-analysis, for example, use is made of a concept called "positive transference"—which means in plain words the establishment of implicit confidence on the part of the patient in his physician. The Freudians, following their general train of thought, consider that a part of the "libido" (of basically sexual origin) is transferred to the physician. The patient, in fact, almost "falls in love" with his (or her) doctor. Towards the end of the course of treatment an opposite process, "negative transference", takes place. The patient, who is beginning to find his own feet, gradually as it were falls out of love with the physician. A revulsion of feeling, almost amounting in some cases to hatred, takes place. Eventually the "libido" is transferred to normal, socially useful objects, and the patient is fit to go out alone into the world.

But psycho-analysis is a difficult, expensive and lengthy process. The physician is a busy, highly-trained and well-paid person. The action and reaction between him and his patient can thus only take up a comparatively small part of the patient's life, and many adverse factors can intervene to spoil the whole procedure. But if the action and reaction can be so arranged as to take place more or less continuously between the patient and his environment, if (as apparently is the case with "situational treatment") the relations between the patient and those around him can be "subtly planned", then surely cheaper and speedier results can be expected.

There is no reason, as far as I can see, why "situational treatment" should not be introduced into mental hospitals. The problem is, of course, the immense inertia inseparable from all large organisations, and the difficulty of training the staff to adopt new methods, especially "subtle" ones. The following extract gives the practical suggestions I made when actually confined myself.

It is not without interest to record the criticism made to me the other evening by a French nurse who is working in this hospital. She told me she had considerable experience of French Mental Hospitals, and that the thing that shocked her here was the lack of individual consideration of each case. Practically all the patients in her ward, she said, had obviously been given up as incurable. Admittedly it was one of the worse wards. But in Paris hospitals, she said, quite a number of the patients would have been getting some sort of treatment—psychological or physical. Given adequate individual attention, it was probable that a reasonable percentage would respond. To abandon the effort to cure them and to concentrate merely on keeping them confined and alive seemed to her wholly wrong.

To a large extent, no doubt, it is a question of numbers. There are something like 1500 patients in this hospital, looked after by some half-dozen resident doctors. These naturally concentrate their curative efforts on the patients most likely to respond to treatment. They are nearly all concentrated in a few wards such as the one to which I have returned as a prize for good behaviour. Patients in the "chronic" wards are only considered when they show marked signs of improvement, or are really ill. At a rough guess, of the 1500 patients in this hospital, about half are thus written off as permanent inhabitants. Many of these are really incurable, sufferers from senile dementia, later stages of general paralysis, and so on. Many more may well be incurable in the present stage of medical knowledge. Others have settled down here and do not particularly want to leave as long as the taxpayers will keep them in relative comfort. Consciously or unconsciously they play up now and then sufficiently to justify their retention medically speaking. Finally there is a really considerable number—probably a hundred or so—of cases where the relatives do not wish to have the patient at home and the authorities are unable to take the responsibility of releasing them without a regular job and a home to go to. The large majority of these are married and do not get on with their wives or husbands as the case may be.

These are perhaps the saddest cases—middle-aged and elderly men and women who have lost hope. Were it not for the devotion of my wife, I might very well be in the same plight myself. I might of course escape and manage to keep hidden for the statutory fifteen days, after which I should be legally free, though in view of the difficulties with ration and identity cards, and of the really terrifying efficiency of the police where inexperienced and relatively harmless people are concerned, this is by no means easy. But I have friends; I have no difficulty in raising money on credit even though my bank accounts are barred, and I have a fairly well-trained and active mind. For those less happily circumstanced the position is well-nigh hopeless.

Altogether I have escaped three times from Mental Hospitals. In each case I was recaptured as soon as I approached any place where I was known. Once I went to my office and was caught; twice, during this last confinement, I went home. My wife did her best to conceal and advise me, but the police were too watchful. Had I changed my name and acted like a criminal on the run I might have got away with it, but I was experimenting rather than attempting to escape for good, and so behaved more or less normally. The fact that I did nothing in the least abnormal when outside did not count in my favour with the hospital authorities when I got back; the bare fact of escaping was regarded, as I have explained, as proof of "insanity". This does not seem wholly fair. Personally I have little doubt that if my wife were not ready to claim me out at the first opportunity, and I was unable to escape, I should have the greatest difficulty in persuading the medical authorities to release me. I might be allowed to have leave here eventually, but at some hospitals I should be regarded as a chronic refractory case and kept there for life. One Medical Superintendent actually said as much.*

One of the most urgent reforms needed in Mental Hospitals is, therefore, systematic reconditioning for civil life and a regular effective way out for all those without relatives willing to take them, or jobs and homes to go to. I have given some thought to this question and would make the following concrete suggestions.

In the first place there should be an extension and overhaul of "occupational therapy". In this hospital there are the usual arrangements for rugmaking, needlework, weaving, carpentry, drawing and painting, and so on. There is a bootmaker's shop, a tailor's shop; a number of men work outside in the gardens or on the farm. The working hours are 9 till 12 noon and 2 till 4 p.m. Patients are encouraged to engage in occupational work, and are paid up to a maximum of 5/- per week for work of a productive nature. For domestic work in the wards payment is also made, averaging between 2/- and 3/- per week.

All this no doubt sounds quite satisfactory. A considerable number of patients find some sort of occupation and potter about in the Occupational Therapy building, in the shops, or on the farm. My impression, however, after working both on the farm

---

* I do not think that this is much of an overstatement, though the Medical Superintendent to whom these extracts were submitted strongly objected to it. There is no doubt that this particular hospital is always anxious to release patients, but the practical difficulties are great.

and in the Occupational Therapy building, was that the whole atmosphere was hopelessly lackadaisical, and that with some notable exceptions the tempo of work was so slow that it could hardly be expected to prepare those concerned for taking jobs outside.

The principal reason for this is the lack of incentive. The slackers get paid as much as those who do their best, and the maximum wage of 5/- is not much more than enough to buy an ounce of tobacco. This is particularly noticeable in domestic work in the wards. The senior nurses who remember conditions in the "bad old days" tell me that it was far easier to get patients to work well then. The charge nurses had an allocation of two or three ounces of tobacco per worker and were allowed to distribute it on the basis of work done. This represented an effective incentive and made it possible to keep even the worst wards far more spick and span than they are today.

"Lunatics" respond to incentive just as much as other people. If there is a satisfactory carrot in front of their noses and an adequate stick behind their backsides, they will work, often very energetically and efficiently. With no stick and, above all, with no carrot to look forward to, they naturally do not bother. Here again modern Mental Hospitals, particularly now that they have been taken over by the Health Service, seem to be the bureaucratic State in miniature.

Many if not most of mental illness are regressions to an adolescent or a childish state of mind. As every nurse or parent knows, the only possible way to train a child in good habits, whether of morality or of work, is by a system of rewards and punishments. The same applies, *mutatis mutandis*, to mental patients.

"Whatsoever thy hand findeth to do, do it with all thy might." Slack and lackadaisical habits both in work and play are little better for mental health than complete idleness. What seems to me to be wanted in Mental Hospitals is a systematic effort based on adequate incentives and the competitive spirit to inculcate keenness—both in work and in games. The resources and personnel are all available; it is merely a question of organisation and of a properly thought-out system. The following memorandum, which I wrote for one of the Charge Nurses while confined in the Refractory Ward, may be of some interest in this connection.

"MEMO to Mr ——

Rough scheme to improve the morale of Y and other Wards by incentives and by inculcating the team spirit throughout.

1 *General*

Mental patients in a refractory ward like Y are the toughest problems in any Mental Hospital. They are mostly introverted schizophrenics; they sit or walk around lost in the mazes of their own incomprehensible phantasies; it is practically impossible by the usual methods to interest them in anything outside themselves.

It seems to me that there are only two exceptions to this general rule:—

(a) All patients—or practically all—can be interested in the satisfaction of their own instinctive urges, generally for food or for money with which these can be bought.

(b) A considerable number of patients can be interested in the work of the ward, particularly if the incentives provided in cash or kind are adequate, as at present they are not. Now the work is mostly done by two or three willing workers who like the occupation. Occasionally the staff manage to rouse some of the others, but not for long; they soon relapse.

It seems to me that insufficient use is made of competition and incentive in general, and that it should also be possible to inculcate the team spirit—thus bringing the powerful herd instinct into play.

2   Practical Details

Take for example the above question of ward work. Even a ward of a Mental Hospital has a certain esprit-de-corps—however rudimentary it may be. There is a certain sense of "belonging" to the ward. Surely every effort should be made by the authorities to encourage this? At present, while the charge nurses certainly take pride in their wards and mostly do their best, they seem to get little encouragement.

Why should not regular inspections by the Medical Superintendent take place, say every Sunday, like the Captain's Sunday inspection in the British Navy? In this case it would be very important for the inspecting Medical Officer not merely to go round formally with the Charge Nurse, but to single out individually those who had done good work and commend them. A weekly prize of cigarettes or tobacco—or unrationed sweets—could easily be provided for distribution to the workers in the tidiest, cleanest and best-decorated ward. In view of the fact that a patient in a Mental Hospital costs the Health Service about £5 per week, the relative cost of such a distribution would be infinitesimal. Provided the prize was adequate, there would be keen competition for it, and within the wards the force of public opinion would be brought to bear on slackers.

Esprit-de-Corps and the team spirit could equally well be fostered in games, as in a Service organisation or a public school. In this hospital many games are played—cricket, football, tennis, badminton, table tennis, as well as draughts, dominoes, chess and

ganisations have to deal with prisoners who have been pushed out into the world; there they are, and if they are to be prevented from once more preying on the community something has to be done about them. But a Mental Patients' Aid Society would have to go into Mental Hospitals and Homes and arrange for them to come out, which is very different. There are Social Service workers who do something of the kind, but my impression, rightly or wrongly, is that they could be allowed considerably more scope.

To the minds of the vast majority of people even today, "lunatics", mental patients, are a different order of beings. Asylums are called Mental Hospitals; the term "lunatic" is more or less banned; and even the word "mental" is avoided whenever possible. Yet the old attitude remains.

The average mental patient, at any rate in the better wards, is quite indistinguishable except to trained observation from the ordinary "sane" man-in-the-street. Now and then one notices some minor eccentricity; occasionally there are little outbursts of temper; and there is a certain indefinable air of listlessness which seems inseparable from Mental Hospitals. But that is all. The border-line between "sanity" and "madness" is extraordinarily hard to define.

In my own case I am quite unable to define it. Sometimes, in elation or depression, I am certifiable as "of unsound mind" according to normal medical practice; at other times I am not. As a matter of experience I can readily distinguish the two states. But I am always the same person; I am always fully aware of what I am doing—except for the two minor bouts of amnesia recorded in earlier chapters; and I am always fully aware of the legal aspects of my acts. Morally, I must admit, my attitude is apt to change; in extreme elation a strong sense of "guidance" tends to make me rather a law to myself. I doubt very much, however, whether I could be regarded on a strict interpretation of the famous Macnaghten Rules laid down by the judges for criminal responsibility as not responsible for my actions, even in acute mania. Not only do I know what I am doing, but I know whether it is right or wrong. As a matter of fact, while I have committed many sins when "sane", when "mad" I have done many eccentric things, some foolish things, and things contrary to ordinary civilised usage, but nothing of which I am in the least ashamed in the moral sense.

It is therefore possible that much greater stress could well be laid on the moral and religious aspects of behaviour as a part of mental treatment than is in fact the case. In so far as mental patients are suffering from regression to a childish state of mind, moral training such as that given by nurses and parents can be very helpful, and it is in fact given in the natural course of events by the nurses in charge.

But in this hospital at any rate the religious aspect is hopelessly neglected. There is a salaried clergyman of the Church of England who holds services on Sundays and is sometimes to be found helping in the library. Yet when I went to him and said that my mental troubles were largely connected with religion, and that I should like to have the opportunity of a talk in private, he only told me to address an official letter to "The Chaplain", setting out my problems. I did so, but never even had an answer. Only once has this chaplain visited a ward in which I was confined, and on that occasion I asked him for a couple of library books. They never arrived.*

Religion has, I am convinced, a great part to play in the scientific treatment of mental disease. At present the parsons and psychologists are still to a considerable extent at loggerheads. Owing to the enormous part which "visions" and religious delusions play in insanity the doctors tend to be afraid of it and to discourage its manifestations. In a Mental Hospital it is in the highest degree unwise to say one's prayers in public, and it is best not to publish the fact that one reads the Bible. Yet it is my own experience, which I have tried to describe in this book, that only through religion, through a thorough and true understanding of it, and an acceptance of the Spirit in humility and faith, can a cure of religious "delusions" be achieved. By other methods they can be suppressed, only in all probability to recur again.

What I have attempted to do is to face the facts of my inner life, to accept them—"hallucinations", "illusions", and flights of ideas, however apparently absurd—and to adapt them to "reality". I have taken them as the voice of the Spirit, which, as already sufficiently explained, I regard as largely synonymous with "instinct" and the "Unconscious"; I have checked them as far as was possible by my reason; and I have acted on them in such directions as are socially possible.

Whether that is the act of a "sane" or of an "insane" man. I do not know. It is certainly what many people, great and small, have done in the past with considerable success, though no doubt many of them would nowadays be confined in Mental Hospitals. Though I am, of course, fully aware that my most striking inner experiences have come to me when I was medically speaking "insane", I would not have missed them for anything. I am what I am largely by virtue of them. By study, prayer and sublimation, I believe that I have been led to turn them to useful ends, and that now, at last, I have come to the end of the road and achieved a definite aim. As so often before in history, God has turned in my innermost soul evil—or what might have been evil—into good.

* The Medical Superintendent has subsequently told me that the Chaplain was very helpful when religious assistance was really necessary. I can only give my own experience.

If this has been possible for me, and readers of this book will perhaps be in a position to judge to some extent whether it has been so, then it must be equally possible for others. I believe it to be fundamentally wrong to tell mental patients that their inner experiences—of whatever kind—are "delusions". Those experiences are messages, as it were, of the Unconscious, and are sent to help them. But they require to be properly understood and rightly used.

I would go so far as to suggest that the inner experiences of the greatest prophets, leaders and geniuses are of precisely the same essential nature as those of the most disorderly lunatic. The only difference is that in the one case the leader or prophet possesses the necessary spiritual and intellectual qualities to understand and use those experiences, whereas the lunatic does not. And the problem of the right use of these experiences, of these messages of the Unconscious or Spirit, is primarily religious.

If that problem can be solved, it may well be that in our Mental Hospitals an immense reservoir of real talent, not to say of genius, will be found to be lying fallow. That there is wisdom in madness, that the "mad" have access to regions of true knowledge which are inaccessible to "normal" people is one of the oldest ideas of humanity. "Genius is akin to madness" is a phrase which expresses this idea, which is certainly as old as Socrates and Solomon. "And I gave my heart to know wisdom, and to know madness and folly." If only mental patients, who almost invariably suffer from an acute inferiority complex owing to their trouble, could be told that their experiences were valuable, provided they learnt to use them, I am convinced that startling results could be achieved.

Nothing is more infuriating for a mental patient in the grip of overwhelming inner experiences arising out of his Unconscious than to be told that they are merely the result of his "illness", or "madness". His whole being rises up in revolt against the very idea, and all the innumerable defensive mechanisms of the human psyche, such as rationalisation, are immediately brought into play. The natural result is to make the patient in his innermost soul want to be "insane", since he is led to believe that "sanity" involves the rejection of inner experiences to which he has become deeply attached.

In this sense I have no hesitation in saying that I myself want to remain "insane". I have not the slightest intention of returning to "sanity" if that means rejecting my own inner experiences. If I were to make the attempt, as I have done in the past, to reject or repress my manic consciousness, experience tells me that it would only return in a comparatively uncontrollable form. Only if I accept my experiences, my manic consciousness, *in toto* and resolutely adapt them to "reality", does it seem to me that there is any hope of a permanent cure.

Broadly speaking, of course, modern psychology is working along these lines. But it still seeks rather to remove "delusions" by showing the patient how they arose than to make effective use of them. It may be argued that most "delusions", being false beliefs, cannot be used. What, for example, can be done with a patient who believes that he is possessed of immense power—a sort of god?

From my own experience I would suggest that delusions of power are among the most useful of all delusions. They are merely an extreme manifestation of the will to power, success and recognition which Adler regards as the mainspring of all human activity, and is in any event one of the most important driving-forces behind it. They are a return in adult life of the expansion of spirit, the daydreams of success, which are a common experience of all adolescents with a spark of ambition. But as a rule the frustrations of real life have caused them to assume the irrational form of a belief that the power and success is actual rather than merely potential. If only such patients could be given insight into their own cases, could be shown that they are merely falsely interpreting messages and wrongly using powers that are really there, available for use, their attitude might be wholly changed. It may well be that in many mental patients there are latent powers far beyond those of so-called "normal" people. To tell them this would flatter their egos and encourage them to make efforts to develop those powers.

William James has discussed, in his *Textbook of Psychology*,[*] a phenomenon which bears intimately on this point. In childhood and adolescence, he writes, various instincts develop at various times, and it is vitally important that the child or adolescent should have the opportunity to use and fire that instinct, or it will atrophy. "If a boy grows up alone at the age of games and sports, and learns neither to play ball nor to row, nor sail, nor ride, nor skate, nor fish, nor shoot, probably he will be sedentary to the end of his days; and, though the best opportunities be afforded him for learning these things later, it is a hundred to one but he will pass them by and shrink back from the effort of taking those necessary first steps, the prospect of which, at an earlier age, would have filled him with eager delight. . . . Outside of their own business," James goes on, "the ideas gained by men before they are twenty-five are practically the only ideas they shall have in their lives. They *cannot* get anything new."

In some forms of insanity, including especially mania, this ripening of the instinct, this eager readiness to absorb and learn new things, to become interested in fresh games, sports and forms of work, seems to recur. It certainly does in my own case. I have, in actual fact, learnt more while confined in Mental Hospitals than

* Published by Macmillan, p. 405.

anywhere else, including my School and University. I have learnt drawing, shorthand, some languages, studied philosophy and psychology as deeply as I was able, collected and systematically written down and filed innumerable scraps of information on all sorts of subjects, and, above all, read in the book of human nature, which is as it were exposed in the raw. I know the history, background and medical diagnosis of many of the patients in the wards I have been in. Finally I have written this book.

If I can do these things, others must be able to do them too. That I could not have done them without the regression to adolescence and childhood and the attendant re-ripening of the instincts which this involves, I have no doubt whatever. It seems to me that the regression of "insanity", far from being the disease it is represented to be, is of immense value. It is, in fact, a sort of rebirth. It offers the possibility of a completely fresh start. Through "insanity" it is virtually possible—in Gospel language—to enter again into our mothers' wombs and be born once more. We can plan our lives afresh like children on a basis of as much wishful thinking as we like—provided always that we are ready to face reality and take the necessary steps to realise those dreams. To explain to us mental patients what is realisable and what is not in the given circumstances, and to guide our energies into channels which may be of value, should be the task of the physician. His method should be "situational treatment", considered in the very widest sense imaginable.

It may very well be that the above suggestions will seem somewhat trite to experienced physicians and psychiatrists in Mental Hospitals. There is nothing revolutionary about most of them. What I am pleading for is rather a revolutionary attitude of mind. I do claim that there is a value in so-called "mental" disease which, though it is already recognised in exceptional circumstances, such as those of great poets and artists, should be much more widely admitted and actually utilised for mental treatment. As Dostoievsky felt concerning his pre-epileptic auras, I would not have desired to miss my "abnormal" experiences for anything else in the world. Nor have I any ambition to be "normal", either in action or, more particularly in thought. All I want is to learn to adapt my "abnormality" to the conditions of the world around me. I deliberately want to be "mad", and in practice I strive as hard as I can to retain in "stable periods" the thoughts and feelings of my "madness". I reject nothing; I repress nothing. And because I repress nothing, it is my hope and belief that the surprises which used to lurk as it were in my Unconscious ready to overwhelm me with the dammed-up force of mania or depression as the case might be will remain under the control of my reason. Whether I shall be successful, time alone can show, but as a method of psychological treatment or self-treatment, I believe this to be more or less novel. To illustrate what I mean, I give here a short essay by a schizophrenic patient of my acquaintance, together with my comments.

A SCHIZOPHRENIC ON HIS NATURE

The schizophrenic is noted for his habit of giving evasive and irrelevant answers to simple questions. The reasons for this are:—

(a) *His morbid powers of association*

The questioner may use a word which the schizo associates with something unpleasant. The word then calls up a feeling of guilt or fear in the schizo, and he attempts to cover his feeling by quickly changing the subject; or (like the octopus) sends out an inky cloud of disjointed sentences, and escapes in the resulting confusion. The associations may be verbal (puns or rhymes) and hence *conscious*; but more often the schizo is not aware of the connection between the question and his unpleasant feeling.

(b) *Impatience*

The schizo's thoughts are always hurrying and jostling one another. (He is seeking the final and absolute answer to all his problems.) Therefore he may anticipate a question and answer it in advance. He considers his questioner slow and stupid if he fails to understand.

Another typical symptom of schizophrenia is the patient's habit of "tying himself into knots" or adopting unnatural and rigid postures. The reasons for this are as follows:

The patient believes himself to be the prey of terrifying cosmic forces: the nurse in his little cubicle seems to be directing the world through space: the radiator emits atomic power. One minute he is "Lord of Creation", the next he has changed to a "reincarnation of Judas", or he might be Satan himself. He is terrified and elated by turns. The people around him are either going to crown him or kill him.

When the savage found himself menaced by Nature (lightning, blizzards, drought, etc.) he resorted to magic to overcome these forces. The schizo's contortions are a similar attempt to protect himself from an imagined catastrophe.

The right-hand side of the body may signify good luck and the left-hand bad. He will then take care to keep his right leg crossed over his left, for example, or his right shoulder raised. He looks around the room for symmetrical objects, and, if these are changed so that the left-hand side predominates, he sweats with terror, and so on. Or he raises his hands towards the electric light, imagining it to be a source of cosmic energy. He seems to feel power flowing into his finger-tips from the light.

Another cause of the schizo's rigid postures can be understood by reading Kafka's story *The Father*. His perfect stillness is a symbolic state of death. His miming of the actions of others is an abnegation of the will, designed to placate the Father. Ideas of this kind always remain with the schizo; in the dormant stages of his illness, however, he will play at being normal.

In my opinion as a layman, the key to the treatment of a state of mind of this kind is contained in the last sentence. It is fundamentally unsound to try to teach mental patients to be "normal"; what is necessary is to teach them to play satisfactorily at being "normal", so that they may live both in the world of "reality" and in their dreams. For their dreams are just as true and "real" as "reality" itself. They are, in fact, "actual".

I have no hesitation in saying that I am myself "playing at being normal" in this sense. Moreover, my own apprehensions of Actuality have many similarities with those of my schizophrenic friend. I clearly sense, for example, the symbolic nature of Actuality, though sometimes my sense is stronger than at others. My Unconscious is constantly "talking" to me through symbols and associations of the kind described, and I take care to pay careful attention to it. All I endeavour to do is to relate it to my "rational" apprehensions. When it is a question of action, particularly an important action, I prefer not to act unless I can get the "irrational" and the "rational" to coincide, rather as some optical instruments require two images to be made to coincide before the reading is taken. In the terminology of the Theory of Actuality this probably means that adequate contact between Positive and Negative has been made. I tend to "follow my hunches" unless they are obviously irrational and likely to lead to trouble. The Negative knows best.

Another thing that strikes me about the above extract is that the writer is obviously trying to do much the same as I have aimed at in this book. He is "seeking the final and absolute answer to all his questions". He will not wholly find it; I have certainly not done so. But to a limited and not wholly inadequate extent it can be found if the irrational impulses and thoughts of the Negative are wholeheartedly accepted and incorporated into Positive rational life.

In this book I have tried to show ways in which this can be done. That is why I feel the book may prove of clinical value for the treatment of mental troubles and for the comfort of mental patients. A number of fellow-sufferers have already read it, or parts of it, and tell me they have found it helpful. If I were to call it "A Manual for the Right Use of Lunacy" it would express the idea I am trying to convey. When doctors cease trying to "cure" lunatics of "delusions" the asylums will begin to empty themselves.

REACTIONS TO SPECIFIC TREATMENTS

1. *Psychological Treatment*

The only systematic psychological treatment I have received was a week's course of Individual Psychology on the principles of Adler. This was given me in 1937, during an early stage of my illness, at a well-known nursing-home near London. I was at the time in a depressive phase suffering from severe insomnia and suicidal impulses.

The object of the psychologist who treated me, giving me an hour's conversation every day, was to make me face up both to my external difficulties in the real world and to the inner troubles of my soul. Following the Adlerian method, he endeavoured to establish my true *Lebenszweck* or life-goal, and to put me on the road towards its achievement. The method, however, failed completely. By the end of the week I was violently suicidal, having gone from bad to worse. My wife rescued me and took me back to the nursing-home where I had been before. There plenty of bromide and no psychology, or at any rate no systematic psychology, gradually enabled me to swing out of the depressive phase and caused my fears to subside of themselves.

Looking back, I would say that, although the Adlerian method was hopeless for me at that stage of my illness, primarily because I could not bring myself to face up to or to confide in the doctor the fundamental religious problems which were at the root of my troubles, I have actually adopted the Adlerian method of Individual Psychology in this book. I am in fact, trying to the best of my ability to reconcile the difficulties and failures of my real situation with the whole inner life of my soul.

For that purpose, both the horrors of my depressive periods and the ecstasies of my manic periods seem to me to have been necessary. In particular, I feel that to have plumbed the depths of depression as described in Chapter III was an essential part of my cure. As stated, I am inclined to the view that this is due to the very thoroughness of my experience. I have, as it were, been in Hell, where my sins seem to have been expiated, and since then no Hell has any terrors for me. This conviction seems to be shared by my Unconscious at the deepest levels. I can find no other satisfactory reason for my somewhat unusual experience; according to most authorities the tendency towards depression in manic-depressive cases increases in later life, while that towards elation decreases.

It is precisely because I have experienced the catharsis of the Horrific Vision followed by the stimulus of its opposite that I seem to have gained the courage to face life again at the age of fifty. I am rather like the donkey in a famous article published not long ago in *The Economist*. Man, said the writer, needs both a carrot and a stick, if he is to give of his best. In a way, I have seen both the stick and the carrot of Eternity. On one thing I am quite determined, and that is to act as far as I can as my Master tells me. I prefer the carrot.

The relevance of this little digression to the question of Individual Psychology may not be immediately apparent. It is that Individual Psychology at any rate cannot afford to ignore the religious aspect. It demands the parson as well as the psychologist. With all due respect to the very kind and well-meaning doctor who treated me, he was not much use as a father-confessor. I needed absolution, and he had none to give. It was not much use telling me to pull myself together and forget my sins, nor to say that they were not very important, and that the worry about them was merely a symptom of my illness, when I could see the gulf of Hell yawning ahead. Furthermore, I am inclined to the view that Individual Psychology might be even more useful for those who have really "been through the mill" of a serious psychosis than for neurotic cases on the borderline, provided always that the religious angle is given adequate attention.

2. *Physical Treatments*

As well as ordinary sedative treatments with bromide, barbiturics, paraldehyde, etc., I have had one course of systematic "prolonged narcosis". This was during the first manic period in 1947. The narcosis proper lasted for three weeks. Its effect was possibly to shorten to some extent the duration of the manic swing, which normally lasts with me some six months and in this case took about half this period. It recurred, however, in the autumn, which seems to indicate that the cure was incomplete.

Much more effective was electrical convulsion therapy (ECT). One course was carried out at a Military Hospital at Hamburg in August 1947, the other at the public Mental Hospital where I am writing this. The results of the two treatments were widely divergent and deserve, I think, some attention.

The Military Hospital gave me only two convulsions. At the time I was in a state of acute mania, seeing continual illusions, imagining everybody around me to be resurrected historical personages and convinced that I was destined to start then and there a movement that would save the world. The two convulsions were sufficient to break up the whole related syndrome of vision and phantasy, and within a little more than two months I was discharged as cured. I had no recurrence for two years.

Here, on the other hand, my state was of not very severe hypomania. I was given a course of six convulsions and discharged about a month after the last of them. I found at once that my symptoms were recurring and returned the following day to the hospital. I then had one more convulsion, after which I refused treatment since it appeared to me that I was as it were being "bumped" from elation to depression without any proper investigation of my real mental state, and I feared a recurrence of the suicidal depression of ten years earlier. The question arises why two convulsions in Hamburg were sufficient to cure acute mania, while seven convulsions did not suffice to cure much milder hypomania.

The modern physical methods of psychiatric treatment, such as ECT, Insulin Therapy, etc., have been discovered purely empirically. They have been found to produce results and they have therefore been used, but little is known about how and why they work.

Introspectively, ECT appears to shift my observing ego from one state of consciousness to another, or using another metaphor, to push one state of consciousness below the "threshold" of observation and replace it with another. In Hamburg this process was startlingly distinct. As I awoke from the period of unconsciousness which follows the convulsion, I could actually feel the phenomena of elation being pushed away from my consciousness. It was apparently analogous to the process which takes place in the mind as one awakes from sleep. The dream gives place to a drowsy state in which the ideas and phantasies of the dream remain fairly clear and only gradually give place to full waking consciousness. Consciousness drives the Unconscious away. In this case, however, the process, instead of only taking a few minutes, took several days. I really felt as if my elated phantasies were being pushed away from my brain down the spinal column by some sort of force. At the same time I felt the aching stiffness in my back which is the usual accompaniment of ECT.

In this hospital my impressions were less distinct. The full course of six convulsions seemed to disturb my whole nervous system and at the same time to have a less clearly defined effect than the two convulsions at Hamburg. At times I seemed seriously depressed, at others more or less elated. The additional convulsions certainly appeared to make me much less stable than I had been at Hamburg. I am inclined to think from my own experience that a course of ECT should be as short as is sufficient to produce the necessary effect on the patient's mind. Apart from the fact that ECT can sometimes produce destructive effects,* in manic-de-

---

* This is admitted by Messrs. Sergeant and Slater, in their "Introduction to Physical Methods of Psycho-Therapy", although they are wholehearted advocates of the methods.

pressive cases it is quite common for depression relieved by ECT to pass over into hypomania, or vice-versa, and the new state has then to be cured by further convulsions and so on. It would therefore be of great value if some method could be devised of establishing precisely what effect the treatment is having on the patient's mind. Is it possible, by objective methods, to measure the underlying psychological state, in order that the physical treatment can be stopped at the right moment or adjusted accordingly? There are in fact a number of objective psychological tests, but I do not know to what extent they are used for the purpose in question. The tests were applied to me (see Appendix C), but only when I was on the verge of discharge, not when I was under treatment.

RESULTS OF SZONDI AND RORSCHACH TESTS

(Carried out on Mr. John Custance in July, 1950.)

Szondi Results.

Instinct Class $= \dfrac{\text{S.E.}}{\text{M}}$

Symptomatic $=$ E.S.(D)
Submanifest $=$ K.P.
Root Factor $=$ M.
Proportional relations of latencies

$$= \frac{\text{Hy}+}{3} \frac{\text{H}-}{3} \frac{\text{M}+}{3} = \text{Triequal}$$

Tendency tension $= 1.4$
Ego pictures 2A's, 1B_1, 2C_1, 1Ep_2

Rorschach Results

Total Responses $= 27$
Total time $= 857$ secs.
T/R $= 31.7$ secs.
Qv. Time cards I $= 24$ secs.
,, ,, II $= 17$ secs.
Total F% $= 60\%$
A% $= 40\%$
P $= 15$
O $= 12$
(H $+$ A) : (Hd $+$ Ad) $= 15 : 3$
EC $= 6$
M : EC $= 4 : 6$
(FM $+$ m) : (Fc $+$ c $+$ C^1) $2 : 0$
Mo. on last 3 cards $= 40\%$

W : M.   10 : 4
Succession = Rigid
Manner of Approach :
W 37% D. 26% d 33% S. 3%
Estimate of Intellectual level = very superior